Determinants of Financial Development

Determinants of Financial Development

Yongfu Huang
University of Cambridge

© Yongfu Huang 2011

All rights reserved. No reproduction, copy or transmission of this
publication may be made without written permission.

No portion of this publication may be reproduced, copied or transmitted
save with written permission or in accordance with the provisions of the
Copyright, Designs and Patents Act 1988, or under the terms of any licence
permitting limited copying issued by the Copyright Licensing Agency,
Saffron House, 6-10 Kirby Street, London EC1N 8TS.

Any person who does any unauthorised act in relation to this publication
may be liable to criminal prosecution and civil claims for damages.

The author has asserted his right to be identified as the author of this work
in accordance with the Copyright, Designs and Patents Act 1988.

First published in 2011 by
PALGRAVE MACMILLAN

Palgrave Macmillan in the UK is an imprint of Macmillan Publishers Limited,
registered in England, company number 785998, of Houndmills, Basingstoke,
Hampshire RG21 6XS.

Palgrave Macmillan in the US is a division of St Martin's Press LLC,
175 Fifth Avenue, New York, NY 10010.

Palgrave Macmillan is the global academic imprint of the above companies
and has companies and representatives throughout the world.

Palgrave® and Macmillan® are registered trademarks in the United States,
the United Kingdom, Europe and other countries.

ISBN: 978–0–230–27367–2 hardback

This book is printed on paper suitable for recycling and made from fully
managed and sustained forest sources. Logging, pulping and manufacturing
processes are expected to conform to the environmental regulations of the
country of origin.

A catalogue record for this book is available from the British Library.

A catalog record for this book is available from the Library of Congress.

10 9 8 7 6 5 4 3 2 1
20 19 18 17 16 15 14 13 12 11

Transferred to Digital Printing in 2014

To Benrun and Benpei

Contents

List of Figures x

List of Tables xi

List of Abbreviations xiii

Preface xvii

1 Introduction 1
  1.1 Background 1
  1.2 Origins of financial development: A review 3
    1.2.1 Institutions 3
    1.2.2 Policy 5
    1.2.3 Geography 6
    1.2.4 Other variables 7
  1.3 Structure of the book 7

2 General Determinants of Financial Development 10
  2.1 Introduction 10
  2.2 The data 13
    2.2.1 Samples 14
    2.2.2 Measures of financial development 14
    2.2.3 The potential determinants 16
  2.3 Empirical strategy 20
    2.3.1 Bayesian Model Averaging 21
    2.3.2 General-to-specific approach 22
  2.4 Empirical results (I): Overall financial development 24
    2.4.1 Some stylized facts 24
    2.4.2 What are the main determinants of *FD*? 27
  2.5 Empirical results (II): Specific financial developments 36
  2.6 Conclusions 46
  Appendix text 48
  Appendix tables 49

3 Private Investment and Financial Development 64
  3.1 Introduction 64
  3.2 The data 67
  3.3 Analysis on data for five-year averages 69

		3.3.1	Methodology: System GMM	69
		3.3.2	Empirical results	73
	3.4	Analysis on annual data		77
		3.4.1	Methodology: Common factor approach	78
		3.4.2	Panel unit root tests	81
		3.4.3	Panel cointegration tests	84
		3.4.4	Estimation on annual data	85
	3.5	Conclusion		92
	Appendix tables			94
	Appendix figures			99
4	**Political Institutions and Financial Development**			**101**
	4.1	Introduction		101
	4.2	Institutions, democratization and finance		102
	4.3	The measures and data		104
		4.3.1	The sample	104
		4.3.2	The measure and data for financial development	105
		4.3.3	The measure and data for institutional improvement	106
	4.4	Methodology		106
	4.5	Evidence		109
		4.5.1	Preliminary evidence	109
		4.5.2	Regression results	114
	4.6	Conclusion		121
	Appendix tables			123
5	**Financial Reforms for Financial Development**			**125**
	5.1	Introduction		125
	5.2	Methodology		127
		5.2.1	Model specifications	127
		5.2.2	Econometric methods	131
	5.3	Empirical evidence		133
		5.3.1	Analysis on the original dataset	134
		5.3.2	Analysis on a larger dataset	143
	5.4	Discussions		147
	5.5	Conclusion		149
	Appendix tables			151
6	**Geographic Determinants of Carbon Markets (CDM)**			**161**
	6.1	Introduction		161
	6.2	Data and stylized facts		164

6.3	Econometric method: Spatial econometric approach	168
6.4	Empirical evidence	171
6.5	Concluding remarks	178
	Appendix table	180

Conclusion   181

Notes   183

Bibliography   194

Index   203

Figures

2.1	Scatter plots of institutions and financial development	25
2.2	Scatter plots of policy and financial development	26
2.3	Scatter plots of geography and financial development	27
2.4	Median Liquid Liability by different country group over 1960–2003	28
4.1	Financial development ten years before and after democratization	113
4.2	Volatility of financial development ten years pre/post-democratization	113
6.1	Scatter plots of CDM and geography	166
6.2	CDM and resource endowments	167
6.3	CDM and distance to biggest and smallest host countries	172

Tables

2.1	Determinants of *FD* by using BMA	30
2.2	Determinants of *FD*	32
2.3	Top ten models and their posterior probabilities for *FD*	34
2.4	Geography, policy, institutions and *FD*	35
2.5	Determinants of *FDBANK*	38
2.6	Determinants of *FDSTOCK*	40
2.7	Determinants of *FDEFF*	42
2.8	Determinants of *FDSIZE*	44
3.1	Does private investment cause financial development? 1970–98 (five-year-average data)	74
3.2	Does financial development cause private investment? 1970–98 (five-year-average data)	75
3.3	Unit root tests in heterogeneous panels	83
3.4	Panel cointegration tests between *FD* and *PI*	85
3.5	Does private investment cause financial development? 1970–98 (Annual data)	90
3.6	Does financial development cause private investment? 1970–98 (Annual data)	91
4.1	Change in *FD* standardized before and after democratization	111
4.2	Institutional improvement and financial development (whole sample), 1960–99	115
4.3	Institutional improvement and financial development (lower-income countries), 1960–99	117
4.4	Institutional improvement and financial development (ethnically diverse countries), 1960–99	119
4.5	Institutional improvement and financial development (French legal origin countries), 1960–99	120
5.1	Within estimates: Benchmark specification (Equation 4) (A, B)	135
5.2	Within estimates: Alternative specification (Equations 5 and 6)	137
5.3	Within estimates: Alternative specification (Equation 8)	138
5.4	Error dependence across countries and over time considered separately (A, B, C)	140

5.5	Augmented dataset with Chinn-Ito measure (2006) (A, B, C)	145
6.1	Moran's I and Geary's C for CDM	173
6.2	Geography and CDM (by inverse-distance weights)	175
6.3	Geography and CDM (by binary weights)	177

Abbreviations

2SLS	two-stage least squares estimator
ADF	augmented Dickey-Fuller test
AM	Abiad and Mody (2005)
AREA	land area of a country in square km
AR(1)	first-order autoregression
ARDL	autoregressive distributed lag
ASIA	dummy variable for Asian countries
BACE	Bayesian averaging of classical estimates
BMA	Bayesian model averaging
BMP	black market premium (%)
BTOT	index of commercial/central bank
CCE	common correlated effect approach
CCEMG	common correlated effect mean group estimator
CCEP	common correlated effect pooled estimator
CDM	clean development mechanism
CER	certified emission reductions
CIVLEG	dummy variable for civil law legal origin
COMLEG	dummy variable for common-law legal origin
CRIGHT	index of creditors' rights
CTRADE	natural log of the Frankel-Romer measure of predisposition to external trade
DGP	data-generating process
DURABLE	index of political stability
EBA	extreme bounds analysis
ELEV	elevation in metres above sea level
ETHNIC	index of ethnic fractionalization
ETHPOL	index of ethnic polarization
EURFRAC	index of European first language
EURO1900	percentage of population in 1900 European or of European descent
EXPMANU	dummy variable for manufactured goods exporting countries
EXPPRIM	dummy variable for fuel and non-fuel primary goods exporting countries
EXPSERV	dummy variable for service exporting countries

FD	index of overall financial development
FDBANK	index of extent of bank-based intermediation
FDBOND	index of bond market development
FDEFF	index of financial efficiency
FDSIZE	index of size of financial system / financial depth
FDSTOCK	index of measure of stock market development
FL	index of financial liberalization
FREE	averaged indices of civil liberties and political rights
GDN	World Bank Global Development Network Database
GDP	gross domestic product
GDP03	initial GDP per capita in 2003
GDP90	initial GDP per capita /initial income in 1990
Gets	General-to-specific approach
GMM	generalized method of moments estimator
GS2SLS	generalized two-stage least squares estimator
GUM	general unrestricted model
HINFL	dummy variable for periods of high inflation
INCLOW	dummy variable for low-income countries
INCMID	dummy variable for middle-income countries
IC	information criterion
KKM	index of governance
LAC	dummy variable for Latin American countries
LANDLOCK	dummy variable for landlocked countries
LANGUAGE	index of language fractionalization
LATITUDE	absolute latitude of a country from the Equator
LEG_FR	dummy variable for French legal origin countries
LEG_GE	dummy variable for German legal origin countries
LEG_SC	dummy variable for Scandinavian legal origin countries
LEG_UK	dummy variable for British legal origin countries
LLY	index of liquid liabilities
LR	long-run
LSDV	Least Squares Dummy Variable estimator
LSDVC	corrected LSDV estimator
MC^3	Markov Chain Monte Carlo technique
MCAP	index of stock market capitalization
MEDSHARE	index of market share of state-owned media
MG	mean group estimator
MINDIST	minimum distance from USA, Japan and Belgium
NIM	index of net interest margin
OLS	ordinary least squares estimator

OPENC	trade openness (at current prices) or the sum of exports and imports over GDP
OVC	index of overhead costs
PC	principal components
PcGets	Gets computer algorithm
PCI	index of political constraints
PIPs	posterior probabilities of inclusion
PMG	pooled mean groups estimator
PMP	posterior model probabilities
POLITY2	index of democracy from Polity IV Database
POP03	initial population in 2003
POP90	initial population in 1990
POP100CR	share of population in 1994 within 100 km of coast or ocean-navigable river
PMP	posterior model probability
PRIVO	index of private credit
R	a free software environment for statistical computing and graphics.
REGEAP	dummy variable for East Asian and Pacific countries
REGLAC	dummy variable for Latin American countries
REGEMENA	dummy variable for Middle Eastern and North African countries
REGSA	dummy variable for South Asian countries
REGSSA	dummy variable for Sub-Saharan African countries
REGWENA	dummy variable for Western European and North American countries
RELIGION	index of religious fractionalization
RESCOFF	dummy variable for coffee/cocoa natural resources exporting countries
RESDIFF	dummy variable for diffuse natural resources exporting countries
RESPOINT	dummy variable for point source natural resource exporting countries
RMSE	root mean square error
RSS	residual sum-of-squares
SDBMP	std. dev. (or volatility) for the black market premium
SDGR	std. dev. for annual growth rate real, chain-weighted GDP 1960–89
SDPI	std. dev. for annual inflation 1960–89
SDTP	std. dev. for volatility of GDP per capita growth of trading partners

SDTT	std. dev. for volatility of the terms of trade index for goods and services
SRIGHT	index of shareholders' rights
SSA	dummy variable for Sub-Saharan countries
SYS-GMM	System generalized method of moments estimator
TOPEN	index of trade openness policy
TOR	index of turnover ratio
TVT	index of total value traded
USINT	index of US Treasury Bill rate
WG	within groups estimator
YRSOFFC	dummy variable for the first year in office

Preface

While it is clear that financial depth has a positive effect on economic growth, the questions of what determines financial development and how to develop financial markets remain imperfectly understood. More specifically, economists still have an insufficient understanding of the following key issues. What brings about the emergence and development of financial markets? What are the reasons why different financial structures, bank-based or market-based, exist in countries where similar levels of economic development have been reached? What accounts for the differences in the levels of financial development in countries like the OECD member countries which have similar income levels, and geographic conditions? The world witnessed the worst financial crisis and climate crisis of our age during the period 2007–09. This highlights the significance of the research into what is essential to the development of financial markets and what is key to develop carbon markets for tackling climate change.

Against this background, my book seeks to investigate the fundamental determinants of the development of financial markets and carbon markets. It starts with a general examination of the determinants of financial development in Chapter 2 and moves on to specific studies in the following chapters. Chapters 3 and 4 examine two specific determinants of financial development in the context of globalization. To be more specific, Chapter 3 provides an exhaustive analysis of the causality between aggregate private investment and financial development from the economic point of view while Chapter 4 explores the determinants of financial development from a political perspective, namely, the impact of institutional improvement on financial development. Chapter 5 looks at what induces governments to undertake reforms aimed at boosting financial development. Chapter 6 is concerned with the development of carbon markets, which is a newly developed/recently emerging area for both research and practice. It examines what could explain the uneven development of carbon markets in developing countries from a geographic point of view, with an aim of encouraging further research into other determinants of carbon market development.

This book constitutes a unique addition to the expanding literature in this field, and its contribution is highlighted by its title. It could be the first comprehensive book of this kind to explore this subject systematically by using various recently developed econometric methods. It provides a very general but comprehensive overview of modern financial development theory and incorporates cutting-edge research in this field, along with a huge number of relevant literature citations. This book also presents the latest thinking on how to develop financial and carbon markets. The findings of this book have rich implications for the conduct of macroeconomic policies in developing countries in an integrated global economy.

This book is suitable for the students of financial development and climate change at the advanced undergraduate or graduate level, for economists and applied econometricians who are interested in economic and financial development, financial liberalization and climate change and for policy-makers and government agencies. This research topic will continue to be of great interest to academics and practitioners across the globe, which is underlined by the number of recent international conferences and symposia devoted to the financial and climate crises.

I would like to avail myself of this opportunity to extend my sincere thanks to all those who have made my research into these issues and my writing of this book a truly fulfilling and unforgettable experience. It goes without saying, or it should, that there are various people without whom this book would never have been possible.

A great debt of gratitude is owed to my PhD supervisor, Professor Jonathan Temple, for giving me his time, insights, enthusiasm, incredible help and constant support. His remarkable insights into various development issues, his erudition in economics and his willingness to discuss and blue-sky with me, have enriched both my academic life and this book. Also, high tribute should be paid to my Centre Director at Cambridge University, Dr Terry Barker, who has kindly advised me on various climate change issues, for example, the last chapter of this book. His generous support and assistance have been of inestimable worth to the conduct of my research and the accomplishment of this book. If this book looks good, it is only because of their insightful suggestions and invaluable help.

A number of academic members were no less critical to my research during the years of the preparation of this book. It would be impossible to give a comprehensive list, but I would like to thank Professor Stephen Bond and Professor Frank Windmeijer for their expert comments and advice. Dr Sonia Bhalotra, Dr Edmund Cannon, Dr David Demory and Dr Andy Picking (in alphabetical order) kindly provided thought-provoking input during my research at Bristol. I am also deeply indebted to Professor Philip Arestis, Professor Hashem Pesaran, Dr Mark Roberts and other colleagues at Cambridge from whom I have greatly benefited in terms of valuable suggestions.

I owe a special debt of gratitude to Professor Yuguang Yang at Fudan University, who has played an important role in the course of my career development. His professional conscientiousness (or rigorousness), positive attitude and strong thirst for knowledge have inspired me to go forward over the years. My appreciation also goes to my close friends from Fudan University, Youqiang Li, Zhiqun Lin, Zhuwu Xu, Muqing Zheng and Xiaoxin Zhou (in alphabetical order) among others for their heartfelt sincerity, encouragement and help in various circumstances.

I would like especially to acknowledge Taiba Batool and Gemma Papageorgiou at Palgrave Macmillan and Cathy Lowne, who have been remarkably patient and helpful and whose expert jobs have helped to make this book a reality. I also highly appreciate the contribution to the book made in various ways by other people at Palgrave Macmillan. The stamp of their illuminating advice and careful checking appears on every page of my book.

On a personal note I wish as always to thank my beloved family for their constant encouragement, unwavering support and love. From the earliest time I can remember, my parents have instilled in me a love of learning that has only grown over time. The incredible help and love of my sister and brother enabled me to go through frustration and depression. Their patience is legendary. To all these and more, I shall be eternally grateful.

Yongfu Huang
Cambridge, March 2010

1
Introduction

1.1 Background

Among the profound evolutions in development economics in recent decades has been the renewed interest in, and growing contributions on, the role of financial systems in economic development. While it is clear that a positive effect exists between financial depth and economic growth, the questions of what determines financial development and how to develop financial markets remain imperfectly understood.

Research on the role of financial development in growth can be traced back at least to Bagehot (1873) who claims that large and well-organized capital markets in England enhanced resource allocation towards more productive investment. Other historical antecedents before 1970 include, among others, Schumpeter (1911), Hicks (1969) and Goldsmith (1969). Schumpeter (1911) emphasizes the critical role of a country's banking system for economic development in mobilizing savings and encouraging productive investment. Hicks (1969) highlights the importance of financial markets in the process of industrial revolution with an observation that the development of financial systems facilitates the applications of new technologies and innovations. Goldsmith (1969) finds evidence of a positive link between financial development and economic growth from a comparative study with data for 35 countries over the period 1860–1963.

Over the past three decades, the financial repression and financial development framework proposed by McKinnon (1973) and Shaw (1973) has been the main intellectual basis of financial market analysis and policy advice. Before the 1970s most developing countries had been financially repressed in the sense that their financial systems had imposed upon them discriminatory taxation in the form of low interest

2 Determinants of Financial Development

rate policies, high reserve requirements and high inflation rates. Keynes (1936) and Tobin (1956) are among the various justifications for maintaining these policies. The McKinnon-Shaw model of financial repression formulates the phenomenon of financial repression and points out that financial repression reduces both the quantity and quality of aggregate investment in the economy in the sense that a lower deposit rate of interest discourages households from holding deposits that would be used to finance productive investment. The policy implication of the McKinnon-Shaw model is that government's repressive policies towards financial systems (such as interest rate ceilings, high reserve requirements and credit control) retard financial development, and therefore economic growth. On the contrary, financial liberalization and financial development can stimulate investment and its productivity, and ultimately foster economic growth. Since 1973, the McKinnon-Shaw model has influenced financial sector policies in many developing countries considerably.

Motivated by the McKinnon-Shaw model, a number of studies in this area have been undertaken, such as Kapur (1976) and Mathieson (1980) among others. However, these works in general treat financial intermediation and financial institutions as exogenous. The last two decades have witnessed a resurgence of interest in the relationship between financial development and economic growth which incorporates the insights of endogenous growth models. These works include Townsend (1979), Diamond (1984), Gale and Hellwig (1985), Williamson (1986, 1987), Bencivenga and Smith (1991), Greenwood and Jovanovic (1990), Saint-Paul (1992), King and Levine (1993) and Bernanke *et al.* (1999) among others.

Apart from a standard Arrow-Debreu framework, these studies make use of the assumption of information asymmetry between lenders and borrowers, producing significant findings. Due to the presence of information asymmetries, the problem of adverse selection and moral hazard might arise, since the borrowers (typically entrepreneurs) have incentives to hide their actual (or expected) return on their investment, calling for costly state verification. The financial contract and financial intermediation are therefore endogenously determined. Not only do these models demonstrate how financial intermediaries emerge, they also analyse how financial intermediation promotes economic growth. The inherent functions of financial systems, including mobilizing savings to their highest valued use, acquiring information, evaluating and monitoring investment projects and enabling individuals to diversify away idiosyncratic risk, have been widely believed to encourage productive investment and therefore total factor productivity.[1]

Introduction 3

Given the broad consensus on the substantial role of financial development in economic growth, it is of great practical importance to understand the origins of financial development. Economists still have an insufficient understanding of what brings about the emergence and development of financial markets, what are the reasons why different financial structures, bank-based or market-based, exist in countries where similar levels of economic development have been reached and what accounts for the differences in the level of financial development in countries like the OECD member countries which have similar income levels and geographic conditions.

This research seeks to investigate the political, economic, policy and geographic determinants of the development of financial markets. In addition, it attempts to examine the causality between financial development and another important aspect of economic activities, namely aggregate private investment. It also aims to explore the consequences of political liberalization in terms of institutional improvement for financial development and whether we should expect any changes in the political system, from autocracy to democracy for example, to exert any influence on the speed of financial development. It then studies what stimulates governments to initiate reforms aimed at financial development. This research ends up in the last chapter by studying the determinants of carbon markets in developing countries from a geographic perspective.

The following section provides a brief review on the determinants of financial development. Section 1.3 describes the structure of the book.

1.2 Origins of financial development: A review

Recent years have witnessed burgeoning research into the potential determinants of financial development. This section briefly outlines the main possible determinants of financial development, including institutional factors, macroeconomic factors, geographic factors and others which have been studied in the literature.

1.2.1 Institutions

Research on the role of institutions in financial development has been considerable, especially research on the effects of the legal and regulatory environment on the functioning of financial markets. A legal and regulatory system involving protection of property rights, contract enforcement and good accounting practices has been identified as essential for financial development. Most prominently, La Porta *et al.* (1997,

1998) have argued that the origins of the legal code substantially influence the treatment of creditors and shareholders, and the efficiency of contract enforcement. They document that countries with a legal code like Common Law tend to protect private property owners, while countries with a legal code like French Civil Law tend to care more about the rights of the state and less about the rights of the masses. Countries with French Civil Law are said to have comparatively inefficient contract enforcement and higher corruption, and less well-developed financial systems, while countries with a British legal origin achieve higher levels of financial development. Among others, Mayer and Sussman (2001) emphasize that regulations concerning information disclosure, accounting standards, permissible banking practice and deposit insurance do appear to have material effects on financial development.

Beck et al. (2003)'s application of the settler mortality hypothesis of Acemoglu et al. (2001) to financial development is another significant work in this context. They argue that colonizers, often named as extractive colonizers, in an inhospitable environment aimed to establish institutions which privileged small elite groups rather than private investors, while colonizers, often named as settler colonizers, in more favourable environments were more likely to create institutions which supported private property rights and balanced the power of the state, therefore favouring financial development. Both the legal origin theory of La Porta et al. (1997, 1998) and Beck et al. (2003)'s application are related to colonization, but the former is more concerned with how colonization determines the national approaches to property rights and financial development, whereas the latter is more about the channel via which colonization influences financial development.

The recently developed "new political economy" approach regards "regulation and its enforcement as a result of the balance of power between social and economic constituencies" (Pagano and Volpin, 2001). It centres on self-interested policy-makers who can intervene in financial markets by either overall regulation or individual cases for purposes such as career concerns and group interests. Rajan and Zingales (2003) emphasize the role of interest groups, and especially the incumbent industrial firms and the domestic financial sector, in the process of financial development. They argue that, in the absence of openness, incumbents have strong incentives to block the development of a more transparent and competitive financial sector which undermines the incumbents' vested interests and relationships. When both trade openness and financial openness are encouraged, the incumbents have incentives to support financial development from which more funds can be sought to meet foreign competition and new rents can be generated to compensate partially for their loss of incumbency.

Generally speaking, institutions might have a profound impact on the supply side of financial development. The level of institutional development in a country to some extent determines the sophistication of the financial system.

1.2.2 Policy

The policy view highlights the importance of some macroeconomic policies, openness of goods markets and financial liberalization in promoting financial development. The significant effect of policy on financial development could be working through either its demand side or its supply side.

Some major national macroeconomic policies such as maintaining lower inflation and higher investment have been documented as being conducive to financial development. Huybens and Smith (1999) theoretically and Boyd et al. (2001) empirically investigate the effects of inflation on financial development and conclude that economies with higher inflation rates are likely to have smaller, less active and less efficient banks and equity markets. Some recent work has supported the view that policies which encourage openness to external trade tend to boost financial development (Do and Levchenko, 2004).

In addition, research has been carried out to study the effects of financial liberalization on financial development over the past three decades, following the McKinnon-Shaw model (McKinnon, 1973; Shaw, 1973), which concludes that while financial repression reduces the quantity and quality of aggregate investment, financial liberalization can foster economic growth by increasing investment and its productivity. The positive link between domestic financial liberalization and financial development is supported by evidence (World Bank, 1989), although domestic financial liberalization is not without risks (Demirgüç-Kunt and Detragiache, 1998). Research on the positive correlation between external financial liberalization, especially capital account openness, and financial development is discussed in the panel data studies of Bailliu (2000) and Chinn and Ito (2006), although potential destabilizing effects may also exist. Claessens et al. (1998) present evidence that opening banking markets improves the functioning of national banking systems and the quality of financial services, with positive implications for banking customers and lower profitability for domestic banks. Laeven (2000) examines whether the liberalization of the banking sector may help to reduce financial restrictions and the external cost of the capital premium, stimulating investment and financial development. Bekaert *et al.* (2002) provide evidence that opening up the stock market to foreign investors renders stock returns more volatile and more highly correlated with the world market return.

1.2.3 Geography

There is less work directly addressing the potential correlation between geography and financial development in comparison to that for policy and institutions. However, much research attention has been paid to the importance of geography for general economic development, emphasizing three aspects in particular.

The first group is concerned with the correlation between latitude and economic development. Countries closer to the equator typically have a more tropical climate. On the one hand, research by Kamarck (1976), Diamond (1997), Gallup *et al.* (1999) and Sachs (2003a, 2003b) suggests that tropical location may lead directly to poor crop yields and production due to adverse ecological conditions such as fragile tropical soils, unstable water supply and prevalence of crop pests. On the other hand, tropical location can be characterized as an inhospitable disease environment, which is believed to be a primary cause for "extractive" institutions (Acemoglu *et al.*, 2001).

A second strand of research relates to countries being landlocked, distant from large markets or having only limited access to coasts and rivers navigable to the ocean (Sachs and Warner, 1995a, 1995b, 1997; Easterly and Levine, 2003; Malik and Temple, 2009). As natural barriers to external trade and knowledge dissemination, geographic isolation and remoteness to some extent determine the scale and structure of external trade in which countries engage. The potential to enter a large economic market and exploit economies of scale may be limited by particular geographic circumstances. The ability to develop a competitive manufacturing sector may be constrained when some intermediate inputs for the production of manufactured goods need to be imported from distant markets. As the main feature of external trade for these countries, the limited range of primary commodities exported determines the vulnerability of these countries to external shocks.

The last strand of research focuses on the link between resource endowment and economic development. Diamond (1997) suggests that countries with a richer endowment of grain species have more potential for high-yielding food crops and technological development. Isham *et al.* (2005) argue that a developing country's natural resource endowment affects its economic development through an unique channel in which natural resource endowment is linked to different export structures, different export structures determine institutional capacities towards coping with external shocks and finally institutional quality is reflected in the level of GDP per capita. Easterly and Levine (2003) argue that the natural endowment of tropics, germs and crops indirectly influences income through the impacts of these on institutions.

In general, geography is likely to work mainly through the demand side of financial development, although it may affect its supply side by influencing the quality of institutions. For instance, the production of particular agricultural products or primary goods and exploitation of some natural resources could reduce the demand for external finance, relative to other countries at a similar level of GDP per capita.

1.2.4 Other variables

Other variables considered as determinants of financial development are economic growth, the income level, population level and religious, language and ethnic characteristics, etc. Greenwood and Jovanovic (1990) and Saint-Paul (1992) document that as the economy grows, the costs of financial intermediation decrease due to intensive competition, inducing a larger scale of funds available for productive investment. The importance of income levels for financial development has been addressed in Levine (1997, 2003, 2005). In considering banking sector development in 23 transition economies, Jaffee and Levonian (2001) demonstrate that the level of GDP per capita and the saving rate have positive effects on the banking system structure as measured by bank assets, numbers, branches and employees.

Stulz and Williamson (2003) stress the impact of differences in culture, proxied by differences in religion and language, on the process of financial development. They provide evidence that culture predicts cross-country variation in protection and enforcement of investor rights, especially of creditor rights. The evidence also shows that the influence of culture on creditor rights protection is mitigated by the introduction of trade openness. Djankov *et al.* (2003) shed light on the role of state ownership of the media in the extent of financial development.

1.3 Structure of the book

This research starts from a general examination of fundamental determinants of financial market development, and moves on to specific studies as to the effects of aggregate private investment and institutional improvement on financial development. It ends up with a study on the geographic determinants of carbon market development in developing countries, mainly the Clean Development Mechanism (CDM) markets.

The structure of this book is outlined as follows:

Chapter 2 is concerned with the main determinants of cross-country differences in financial development. Two prominent tools for addressing model uncertainty, Bayesian Model Averaging and General-to-specific approaches, are jointly applied to investigate the financial development effects of a wide range of variables taken from various sources. The analysis suggests that the level of financial development in a country is mainly influenced by the latter's overall level of development, the origins of its legal system and the quality of its institutions.

Chapter 3 provides an exhaustive analysis of the causality between financial development and another important aspect of economic activities, namely aggregate private investment. It uses recently developed panel data techniques on data for 43 developing countries over the period 1970–98. GMM estimation on averaged data, and a common factor approach on annual data allowing for global interdependence and heterogeneity across countries, suggest positive causal effects going in both directions. This finding has rich implications for the development of financial markets and the conduct of macroeconomic policies in developing countries in an integrated global economy. GMM results based on averaged data appear in the *Journal of Statistics: Advanced in Theory and Applications*, 2009, 2(2), whilst GMM results based on annual data appear in an *Empirical Economics* Special Issue on "New Perspectives on Finance and Development", 2010.

Chapter 4 studies the effect of institutional improvement on financial development in two steps. It examines whether political liberalization in terms of institutional improvement promotes financial development, using a panel dataset of 90 developed and developing countries over the period 1960–99, revealing a positive effect on financial development at least in the short run, particularly for lower-income countries, ethnically divided countries and French legal origin countries. The results of this chapter appear in *World Development*, 2010 38(12).

Chapter 5 studies what induces governments to undertake reforms aimed at financial development. Its starting point is Abiad and Mody (2005). Rather than their ordered logit technique, it uses a within groups approach allowing for error dependence across countries and over time. This chapter finds that policy change in a country is negatively rather than positively associated with its liberalization level, while the regional liberalization gap appears less relevant. On the effects of shocks and crises, it suggests that some of the Abiad and Mody (2005) findings are robust, but others are fragile. Furthermore, it claims that the extent of democracy is important for this analysis, and identifies a negative effect of the extent of democracy on policy reform. Some results of this chapter appear in the *Journal of Applied Econometrics*, 2009, 24(7).

Chapter 6 examines whether certain geographic endowments matter for the CDM market development. It suggests that CDM credit flows in a country are positively affected by those in its neighbouring countries. Countries with higher absolute latitudes and elevations tend to initiate more CDM projects, whereas countries having richer natural resources do not seem to undertake more CDM projects. This finding sheds light on the geographic determinants of uneven CDM development across countries, and has implications for developing countries in terms of international cooperation and national capacity building for effective access to the CDM.

2
General Determinants of Financial Development

2.1 Introduction

This chapter attempts to examine systematically the factors that might account for cross-country differences in financial development. It employs two modern quantitative methods, Bayesian Model Averaging (BMA) and General-to-specific (Gets) approaches, to gauge the robustness of a selection of possible determinants of financial development. Special emphasis has been placed on the contributions that institutions, policy and geography may have in developing financial markets.

First, we take a look at some simple contrasts in the financial development experience. The United Kingdom and France have similar levels of GDP per capita, democratic institutions and geographic characteristics in terms of latitude, access to the sea and distance from large markets. Nevertheless, they follow different legal traditions, reflected in different legal practices towards the protection of private property rights. In the 1990s, stock market capitalization to GDP ratio in the UK was more than three times higher than that in France, while the ratio of private credit to GDP in the UK (112%) was noticeably higher than the same ratio in France (89%). How much of the difference in financial depth between the UK and France is due to the difference in their legal traditions and practices?

The financial development experience in Latin American countries provides an enlightening example of the possible role of macroeconomic policies in financial development given the similarities of geographic conditions, institutional development and cultural characteristics. After implementing market-oriented policies in the 1970s and establishing prudential regulations in the 1980s, Chile achieved remarkable growth in financial intermediary development and stock market capitalization, and has been regarded as the financial leader in Latin America since the mid-1980s. In the 1990s both the ratio of liquid liabilities to GDP and the ratio of private credit to GDP in Chile were 50 percentage points higher than those of Brazil, the second best country in the region. Stock market capitalization as a fraction of GDP in Chile in the 1990s was 78%, at least three times larger than that in any other Latin American country. How much of the success of Chilean financial development is due to better macroeconomic policies?

In the 1990s the ratio of credit issued to the private sector to GDP in Canada was 94%, more than four times higher than that in Mexico of 23%. Stock market capitalization as a fraction of GDP in Canada in 1990s was 65%, more than twice as high as in Mexico (31%). Canada and Mexico share a number of similarities in terms of geographic endowments and institutional development. More specifically, both of them have access to the sea, have a long border with the biggest developed country, have a large land area and a democratic political system, etc. However, among other factors, Canada and Mexico apparently differ in income level and latitude, which is associated with historical dominance of tropical cash crops in Mexico and grain in Canada. How much of the difference in financial depth between Canada and Mexico is due to the difference in income level and how much is due to their geographic endowment, and its long-run effects on institutions?

Exploring what determines financial development has become an increasingly significant research topic in recent years. Examples are La Porta *et al.* (1997, 1998), Beck *et al.* (2003), Rajan and Zingales (2003) and Stulz and Williamson (2003) to mention a few. La Porta *et al.* (1997, 1998) have made a significant contribution to this topic with regard to the legal determinants of financial development. By applying the settler mortality hypothesis of Acemoglu *et al.* (2001) to financial development, Beck *et al.* (2003) address how institutions matter for financial development. The Rajan and Zingales (2003) interest groups theory argues that politics matter for financial development. Stulz and Williamson (2003) illustrate that culture matters, although it may be tempered by openness. As to the role of policy, among others, Baltagi *et al.* (2009) study the importance of trade openness, whilst Chinn and Ito (2006) focus on the effect of financial openness.

Besides this, there is a large body of research aiming to identify the determinants of financial development, ranging from some emphasizing macroeconomic factors such as inflation, the income level (in terms of GDP per capita) and the saving rate to others stressing institutional and geographic factors. Since the relevant economic theories provide limited guidance on the specification of a cross-country regression for financial development, it is not clear which of these factors, acting relatively independently, plays the primary role in determining financial development when they are all taken into consideration. Formally speaking, there is a model uncertainty problem concerning which variables should be included in the model to capture the underlying data-generating process.

When facing a situation where a vast literature suggests a variety of economic policy, political and institutional factors as determinants of long-run average growth rates, Levine and Renelt (1992) raised a concern over the robustness of existing conclusions in cross-section growth regressions. They found that only a few variables can be regarded as robust determinants of growth and almost all results are "fragile". They suggested applying a version of "extreme bounds analysis" to the problem of model uncertainty. Motivated by this influential work, Sala-i-Martin (1997a, 1997b), Fernandez et al. (2001) and Sala-i-Martin et al. (2004) are significant works among others that have investigated the contributions of various factors to cross-country growth. These works have emphasized the Bayesian method as a potential technique for addressing model uncertainty.

Empirical research on the determinants of financial development encounters a similar model uncertainty problem to that on economic growth. This chapter is the first attempt to study extensively the structural determinants of financial development using a large array of variables, by jointly applying BMA and the so-called LSE Gets approach, which is another modern method aiming to recover the true data-generating process. The Gets method has been recently developed and advocated by David Hendry and other practitioners (Hoover and Perez, 1999; Krolzig and Hendry, 2001 and Hendry and Krolzig, 2005 for example). To date, BMA and Gets have become more and more popular for the purpose of model selection, although the theory of econometric model selection is still underdeveloped.

Not only will this chapter look at each individual factor, but it also pays special attention to the roles of institutions, policy and geography in the process of financial development.[2] There has been substantial research on the role of institutions, policies and geography in the process of economic development in which much work regards institutions as the fundamental factor in long-run growth (Acemoglu et al., 2001; Dollar and Kraay, 2003; Easterly and Levine, 2003 and Rodrik et al., 2004). In particular, research by Easterly and Levine (2003) and Rodrik et al. (2004) highlights the dominant role of institutions over those of geography and policy. They argue that geography and policy affect economic development through institutions by influencing institutional quality, and the direct effect of geography and policy on development becomes weaker once institutions are controlled for. Is this also the case for financial development?

In three aspects, this chapter exhibits distinct innovations and strengths. First, it considers a wider assortment of economic, political and geographic variables than any previous study. The second aspect is its joint application of the BMA and Gets procedures, which combines the strengths of each method. By jointly applying two modern methods using a wide range of variables, more reliable conclusions can be expected. Third, since, as pointed out by Levine (2005), there is no uniformly accepted proxy for financial development currently available, this paper constructs a composite index of financial development using principal component analysis, which enables us to look at different dimensions of financial development including overall financial development, financial intermediary development, stock market development, financial efficiency development and financial size development (usually called "financial depth").

The analyses based on the BMA and Gets procedures lead to the following findings. Institutions, macroeconomic policies and geography, when taken as groups, together with cultural characteristics and the income level of a country, are significantly associated with the level of financial development. Of 39 variables taken individually, legal origins, a government quality index, a trade policy index, land area, initial GDP, initial population and the population fraction of speakers of the main Western languages are found to be important determinants of financial development. In particular, this research highlights the dominant roles played by initial GDP, legal origin and institutional quality in the process of financial development.

The following section includes a description of the data. Section 2.3 discusses the empirical strategy and is followed by the empirical results of both BMA and Gets in Section 2.4. Section 2.5 summarizes the conclusions.

2.2 The data

This section describes the sample of countries on which this study is undertaken, and the measures of financial development and potential determinants. Appendix Table A2.1 contains the description and sources of these variables and Appendix Table A2.2 presents summary statistics.

2.2.1 Samples

This study mainly investigates key determinants of five specific indices of financial development discussed in more depth below. For each financial index, there are three samples on which the investigation is based: the whole sample, a developing country sample and a smaller sample for which the La Porta *et al.* (1998) data are available. The whole sample is the main focus of the analysis. The developing countries in the settler mortality dataset of Acemoglu *et al.* (2001) form the main part of the developing country sample here. Looking at the smaller La Porta *et al.* (1998) sample makes it possible to examine whether differences in legal tradition, reflected in the protection of shareholders' and creditors' rights, determine cross-country differences in financial development. The countries included are listed in Appendix Table A2.3.

Note that the transition economies and small economies with a population of less than 500,000 in 1990 are excluded from the sample. The information on the transition economies and population size is from the World Bank Global Development Network Database (GDN) and the Penn World Table 6.2 from Heston *et al.* (2006), respectively.

2.2.2 Measures of financial development

Since there is no single aggregate index for financial development in the literature, we use principal component analysis based on widely used indicators of financial development to produce new aggregate indices.

Essentially the principal components analysis takes N specific indicators and produces new indices (the principal components) $X_1, X_2,...X_N$ that are mutually uncorrelated. Each principal component, as a linear combination of the N indicators, captures a different dimension of the data. Typically the variances of several of the principal components are low enough to be negligible, and hence the majority of the variation in the data will then be captured by a small number of indices. This chapter uses the first principal component, which accounts for the greatest amount of the variation in the original set of indicators, in the sense that the linear combination corresponding to the first principal component has the highest sample variance, subject to the constraint that the sum-of-squares of the weights placed on the (standardized) indicators is equal to one.

The conventional measures of financial development on which the principal component analysis is based are as follows.[3]

The first measure, Liquid Liabilities (*LLY*), is one of the major indicators used to measure the size, relative to the economy, of financial intermediaries, including three types of financial institutions: the central bank, deposit money banks and other financial institutions. It is calculated as the liquid liabilities of banks and non-bank financial intermediaries (currency plus demand and interest-bearing liabilities) over GDP.

The second indicator, Private Credit (*PRIVO*), is defined as the credit issued to the private sector by banks and other financial intermediaries divided by GDP, excluding credit issued to government, government agencies and public enterprises, as well as the credit issued by the monetary authority and development banks. It measures general financial intermediary activities provided to the private sector.

The third, Commercial-Central Bank (*BTOT*), is the ratio of commercial bank assets to the sum of commercial bank and central bank assets. It proxies the advantage of financial intermediaries in channelling savings to investment, monitoring firms, influencing corporate governance and undertaking risk management relative to the central bank.

Next are two efficiency measures for the banking sector. Overhead Costs (*OVC*) is the ratio of overhead costs to total bank assets. The Net Interest Margin (*NIM*) equals the difference between bank interest income and interest expenses, divided by total assets. A lower value of overhead costs and net interest margin is frequently interpreted as indicating greater competition and efficiency.

The last are three indices for stock market development.[4] Stock Market Capitalization (*MCAP*), the size index, is the ratio of the value of listed domestic shares to GDP. Total Value Traded (*TVT*), as an indicator to measure market activity, is the ratio of the value of domestic shares traded on domestic exchanges to GDP, and can be used to gauge market liquidity on an economy-wide basis. Turnover Ratio (*TOR*) is the ratio of the value of domestic share transactions on domestic exchanges to the total value of listed domestic shares. A high value of the turnover ratio will indicate a more liquid (and potentially more efficient) equity market.

The data are obtained from the World Bank's Financial Structure and Economic Development Database (2008) and averaged over 1990–2001. Any country for which fewer than three years of data are available is omitted from the sample.

Appendix Table A2.4 presents the eigenvalues, proportion explained and the eigenvector of each first principal component from which the new indices of financial development are defined. It reports the sample variance of each first principal component (linear combination), the proportion of the variance in the raw data the first principal component accounts for and the coefficient (weight) of each existing standardized measure in the linear combination.

16 *Determinants of Financial Development*

(1) The first is a measure of overall financial development, denoted by *FD*. This is based on eight components, namely Liquid Liabilities, Private Credit, Commercial-central Bank, Overhead Cost, Net Interest Margin, Stock Market Capitalization, Value Traded and Turnover. The first principal component accounts for 49% of the variation in these seven indicators. In Appendix Table A2.4 the coefficients of each financial indicator for *FD* indicate the negative correlations between the Overhead Cost and Net Interest Margin and *FD*, and the positive correlations between the rest and *FD*.

(2) A second measure, *FDBANK*, captures the extent of bank-based intermediation. It uses five indicators, Liquid Liabilities, Private Credit, Commercial-central Bank, Overhead Costs and Net Interest Margin. *FDBANK* accounts for 61% of the variation in these five indicators.

(3) A third measure, *FDSTOCK* is a measure of stock market development, based on Stock Market Capitalization, Value Traded and Turnover. *FDSTOCK* accounts for 66% of the variations in these financial indices.

(4) A fourth measure, *FDEFF*, captures financial efficiency. The four indicators of financial efficiency used are Overhead Cost, Net Interest Margin, Value Traded and Turnover. *FDEFF* accounts for 54% of the total variation in these indicators. Lower values of this index indicate a higher level of financial efficiency.

(5) A fifth measure, *FDSIZE*, based solely on Liquid Liabilities and Stock Market Capitalization, captures the size of financial system (also called "financial depth"). The first principal component of these two measures accounts for 81% of the variation.

2.2.3 The potential determinants

Potential determinants of financial development considered in this analysis are widely selected from various sources. To discover the structural determinants of financial development, they are either those "predetermined" like fixed factors, or those "evolving slowly over time" like some institutional factors which are averaged over 1960–89. All variables that could potentially cause serious endogeneity problems are excluded.[5] The candidate determinants are grouped into four categories as showed in Appendix Table A2.1. The problem of missing data has been addressed by using a set of fixed factors as independent variables to impute the missing data. The fixed factors used include some regional dummies, dummies for income levels and geographic factors for which we have a complete set of data. The imputation procedure is summarized in Appendix Table A2.5.

2.2.3.1 Institutional variables

This analysis firstly considers legal origin dummies from the GDN dataset in the work by La Porta *et al.* (1997, 1998) on the legal determinants of financial development. The relevant variables are the common law legal origin dummy (*COMLEG*) for countries with British legal origin and a civil law legal origin dummy (*CIVLEG*) for countries with French, Germany and Scandinavian legal origins. Two variables closely related to the financial system itself are also considered.[6] Taken from the dataset of La Porta *et al.* (1998), *SRIGHT* is the aggregate index for shareholders' rights ranging from 0 to 6, while *CRIGHT* is the aggregate index for creditors' rights ranging from 0 to 4. These variables measure directly the extent to which the government protects the rights of shareholders and creditors.

In addition, this research makes use of some general institutional indicators. *POLITY2* and *DURABLE* are taken from the PolityIV Database (Marshall and Jaggers, 2009), and averaged over 1960–89. *POLITY2* is an index of democracy, seeking to reflect government type and institutional quality based on freedom of suffrage, operational constraints and balances on executives and respect for other basic political rights and civil liberties. It is called the "combined polity score", equal to the democracy score minus the autocracy score. The democracy and autocracy scores are derived from six authority characteristics (regulation, competitiveness and openness of executive recruitment, operational independence of chief executive or executive constraints and regulation and competition of participation). Based on these criteria, each country is assigned a democracy score and autocracy score ranging from 0 to 10. Accordingly, *POLITY2* ranges from -10 to 10 with higher values representing more democratic regimes. *DURABLE* is an index of political stability, using the number of years since the last transition in the type of regime or independence. The next variable is *FREE*, the average of the indices of civil liberties and political rights from the Freedom House Country Survey (2008) over 1972–89. Higher ratings indicate better civil liberties and political rights such as freedom to develop views, institutions and personal autonomy from government. I also employ *KKM* and *PCI*. The *KKM* measure from Kaufmann *et al.* (2008) is a widely used indicator of the quality of government in a broader sense, derived by averaging six measures of government quality: voice and accountability, political stability and absence of violence, government effectiveness, light regulatory burden, rule of law and freedom from graft. The variable *PCI*, measuring narrowly the constraints on the executive, is derived by Henisz

18 *Determinants of Financial Development*

(2000). The last institutional variable I use is *EURO*1900, the percentage of population that was European or of European descent in 1900, taken from Acemoglu *et al.* (2001). Although missing values for *EURO*1900, *SRIGHT*, *CRIGHT* and the market share of state-owned media (discussed below) are imputed, the variable *EURO*1900 appears only in the developing country sample while the others appear only in the La Porta sample.

2.2.3.2 Policy variables

To examine whether macroeconomic policy variables explain cross-country variation in financial development, this research makes extensive use of five economic volatility indicators and three trade openness indicators. It uses output volatility and inflation volatility to capture macroeconomic mismanagement and fluctuations. The output volatility measure (*SDGR*) is defined as the standard deviation of the annual growth rate of real, chain-weighted GDP per capita over 1960–89 from the Penn World Table 6.2. Inflation volatility (*SDPI*) is defined as the standard deviation of the annual inflation rate over 1960–89 from the World Development Indicators (2008). Taken from the GDN, the volatility of the black market premium (*SDBMP*), volatility of the terms of trade (*SDTT*) and trading partners' output volatility (*SDTP*) are used to reflect the extent of external shocks. *SDBMP* is defined as the standard deviation of the annual black market premium (*BMP*) over 1960–89. *SDTT* is defined as the standard deviation of the first log-differences of a terms of trade index for goods and services. *SDTP* is the standard deviation of trading partners' GDP per capita growth (weighted average by trade share).

To assess the role of trade factors, this research uses dummies for fuel and non-fuel primary goods exporting countries (*EXPPRIM*) and manufactured goods exporting countries (*EXPMANU*) from the GDN. A trade openness policy index, *TOPEN*, available from the database of Harvard University's Center for International Development (Gallup *et al.*, 1999), is utilized to measure the extent of openness to external trade in the presence of government intervention over 1965–90, while the trade share proposed by Frankel and Romer (1999), denoted by *CTRADE*, is employed to capture natural openness to external trade. *CTRADE* is derived by Frankel and Romer (1999) by summing up all bilateral trade with all potential trading partners from a bilateral trade equation that controls for population and land area of the home country and trading partners, the distance between any two trading partners and whether or not the home country is landlocked.

2.2.3.3 Geographic variables

To examine the role of geography, this study takes six regional dummies from the GDN for East Asian and Pacific countries (*REGEAP*), Middle Eastern and North African countries (*REGMENA*), Western European and North American countries (*REGWENA*), South Asian countries (*REGSA*), Sub-Saharan African countries (*REGSSA*) and Latin American and Caribbean countries (*REGLAC*), respectively. It also uses the following two geographic variables from the GDN. The landlocked variable (*LANDLOCK*) is a dummy variable that takes the value of 1 if the country has no coastal access to the ocean, and 0 otherwise. There are 17 landlocked countries in the whole sample. Absolute latitude (*LATITUDE*) equals the absolute distance of a country from the Equator. The closer to the equator the countries are, the more tropical climate they have.[7] Latitude potentially has an institutional interpretation since smaller absolute latitudes are associated with more unfavourable environments, which are associated with weaker institutions according to the settler mortality hypothesis of Acemoglu *et al.* (2001). The land area (*AREA*) in square kilometres for each country, taken from Hall and Jones (1999), is in logs.

This study also makes use of three additional geographic variables. One is *POP100CR* from the database of Harvard University's Center for International Development. It is the 1994 share of population within 100 km of a coast or navigable river for a country. Another is *MINDIST*, based on data from Jon Haveman's International Trade website. This captures the minimum distance from the three capital-goods-supplying centres in the world (USA, Japan and the EU, the centre of the latter represented by Belgium). The study uses the logarithm of the minimum distance from the three capital-goods-supplying centres plus one. These variables might be highly correlated with external trade and manufacturing, since lack of access to coasts or rivers navigable to the ocean and geographic remoteness constitute natural disadvantages to external trade. A further variable for geographic endowment is a dummy for the point source natural resource exporting countries (*RESPOINT*) from Isham *et al.* (2005), who find that, in comparison to manufacturing exporters and exporters of "diffuse" natural resources (e.g. wheat, rice and animals) and coffee/cocoa natural resources, the exporting countries of "point source" natural resources (e.g. oil, diamonds and plantation crops) are more likely to have severe social and economic divisions, and less likely to develop socially cohesive mechanisms and effective institutional capacities for managing shocks.

2.2.3.4 Other variables

Other variables included in this analysis are initial income (*GDP90*), initial population (*POP90*), an ethnic fractionalization index (*ETHNIC*), an ethnic polarization index (*ETHPOL*), a religious fractionalization index (*RELIGION*), a language fractionalisation index (*LANGUAGE*), a European first language index (*EURFRAC*) and the market share of state-owned media, either television or newspapers (*MEDSHARE*).

The inclusion of the level of GDP per capita in 1990 (*GDP90*) is stimulated by work such as Greenwood and Smith (1997) on the feedback from growth in the economy to the development of financial markets. Population size is also closely related to indices of financial development since small countries tend to have higher ratios of liquid liabilities and private credit, having the potential to affect the overall results substantially. *GDP90* and *POP90*, the level of the population in 1990, are from the GDN and used in logs.

The variables *ETHNIC*, *RELIGION* and *LANGUAGE*, taken from Alesina *et al.* (2003), characterize social divisions and cultural differences, as does the variable *ETHPOL*, which is taken from Reynal-Querol and Montalvo (2005) to capture the extent to which a large ethnic minority faces an ethnic majority in a society. The *EURFRAC* measure, taken from Hall and Jones (1999), is the fraction of population speaking one of the major languages of Western Europe (English, French, German, Portuguese or Spanish) as a mother tongue. To some extent, this variable reflects not only the culture of the country, but also the history of colonization. It is therefore closely linked to some other variables like *EURO1900*, *CIVLEG* and *COMLEG*.

The market share of stated-owned media (*MEDSHARE*) is from Djankov *et al.* (2003), which shows that greater state ownership of the media is associated with less political and economic freedom, inferior governance, less developed capital markets and poor health outcomes. Djankov *et al.* (2003) consider two kinds of media state ownership. One is press state ownership, the market share of state-owned newspapers out of the aggregate market share of the five largest daily newspapers (by circulation), and the other is television state ownership, the market share of state-owned television stations out of the aggregate market share of the five largest television stations (by viewer). The index used here is the average of the two media state ownerships.

2.3 Empirical strategy

This section discusses the empirical strategies for dealing with model uncertainty faced by research on the determinants of financial development, with the central focus placed on BMA and Gets approaches.

As summarized in the Introduction, substantial research has been done to explore the origins of financial development, leading to a large number of candidate determinants. Essentially the associated theories, developed under specific settings, are not mutually exclusive, raising concern over the robustness of these candidate determinants in any cross-section regression used to explain financial development.

Usually, the uncertainty about the composition of a regression model is called "model uncertainty". To handle the model uncertainty issue, a number of methodologies have been proposed and widely debated. Among others, the Extreme Bounds Analysis (EBA), BMA and Gets are the most famous methods.

To handle the model uncertainty issue, a number of methodologies have been proposed and widely debated. Among others, the EBA,[8] BMA[9] and Gets[10] are the most widely used methods. Although the BMA and Gets procedures have respective advantages in handling model uncertainty, neither of them is without limits or exempt from criticism.[11] This research chooses to apply the BMA and Gets procedures jointly to handle model uncertainty in this context. The combination of Gets and BMA analyses has the advantage of incorporating their merits while circumventing some of their limitations. In what follows, I set out the methods of BMA and Gets in more detail.

2.3.1 Bayesian Model Averaging

This section begins with a brief review of the development of BMA approach.

Following the seminal work by Levine and Renelt (1992), Sala-i-Martin (1997a,b)[12], Fernandez *et al.* (2001)[13] and Sala-i-Martin *et al.* (2004) are among the significant works using BMA to study the robustness of cross-country growth regressions. Based on work by Raftery (1995), Sala-i-Martin *et al.* (2004) propose a version of BMA called Bayesian Averaging of Classical Estimates (BACE), in which diffuse priors are assumed for the parameters and only one other prior, relating to the expected model size, is required. This approach has generated evidence in favour of Sala-i-Martin (1997a,b)'s original findings as well.

Essentially, BMA treats parameters and models as random variables and attempts to summarize the uncertainty about the model in terms of a probability distribution over the space of possible models. More specifically, it is used to average the posterior distribution for the parameters under all possible models, where the weights are the posterior model probabilities (*PMPs*). To evaluate these, the BMA uses the Bayesian Information Criterion (*BIC*) to approximate the Bayes factors which are needed to compute the posterior model probability, whose derivation is described in the Appendix Text.

Typically, the number of possible models, 2^p given p candidate variables, is large. Most applications of BMA to larger datasets do not average over all possible models, but use a search algorithm to identify the subset of models with greatest relevance. The Occam's Window and Markov Chain Monte Carlo techniques can be adopted for this purpose.[14] The approach developed by Hoeting *et al.* (1996) has the advantage of selecting variables and identifying outliers simultaneously, but requires a larger sample size relative to the regressor set, and so this method will be applied only in Table 2.1 below. The simpler version of BMA used elsewhere in this study follows Raftery *et al.* (1997) which focuses only on the subset defined by the Occam's Window technique and treats all the worst-fitting models outside the subset as having zero posterior probability. Embodying the principle of parsimony,[15] the use of the Occam's Window technique considerably reduces the number of possible models, and in the meantime encompasses the inherent model uncertainty present. Once the Occam's Window technique excludes the relatively unlikely models, the posterior model probabilities for the well-fitting models are then calculated.

Once we have posterior model probabilities, we are ready to implement a systematic form of inference for different quantities of interest. For example, when the interest is one of the regression parameters being present, whether positive or negative, what we need to do is to sum up the posterior model probabilities for all models in which the parameter is non-zero, be it positive or negative. In Sections 2.4 and 2.5 below, on the empirical results, the output of the BMA analysis includes the posterior inclusion probabilities for variables and a sign certainty index. The posterior inclusion probability (PIP) for any particular variable is the sum of the posterior model probabilities for all of the models including that variable. The higher the posterior probability for a particular variable, the more robust that determinant for financial development appears to be. For PIPs greater than 0.20, a sign certainty index rather than sign certainty probability is presented, indicating whether the relationship appear to be either positive or negative.[16]

2.3.2 General-to-specific approach

The Gets modelling strategy starts from the most general unrestricted model (GUM), which is assumed to characterize the essential data-generating process (DGP), applies standard testing procedures to eliminate statistically insignificant variables and ends up with a "congruent" final model, which should be free of significant mis-specification. Hoover and Perez (1999) make important advances in practical modelling, like the multiple-path approach to Gets model selection. Based on these, the PcGets algorithm has been developed to embody the principles of the underlying theory of Gets reductions extensively discussed in Hendry (1995).

The selection of models by PcGets roughly includes three stages.[17]

The first stage concerns the estimation and testing of the GUM. The GUM should be formulated carefully based on previous empirical and theoretical findings, institutional knowledge and data characteristics. The specification of the GUM should be sufficiently general with a relatively orthogonal parameterization for the N candidate regressors. The next step is to conduct a mis-specification test for "congruence" of the initial GUM. The congruence of the initial GUM is maintained through the selection process to ensure a congruent final model. Once the congruence of the GUM is established, pre-search reduction tests are conducted at a loose significance level. The statistically insignificant variables are eliminated both in blocks and individually, and the GUM reformulated as the baseline for the next stage.

The second stage is the search process. Many possible reduction paths are investigated to avoid path-dependent selection. The terminal model emerges from each path when all reduction diagnostic tests are valid and all remaining variables are significant. At the end of the path searches, all distinct terminal models are collected and tested against their union to find an un-dominated encompassing contender. If a unique model results, it is selected; otherwise, the "surviving" terminal models form a union as a new starting point for reduction. The search process continues until a unique model occurs, or the union coincides with either the original GUM or a previous union. If a union made up of mutually encompassing and un-dominated models results, PcGets employs the *BIC* to select the unique final model.

The third stage is the post-search evaluation. At this stage PcGets uses post-selection reliability checks to evaluate the significance of variables in the final model selected in two overlapping subsamples.

Obviously, the choice of critical values for pre-selection, selection encompassing tests and subsample post-selection is important for the success of the PcGets algorithm. It provides two basic strategies, liberal and conservative, for the levels of significance, degree of pretesting and so on. The liberal strategy tries to equate the probability of deleting relevant and retaining irrelevant variables, whilst the conservative strategy tries to reduce the chance of retaining irrelevant variables. The choice of different strategies hence affects the chance of either retaining irrelevant variables or dropping relevant variables. Throughout the chapter, PcGets

24 *Determinants of Financial Development*

is conducted with a more liberal strategy than the default setting of the "liberal strategy" as presented in Appendix Table A2.6,[18] aiming to keep all promising variables in the final model. The final conclusions are then based on the intersection of the BMA and Gets results.

2.4 Empirical results (I): Overall financial development

This section begins studying the determinants of various indices of financial development. The BMA and Gets methods are applied and compared in three different samples (the whole sample, the developing country sample and the La Porta sample) for each index. This section, the central contribution of this analysis, studies the determinants of overall financial development (*FD*). Section 2.5 is concerned with the determinants for four specific indexes of financial development, followed by a study of the determinants of bond market development.

2.4.1 Some stylized facts

As a starting point, it might be useful to look at some stylized facts on the links between some important institutional, policy and geographic variables and *FD*. These figures are based on the whole sample.

Figure 2.1 presents two scatter plots for the links between institutions and financial development. Better institutional quality, captured by *KKM*, and a more democratic regime, captured by *POLITY2*, are associated with higher values for *FD*. The trade policy index denoted by *TOPEN* and Frankel-Romer trade share denoted by *CTRADE* are positively related to *FD* in Figure 2.2. The upper chart of Figure 2.3 indicates that countries closer to the main world market centres achieve a higher level of *FD*, while the lower chart shows that financial markets in countries further from the equator are relatively more advanced.

Figure 2.4 portrays the evolution of averaged liquid liability (*LLY*) over 1960–2003 by different country groups. Note from the upper-left chart that countries in all income groups experienced an increase in *LLY*, although higher-income countries remain at a higher level of financial development than lower-income countries throughout. The upper-right chart shows considerable differences in averaged *LLY* between manufactured goods exporting countries and primary goods exporters in which the latter remain at lower levels or at least partially financially repressed. The lower-left chart shows that the level of *LLY* in West European and North American countries was much higher and more stable than that in other country groups. The development process of *LLY* in East Asian and Pacific countries was much more pronounced relative to that in any other country group. In the lower-right chart, the development performance

General Determinants of Financial Development 25

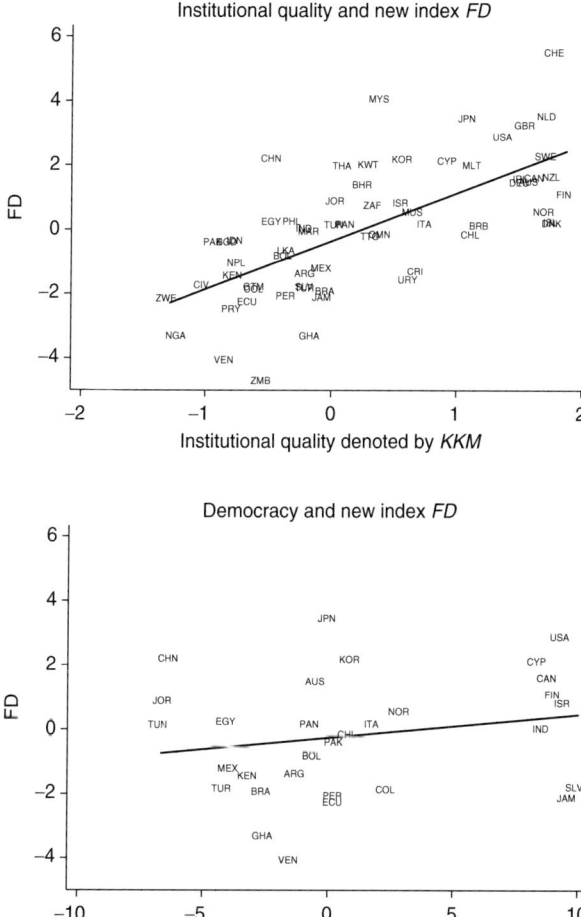

Figure 2.1 Scatter plots of institutions and financial development

Note: Variables and data sources are described in Appendix Table A2.1. These figures show scatter plots of the institutional quality denoted by *KKM*, and the democracy index *POLITY2*, against the new index *FD*.

of *LLY* in common law countries was in general much more gradual, with the whole process stretching over four decades compared to that in civil law countries, which experienced surges in the 1970s and late 1990s, but a decline in the late 1980s.

26 *Determinants of Financial Development*

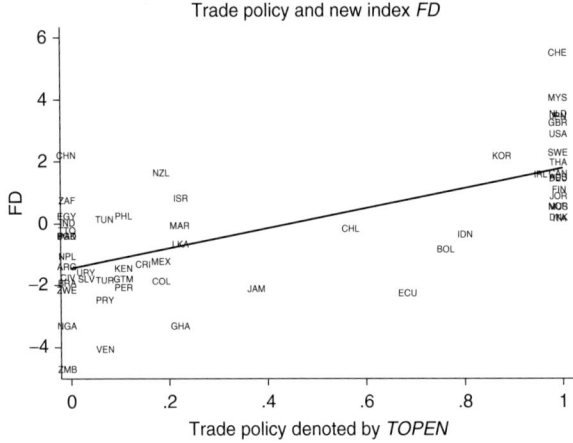

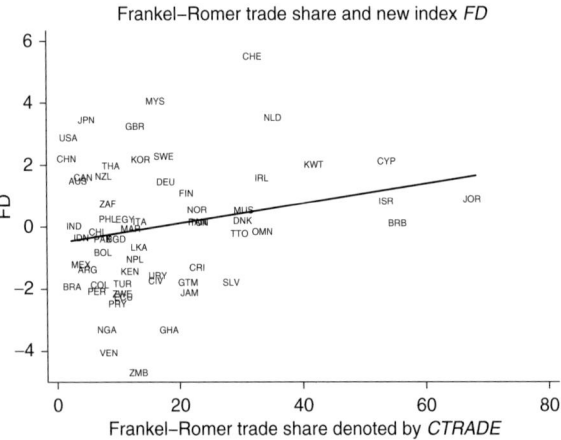

Figure 2.2 Scatter plots of policy and financial development

Note: Variables and data sources are described in Appendix Table A2.1. These figures show scatter plots of the trade policy index from Gallup *et al.* (1999), and the trade share constructed by Frankel and Romer (1999), against the new index *FD*.

The figures above have shown some interesting facts on the determinants of *FD*. However, a clear conclusion on the robustness of any variable presented cannot readily be drawn. The task of the subsequent Section 2.4.2 is to examine these links more systematically.

General Determinants of Financial Development 27

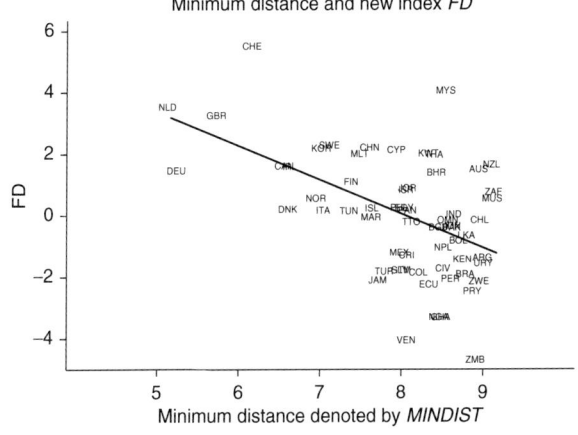

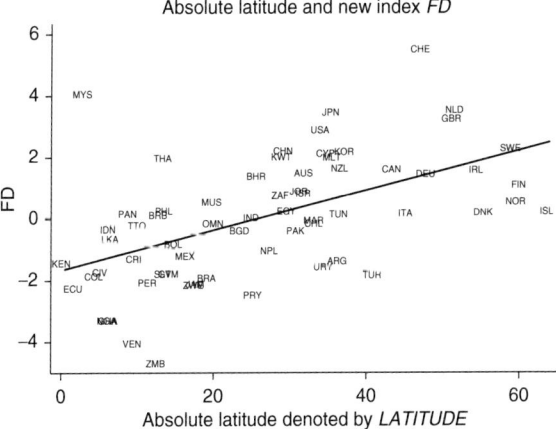

Figure 2.3 Scatter plots of geography and financial development

Note: Variables and data sources are described in Appendix Table A2.1. These figures show scatter plots of the logarithm of minimum distance, and the absolute latitude, against the new index *FD*.

2.4.2 What are the main determinants of *FD*?

As mentioned earlier, much research regards institutions as the fundamental factor in long-run growth, and some even argue that the only effect of geography on development is via institutions (Acemoglu *et al.*,

28 Determinants of Financial Development

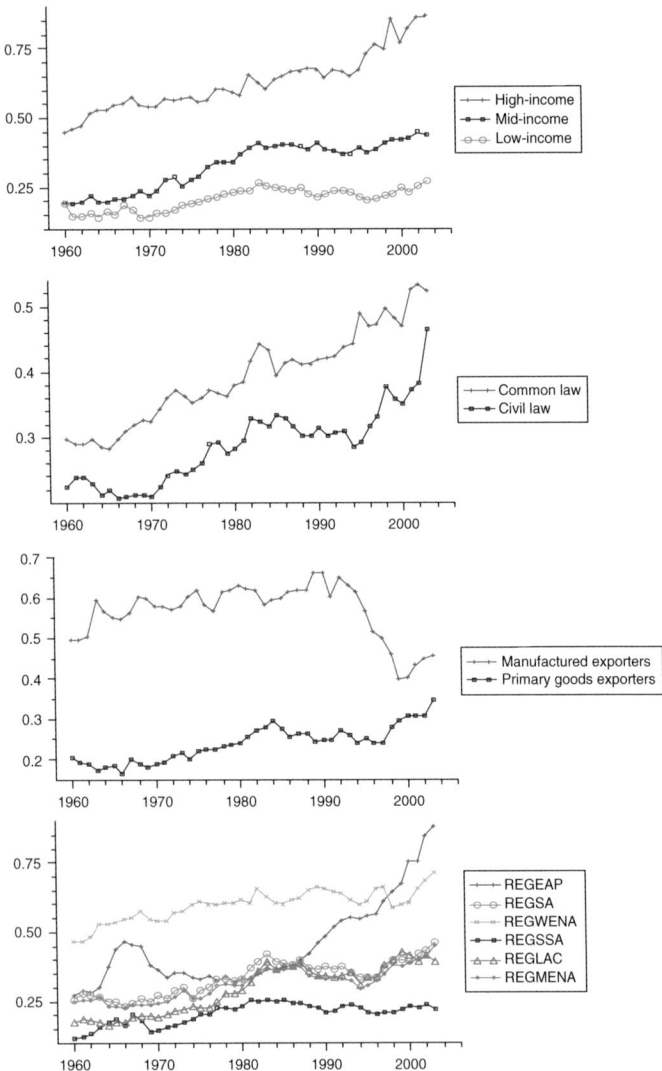

Figure 2.4 Median Liquid Liability by different country group over 1960–2003

Note: Variable descriptions are from Appendix Table A2.1. These figures plot the median liquid liabilities by different income groups in the upper-left chart, countries with different law traditions in the upper-right chart, different exporting countries in the lower-left chart and different regions in the lower-right chart over 1960–2003.

2001; Dollar and Kraay, 2003; Easterly and Levine, 2003 and Rodrik *et al.*, 2004). Before proceeding to study the main determinants of overall *FD*, this section starts by testing the hypothesis of whether any of three determinants (institutions, policy and geography), considered as a whole, dominates the other two.

Table 2.1 reports the BMA results for determinants of *FD*, which is measured over 1990–99, for 64 countries in the whole sample. All possible explanatory variables are grouped into four blocks in the order of "other" variables, geographic variables, policy variables and institutional variables. In addition to including the "other" variables, models 1–3 include any two of the three blocks (geographic variables, policy variables and institutional variables) to examine the combined effects of any two types of determinants on *FD*.[19]

The BMA analysis yields posterior inclusion probabilities (either "PIPs" or "MC^3"),[20] the total posterior model probabilities for the set of models which include a given variable of interest and the sign certainty index ("Sign") of a relationship discussed above. The PIPs are the posterior inclusion probabilities calculated by using the method from Raftery (1995). A sign certainty index is provided where the PIPs are above 0.2. The MC^3 denotes the posterior inclusion probabilities computed by using the Markov Chain Monte Carlo techniques due to Hoeting *et al.* (1996), which conduct variable selection and outlier identification simultaneously. Any MC^3 greater than 0.2 is shown in bold.

Looking at the first block of "other" variables across models, we note that initial income, *GDP90*, appears to be important in almost all models with a high posterior probability of inclusion, meaning that, as expected, the level of GDP per capita is fundamental in explaining the cross-country variation in *FD*. Other variables in this block exhibit varying explanatory power for *FD*. Models 1 and 2 present the effect of geography on *FD* when policy and institutions, respectively, are controlled for. The effect of geography on *FD* doesn't seem to disappear when the institutional variables are present, implying that the usual claim that geography works through institutions is not necesarily true in this context. The two BMA methods show that two regional dummies (*REGSSA* and *REGLAC*) appear to be closely related to *FD*, meaning that a number of developing countries in these regions are associated with higher levels of financial development in the 1990s, conditional on other variables. The regional dummy *REGEAP* and land area (*AREA*) also appear to be important predictors of *FD* when institutions are controlled for. Similarly, policy has a significant effect on *FD* in the presence of geography and institutions (Models 1 and 3). Among others, at least *EXPPRIM* is significant in both

Table 2.1 Determinants of FD by using BMA

	Whole 64 1			Whole 64 2			Whole 64 3		
Variable	PIPs	Sign	MC^3	PIPs	Sign	MC^3	PIPs	Sign	MC^3
CONSTANT	1.000	(−)		1.000	(−)		1.000	(−)	
GDP90	0.466	(+)	0.342	0.941	(+)	**0.488**	0.744	(+)	**0.689**
POP90	0.000		0.026	0.969	(+)	**0.839**	0.941	(+)	**0.517**
ETHPOL	0.004		0.039	0.649	(+)	0.070	0.906	(+)	0.035
ETHNIC	0.000		0.028	0.014		**0.962**	0.000		**0.333**
RELIGION	1.000	(+)	0.029	0.056		0.071	0.099		0.029
LANGUAGE	0.000		0.056	0.036		**0.995**	0.000		**0.962**
EURFRAC	0.000		**0.992**	0.706	(−)	0.040	0.982	(−)	0.089
REGEAP	0.186		0.132	0.726	(+)	**0.958**			
REGMENA	0.314	(+)	0.176	0.006		0.060			
REGSA	0.186		0.110	0.053		0.037			
REGSSA	0.879	(−)	**0.946**	0.642	(−)	0.049			
REGLAC	0.872	(−)	**0.942**	0.385	(−)	0.071			
REGWENA	0.204	(−)	0.175	0.036		0.094			
LANDLOCK	0.000		0.065	0.003		**0.208**			
LATITUDE	0.000		0.056	0.386	(−)	0.063			
AREA	0.073		0.034	0.975	(−)	**0.831**			
MINDIST	0.030		0.032	0.012		**0.623**			
POP100CR	0.051		0.027	0.400	(−)	0.056			
RESPOINT		0.037	0.005	0.025					
TOPEN	0.850	(+)	**0.927**				0.045		**0.309**
CTRADE	0.099		0.049				0.215	(+)	0.050
EXPMANU	0.000		0.030				0.000		0.025
EXPPRIM	0.409	(−)	0.175				0.999	(−)	**0.964**
SDGR	0.000		0.031				0.000		0.069
SDBMP	0.252	(−)	0.192				0.000		0.126
SDPI	0.076		0.030				0.064		0.053
SDTP	0.000		0.023				0.398	(+)	**0.228**
SDTT	0.329	(−)	**0.201**				0.045		0.026
CIVLEG				0.589	(−)	**0.740**	0.461	(−)	**0.867**
COMLEG				0.361	(−)	0.358	0.128		**0.467**
POLITY2				0.291	(+)	0.051	0.258	(+)	0.050
DURABLE				0.300	(+)	0.058	0.022		0.031
FREE				0.020		0.069	0.006		0.084
KKM				0.988	(+)	**1.000**	1.000	(+)	**0.999**
PCI				0.963	(−)	**0.996**	0.924	(−)	**0.953**
EURO1900									
MEDSHARE									
SRIGHT									
CRIGHT									

Note: The dependent variable FD is the aggregate index of overall financial development over period, 1990–99. Variable description is in Appendix Table A2.1. BMA yields the posterior probabilities of inclusion (either "PIPs" or "MC^3"), the total posterior model probabilities for all models including a given variable and the sign certainty index of a relationship ("Sign"). A sign is given to PIPs greater than 0.2. No sign givern means the sign of estimated relationship being uncertain. Any MC^3 greater than 0.2 is in bold. The PIPs is taken from Raftery (1995) while the MC^3 is due to Hoeting et al. (1996) who also identify the outliers.

cases. Neither does the usual claim that policy works through institutions by affecting their quality apply to this context. Models 2 and 3 show that the role of institutions is not altered when geography and policy are controlled for. Note that most of the institutional variables appear to be significant predictors of *FD*, in particular, the *KKM* (governance index) and *PCI* (political constraints index) have a posterior probability of inclusion close to 1.

Overall, Table 2.1 has demonstrated that geography, institutions and policy as a group are all important in the process of financial development, although their effects may be picked up by varied predictors when conditioning on other factors is in place. These results clearly suggest that it would be more appropriate to include all of them in the analysis.

Table 2.2 contains a thorough study of determinants of *FD* by using BMA and Gets in which the above conclusion (in terms of geography, institutions and policy all being important) is embodied. The BMA analysis reports PIPs and the sign certainty index ("Sign") discussed above. The Gets analysis produces the coefficients and t-values for possible determinants in the final model. It also reports the residual sum-of-squares (RSS), the equation standard error or residual standard deviation (sigma), the squared multiple correlation coefficient (R^2) and its values adjusted for degree of freedom $\left(R^2_{adj}\right)$, the log-likelihood value and three information criteria: the Akaike Information Criterion (AIC), the Hannan-Quinn Criterion (HQ) and the Schwarz Criterion (SC). The output also includes three mis-specification tests (Chow test, Normality test and Heteroscedasticity test).[21] The Gets results in Table 2.2 are the final models for three samples, respectively, in Appendix Table A2.7, which clearly shows the variables included in the GUM and in the final model.

In Table 2.2, the BMA analysis for the whole sample yields a subset inclusive of four "other" variables (*GDP90*, *POP90*, *ETHPOL* and *EURFRAC*), two geographic variables (*REGEAP* and *AREA*), four policy variables (*CTRADE, EXPPRIM, SDBMP* and *SDPI*) and five institutional variables (*CIVLEG, COMLEG, DURABLE, KKM* and *PCI*). Given no rejection of the mis-specification tests, the Gets analysis for the whole sample yields a subset inclusive of three "other" variables (*GDP90, POP90* and *EURFRAC*), two geographic variables (*LATITUDE* and *AREA*), one policy variable (*SDTT*) and three institutional variables (*CIVLEG, KKM* and *PCI*). Both the BMA and Gets analyses on the whole sample unanimously suggest that three "other" variables (*GDP90, POP90* and *EURFRAC*), one geographic variable (*AREA*) and three institutional variables (*CIVLEG, KKM* and *PCI*) are the main determinants for *FD*.

Table 2.2 Determinants of FD

Variable	Whole BMA PIPs	Sign	Gets Coeff	t-value	Developing Country BMA PIPs	Sign	Gets Coeff	t-value	La Porta BMA PIPs	Sign	Gets Coeff	t-value
CONSTANT	1.000	(−)	−10.563	−4.074	1.000	(−)	−15.723	−5.932	1.000	(+)		
GDP90	0.946	(+)	1.391	4.403	1.000	(+)	2.049	7.192	0.012			
POP90	0.996	(+)	0.705	5.856	0.994	(+)	0.248	2.855	1.000	(+)	1.314	8.610
ETHPOL	0.999	(+)			0.007				0.039		3.131	4.652
ETHNIC	0.000				0.027				0.942	(+)		
RELIGION	0.004				0.492	(−)			0.067			
LANGUAGE	0.009				0.998	(+)	1.487	2.941	0.054			
EURFRAC	0.998	(−)	−1.287	−3.694	0.002				0.978	(−)	−3.988	−6.216
REGEAP	0.999	(+)			0.001				0.093		−4.224	−3.847
REGMENA	0.001				0.998	(−)			0.868	(+)		
REGSA	0.027				0.062				0.189		−3.000	−4.524
REGSSA	0.029				0.465	(−)	3.353	7.548	0.053			
REGLAC	0.019				0.008				0.069		2.435	3.317
REGWENA	0.002								0.965	(−)	−7.789	−5.614
LANDLOCK	0.009				0.005				0.993	(+)	2.562	3.979
LATITUDE	0.011				0.322	(−)			0.051			
AREA	0.992	(−)	−0.041	−2.948	0.817	(−)			1.000	(−)	−0.416	−4.095
MINDIST	0.003		−0.417	−4.188	0.046				0.241			
POP100CR	0.000				0.377	(+)			0.043		0.015	2.592
RESPOINT	0.023				1.000	(−)	3.353	7.548	0.434	(−)	−2.960	−4.633
TOPEN	0.001				1.000	(+)	1.990	5.192	0.985	(+)	1.854	3.512
CTRADE	0.492	(+)			0.903	(+)			0.050		0.034	2.421
EXPMANU	0.000				0.064						1.246	4.264
EXPPRIM	0.996	(−)			0.002				0.077		1.416	2.597
SDGR	0.000				0.005				0.980	(−)	−0.571	−3.875
SDBMP	0.346	(−)			0.658	(−)	0.120	0.004	4.876			

	PIP	Sign					PIP	Sign		
SDPI	0.700	(+)			1.000	(+)	0.001	2.193	0.504	(−)		−0.035	−5.076
SDTP	0.033				0.445	(−)			0.177			−1.390	−2.263
SDTT	0.130		−0.024	−3.270	0.000				0.037			0.036	3.222
CIVLEG	0.529	(−)	−0.927	−3.396	1.000	(−)	−4.562	−5.239	0.074				
COMLEG	0.205	(+)			1.000	(+)	−3.445	−3.879	0.074			1.687	4.452
POLITY2	0.058				0.992	(−)	0.164	4.382	0.059				
DURABLE	0.764	(+)			0.000				0.686	(+)			
FREE	0.002				0.035				0.035			−0.453	−3.033
KKM	1.000	(+)	1.846	5.064	0.370				0.992	(+)		4.849	9.156
PCI	0.995	(−)	−5.363	−5.184	1.000	(−)	−5.391	−4.026	0.995	(−)		−13.547	−7.002
EURO1900					0.002								
MEDSHARE									0.405	(−)			
SRIGHT									0.753	(+)			
CRIGHT									0.066			−0.374	−3.169
RSS			51.11				17.06					3.78	
sigma			0.97				0.73					0.50	
R^2			0.80				0.86					0.98	
Radj^2			0.77				0.82					0.94	
LogLik			7.20				20.84					47.21	
AIC			0.09				−0.40					−1.11	
HQ			0.22				−0.22					−0.73	
SC			0.42				0.08					−0.05	
Chow test 1			0.66	0.68			0.28						
Chow test 2			8.46	0.01			0.41						
Normality test							1.35	1.76				1.35	0.51
Hetero test													

Note: The dependent variable *FD* is the aggregate index of overall financial development over the period, 1990–99. Variable description is in Appendix Table A2.1. There are 64 observations in the whole sample, 44 observations in the developing country sample and 40 observations in the La Porta sample. BMA analysis yields the posterior probabilities of inclusion (PIPs) and the sign certainty index of a relationship (Sign). No sign given means the sign of estimated relationship being uncertain. Gets analysis yields coefficients and *t*-values for the variables in the final model. See text for the description of PcGets output.

34 Determinants of Financial Development

Table 2.3 Top ten models and their posterior probabilities for FD

	1	2	3	4	5	6	7	8	9	10
GDP90	*	*	*	*	*	*	*	*	*	*
POP90	*	*	*	*	*	*	*	*	*	*
ETHPOL	*	*	*	*	*	*	*	*	*	*
EURFRAC	*	*	*	*	*	*	*	*	*	*
REGEAP	*	*	*	*	*	*	*	*	*	*
AREA	*	*	*	*	*	*	*	*	*	*
CTRADE			*	*	*		*	*		
EXPPRIM	*	*	*	*	*	*	*	*	*	*
SDBMP			*	*	*		*		*	
SDPI	*	*	*	*	*		*	*	*	*
SDTT										
CIVLEG	*	*	*	*		*			*	
COMLEG					*			*		*
DURABLE	*		*	*	*		*	*	*	*
KKM	*	*	*	*	*	*	*	*	*	*
PCI	*	*	*	*	*	*	*	*	*	*
PMP	0.048	0.042	0.042	0.037	0.030	0.028	0.028	0.028	0.028	0.025

Note: This table presents the top ten models for *FD*, ranked by their posterior model probability (PMP) in the whole sample. The variable description is in Appendix Table A2.1.

In Tables 2.1 and 2.2, the BMA procedure has yielded PIPs for all candidate variables. A natural question to ask is about the structure of the models, especially the models with higher explanatory power. Table 2.3 lists the structure of the top ten models for *FD* in the whole sample in terms of posterior model probabilities, serving as a concrete illustration of model selection. A noteworthy point is that all these models have more than ten possible predictors with geographic variables (such as *REGEAP*, *AREA*), policy variables (such as *EXPPRIM*) and institutional variables (like *KKM* and *PCI*) and "other" variables (like *GDP90*, *POP90*, *ETHPOL* and *EURFRAC*) present in all models. However, one should be aware of the dramatic model uncertainty, reflected by less than 5% posterior model probabilities for all top ten "best" models, which indicates the potential importance of the BMA and Gets procedures for model selection as a systematic response to pervasive model uncertainty.

Moving on one step further, OLS regressions are used to estimate some of the best performing models in Table 2.4. The best model, that is the model with highest posterior probability in Table 2.3, is presented in column 4. The "other" variables, like *GDP90*, *POP90* and *EURFRAC*, are

Table 2.4 Geography, policy, institutions and *FD*

	(1)	(2)	(3)	(4)
CONSTANT	−15.159	−8.220	−10.874	−8.056
	[5.87]**	[2.95]**	[3.33]**	[3.16]**
GDP90	1.312	0.990	1.000	0.958
	[6.25]**	[2.65]*	[2.93]**	[3.01]**
POP90	0.521	0.584	0.371	0.512
	[3.66]**	[4.75]**	[3.12]**	[4.72]**
ETHPOL	1.117	1.584	1.029	1.496
	[1.88]	[2.89]**	[1.65]	[3.17]**
EURFRAC	−0.801	−1.138	−1.143	−1.100
	[2.32]*	[3.84]**	[3.68]**	[4.16]**
REGEAP	1.961	1.277		1.239
	[4.61]**	[3.29]**		[3.92]**
AREA	−0.177	−0.457		−0.412
	[1.58]	[4.72]**		[4.41]**
CTRADE	0.044		0.025	
	[4.07]**		[2.01]	
EXPPRIM	−0.609		−0.970	−0.943
	[1.54]		[3.11]**	[4.06]**
SDBMP	−0.001		0.000	
	[3.79]**		[0.22]	
SDPI	0.001		0.001	0.001
	[4.12]**		[3.51]**	[4.50]**
SDTT	−0.010		−0.010	
	[1.20]		[0.93]	
CIVLEG		−1.159	−1.712	−0.600
		[2.22]*	[3.33]**	[2.49]*
COMLEG		−0.656	−0.998	
		[1.28]	[1.96]	
DURABLE		0.018	0.011	0.017
		[1.66]	[0.73]	[1.54]
KKM		1.489	1.237	1.445
		[4.40]**	[3.30]**	[5.12]**
PCI		−4.006	−3.791	−4.258
		[4.29]**	[3.98]**	[4.90]**
Standardized coefficients				
ETHPOL	0.49	0.72	0.45	0.68
EURFRAC	−0.46	−0.62	−0.63	−0.61
AREA	−0.15	−0.29		−0.26
CTRADE	−0.04		−0.05	
SDBMP	−0.06		−0.06	
SDPI	−0.06		−0.06	−0.06
SDTT	−0.07		−0.07	
DURABLE		−0.05	−0.06	−0.05
KKM		0.68	0.55	0.66
PCI		−2.05	−1.94	−2.17
Observations	64	64	64	64
R-square	0.740	0.820	0.790	0.860

Note: The models are estimated by OLS. The dependent variable is *FD*, over 1990–99. The t-values are reported in brackets. Variable descriptions are from Appendix Table A2.1. The standardized coefficients show the change of a standard deviation of *FD* due to a one standard deviation change in a variable for those other than initial GDP and population, binary variables.

*, ** and *** significant at 10%, 5% and 1%, respectively.

found significant in every model. The regional dummy *REGEAP* is significant in all relevant models, showing that the East Asian and Pacific countries are positively associated with higher *FD*. While *AREA* is significant in Models 2 and 4, the standardized coefficient for it is rather small. For the policy variables, *EXPPRIM* is significant in Models 3 and 4, but not for Model 1. *SDPI* is significant in all relevant models, but the standardized coefficient for it is negligible. Three institutional variables, *CIVLEG*, *KKM* and *PCI*, are found to be significantly associated with *FD* in all relevant models. The effects of *KKM* and *PCI* on *FD* are very strong, as shown by the standardized coefficients in the lower section of the table: a one standard deviation change in *KKM* translates into a more than 0.5 standard deviation of the *FD* measure, and even stronger effects for *PCI*.

In sum, on the one hand, the analyses above further confirm that institutions, policy and geography, taken as a group, jointly explain a substantial proportion of the variation in *FD*. On the other hand, the above analyses show that, in comparison to policy and geography, institutions could play a fundamental role in the process of financial development. When taken individually, at least *CIVLEG*, *KKM*, *PCI*, *GDP*90, *POP*90 and *EURFRAC* are found to have a significant influence on financial development. This finding explicitly suggests that, in addition to initial GDP and initial population, the legal origin[22] and institutional quality are the most fundamental determinants of financial development in a country.

2.5 Empirical results (II): Specific financial developments

This section turns to study briefly the determinants of four specific indices for financial development derived by using principal component analysis, namely, financial intermediary development (*FDBANK*), stock market development (*FDSTOCK*), financial efficiency development (*FDEFF*) and financial size development (*FDSIZE*). Bond market development (*FDBOND*) is also studied afterwards. The three samples are investigated for each index in which *EURO*1900 is available only for the developing country sample while *SRIGHT*, *CRIGHT* and *MEDSHARE* are available only for the La Porta dataset sample.

As in the previous section, the Gets model search is conducted with the relatively liberal strategy presented in Appendix Table A2.6.

The determinants of financial intermediary development (*FDBANK*) are reported in Table 2.5. The whole sample has 91 observations, the developing country sample has 70 and the La Porta sample has 40.[23]

General Determinants of Financial Development 37

The BMA and Gets analyses on the whole sample suggest *FDBANK* is positively related to initial income. East Asian and Pacific countries, Middle Eastern and North African countries and South Asian countries witness relative success in financial intermediary development. *MINDIST* is suggested to be important as well. The trade open policy index (*TOPEN*) and Frankel-Romer index (*CTRADE*) are significantly positively signed, suggesting financial intermediary development is boosted by more open trade policies. Three institutional variables (*POLITY2*, *KKM* and *PCI*) are suggested to be determinants for *FDBANK*, consistent with a conventional view that better institutions are associated with better financial intermediary development. The analyses based on the developing country and La Porta samples in general confirm the findings for *GDP90*, *REGEAP*, *REGMENA*, *TOPEN*, *KKM* and *PCI*. In addition, the analyses from the La Porta sample show that shareholders' right and creditors' rights may be closely related to financial intermediary development.

The determinants of stock market development (*FDSTOCK*) are reported in Table 2.6. The whole sample has 81 observations, the developing country sample has 50 and the La Porta sample has 49. The BMA and Gets analyses on the whole sample indicate that *FDSTOCK* is positively related to the initial population and the ethnic polarization index, while it is negatively related to the language fractionalization index (*EURFRAC*).[24] East Asian and Pacific countries experience a rise in stock market development. Land area is also important for *FDSTOCK*. Among other policy factors, *TOPEN* and *SDGR* are almost suggested by two methods to be in the model – this finding is also supported in the developing country and La Porta samples. The usual claim concerning the positive impacts of open trade policy on financial development applies here. The significantly negative effect of output volatility on *FDSTOCK* means that macroeconomic mismanagement might exert an adverse effect on *FDSTOCK*. Three institutional variables (*DURABLE*, *KKM* and *PCI*) are suggested to be the main determinants for *FDSTOCK*. The analyses based on the developing country and the La Porta samples support the idea that more open trade policies and better institutions promote stock market development.

The determinants of financial efficiency (*FDEFF*) are reported in Table 2.7. The whole sample has 79 observations, the developing country sample has 48 and the La Porta sample has 49. Note that the lower value of *FDEFF* is associated with a higher level of financial efficiency development as discussed in Section 2.2.2. The BMA and Gets analyses on the whole sample suggest that *RELIGION* is significantly related to *FDEFF*. East Asian and Pacific countries, South Asian countries, Middle Eastern

Table 2.5 Determinants of FDBANK

	Whole				Developing Country				La Porta			
	BMA		Gets		BMA		Gets		BMA		Gets	
Variable	PIPs	Sign	Coeff	t-value	PIPs	Sign	Coeff	t-value	PIPs	Sign	Coeff	t-value
CONSTANT	1.000	(−)	−2.523	−1.579	1.000	(−)	−4.218	−2.614	1.000	(+)		
GDP90	0.832	(+)	0.449	2.445	0.413	(+)	0.568	2.598	0.175			
POP90	0.017				0.000				0.858	(+)		
ETHPOL	0.012				0.008				0.692	(−)		
ETHNIC	0.001				0.000				0.852	(+)		
RELIGION					0.004				0.203	(−)		
LANGUAGE	0.000				0.000				0.060			
EURFRAC	0.000				0.000				0.326	(−)	−0.967	−2.751
REGEAP	1.000	(+)	1.979	6.770	0.929	(+)	1.879	5.125	0.268	(+)		
REGMENA	1.000	(+)	1.327	4.115	0.928	(+)	2.025	4.534	1.000	(+)		
REGSA	1.000	(+)	2.123	5.019	0.926	(+)			0.344	(+)		
REGSSA	0.001				0.072				0.336	(+)		
REGLAC	0.000				0.072				0.144			
REGWENA	0.001								0.767	(−)	−1.750	−3.295
LANDLOCK	0.008		−0.224	−0.817	0.259	(−)			0.734	(+)		
LATITUDE	0.000				0.000				0.048			
AREA	0.000				0.000				1.000	(−)		
MINDIST	0.804	(−)	−0.205	−2.630	0.000				0.343	(−)	−0.078	−2.270
POP100CR	0.001				0.000				0.257	(−)		
RESPOINT	0.361	(−)			0.321	(−)	−0.680	−2.674	0.770	(−)		
TOPEN	0.703	(+)	0.790	2.118	0.682	(+)			0.969	(+)	1.942	4.213
CTRADE	0.862	(+)	0.020	2.730	0.158				0.949	(−)		
EXPMANU	0.095				0.184							
EXPPRIM	0.126				0.134				0.083			
SDGR	0.000				0.000				0.940	(−)		
SDBMP	0.005				0.035				0.175			

Variable	Whole sample (91 obs) PIP	Sign	Coef	t	Developing (70 obs) PIP	Sign	Coef	t	La Porta (40 obs) PIP	Sign	Coef	t
SDPI	0.001				0.035				0.165			
SDTP	0.000				0.000				0.129			
SDTT	0.109				0.143				0.062			
CIVLEG	0.043				0.013				0.116			
COMLEG	0.182		−0.367	−1.743	0.035				0.107			
POLITY2	0.335	(+)	0.060	2.079	0.059		0.113		0.037		0.691	2.305
DURABLE	0.000				0.000				0.028			
FREE	0.031				0.033				0.024			
KKM	1.000	(+)	0.733	2.709	1.000	(+)	0.753	2.737	1.000	(+)	1.349	4.850
PCI	0.828	(−)		−3.433	0.430	(−)	−4.340	−2.944	0.832	(−)	−3.622	
EURO1900					0.045							
MEDSHARE									0.130			
SRIGHT									0.662	(+)		
CRIGHT									0.729	(−)		
RSS	51.30				51.41				29.21			
sigma	0.82				0.94				0.93			
R^2	0.82				0.65				0.76			
Radj^2	0.79				0.61				0.72			
LogLik	26.08				8.82				6.29			
AIC	−0.27				−0.02				−0.01			
HQ	−0.11				0.08				0.08			
SC	0.12				0.23				0.24			
Chow test 1	1.63				2.27							
Chow test 2	2.94				1.45							
Normality test	0.65	0.72			0.05	0.48			0.93	0.63		
Hetero test	20.25	0.51										

Note: The dependent variable *FDBANK* is the index of financial interdiediary development over the period, 1990–99. Variable description is in Appendix Table A2.1. There are 91 observations in the whole sample, 70 observations in the developing country sample and 40 observations in the La Porta sample. BMA analysis yields the posterior probabilities of inclusion (PIPs) and the sign certainty index of a relationship (Sign). No sign given means the sign of estimated relationship being uncertain. The Gets analysis yields coefficients and t-values for the variables in the final model. See text for the description of PcGets output.

Table 2.6 Determinants of FDSTOCK

	Whole				Developing Country				La Porta			
	BMA		Gets		BMA		Gets		BMA		Gets	
Variable	PIPs	Sign	Coeff	t-value	PIPs	Sign	Coeff	t-value	PIPs	Sign	Coeff	t-value
CONSTANT	1.000	(−)			1.000	(−)	−8.131	−6.444	1.000	(−)		
GDP90	0.183				1.000	(+)	0.645	4.911	0.045		−0.669	−3.836
POP90	1.000	(+)	0.435	8.414	1.000	(+)	0.290	7.118	0.919	(+)	0.732	4.701
ETHPOL	0.985	(+)	0.791	3.379	0.000				0.832	(+)	1.490	2.897
ETHNIC	0.000				0.014				0.009			
RELIGION	0.008				0.974	(+)	0.989	3.567	0.232	(+)		
LANGUAGE	0.039				0.005				0.046			
EURFRAC	0.210	(−)	−0.611	−3.016	0.977	(−)			0.783	(−)	−0.932	−2.783
REGEAP	0.937	(+)	−1.301	−3.001	0.056				0.016		−0.833	−1.689
REGMENA	0.062		−1.653	−4.024	0.021				0.008			
REGSA	0.035		−2.485	−5.434	0.351				0.721	(−)	−2.367	−3.686
REGSSA	0.022		−1.427	−3.245	0.892	(−)	−1.714	−2.791	0.034			
REGLAC	0.000		−1.128	−2.828	0.012	(−)	−1.623	−2.807	0.000			
REGWENA	0.063		−1.716	−3.664			−2.098	−3.419	0.033		−1.258	−2.367
LANDLOCK	0.000				0.007		−1.562	−3.196	0.004			
LATITUDE	0.000				0.000				0.040			
AREA	0.985	(−)	−0.245	−6.484	0.000				0.935	(−)	−0.462	−4.611
MINDIST	0.120				0.000				0.722	(+)	0.173	2.361
POP100CR	0.037				0.006				0.000			
RESPOINT	0.007				0.532	(−)			0.000			
TOPEN	0.191		0.578	2.686	1.000	(+)	0.901	4.497	0.098		0.647	1.361
CTRADE	0.000				0.000				0.081			
EXPMANU	0.901	(+)			0.003				0.165		0.602	1.976
EXPPRIM	0.003				0.000				0.065		0.858	1.948
SDGR	0.141		−0.129	−3.320	0.244	(−)	0.000	−3.172	0.555	(−)	−0.351	−3.908
SDBMP	0.014				0.736	(−)			0.252			

Variable								
SDPI	0.000			0.068			0.076	
SDTP	0.745	(+)		0.001			1.000	(+)	1.847	3.524
SDTT	0.000			0.000			0.000	
CIVLEG	0.002			0.615	(−)		0.006	
COMLEG	0.111		0.582	0.133		0.321	2.212	0.005	
POLITY2	0.010			0.045			0.036	
DURABLE	0.216	(+)	0.013	0.040		3.003		0.688	(+)	0.022	2.619
FREE	0.134			0.164			0.051	
KKM	0.976	(+)	0.701	0.463	(+)	0.161	2.983	0.894	(+)	1.503	4.310
PCI	0.245	(−)	−1.828	0.000			0.006	
EURO1900				0.006		−0.813	−1.681	0.249	(−)	
MEDSHARE								0.108	
SRIGHT								0.002	
CRIGHT									

RSS	14.02		4.27	17.87
sigma	0.47		0.34	0.74
R^2	0.87		0.84	0.78
Radj^2	0.84		0.78	0.68
LogLik	71.04		61.53	24.71
AIC	−1.33		−1.90	−0.36
HQ	−1.13		−1.70	−0.12
SC	−0.83		−1.37	0.26
Chow test 1	1.20	0.33		
Chow test 2	0.88	0.54	1.47	0.23	0.15	0.96
Normality test			9.04	0.01	8.52	0.01
Hetero test	31.22	0.22		

Note: The dependent variable *FDSTOCK* is the index of stock market development over the period 1990–99. Variable description is in Appendix Table A2.1. There are 81 observations in the whole sample, 50 observations in the developing country sample and 49 observations in the La Porta sample. BMA analysis yields the posterior probabilities of inclusion (PIPs) and the sign certainty index of a relationship (Sign). No sign given means the sign relationship being uncertain. Gets analysis yields coefficients and t-values for the variables in the final model. See text for description of PcGets output.

Table 2.7 Determinants of FDEFF

Variable	Whole BMA PIPs	Whole BMA Sign	Whole Gets Coeff	Whole Gets t-value	Developing Country BMA PIPs	Developing Country BMA Sign	Developing Country Gets Coeff	Developing Country Gets t-value	La Porta BMA PIPs	La Porta BMA Sign	La Porta Gets Coeff	La Porta Gets t-value
CONSTANT	1.000	(+)			1.000	(+)	9.145	4.200	1.000			
GDP90	0.010				0.996	(−)	−1.456	−6.307	0.243	(+)	0.661	4.845
POP90	0.041				0.856	(−)	−0.536	−5.097	0.672	(−)	−0.411	−3.726
ETHPOL	0.000				0.987	(+)			0.034			
ETHNIC	0.000				0.027				0.004			
RELIGION	0.375	(−)	−0.789	−1.839	0.061				0.479	(−)		
LANGUAGE	0.000				0.996	(−)	−0.975	−2.279	0.170			
EURFRAC	0.028				0.336				0.894	(+)	1.039	3.902
REGEAP	0.989	(−)	−1.397	−5.028	0.029				0.075			
REGMENA	0.962	(−)	−1.685	−5.377	1.000	(−)	−2.613	−7.077	0.716	(−)	−0.894	−2.535
REGSA	0.986	(−)	−2.326	−5.240	1.000	(−)			0.707	(−)		
REGSSA	0.033				0.006				0.029			
REGLAC	0.037				0.045				0.225	(+)		
REGWENA	0.777	(−)							0.071			
LANDLOCK	0.000				0.021				0.031			
LATITUDE	0.000				0.055				0.001			
AREA	0.021				0.851	(+)	0.411	4.515	0.289	(+)	0.160	2.168
MINDIST	0.066				0.024				0.015			
POP100CR	0.000				0.003				0.028			
RESPOINT	0.103		0.667	2.473	0.996	(+)	1.379	5.697	0.019			
TOPEN	0.052				0.996	(−)			0.030			
CTRADE	0.000				0.088				0.000	(−)		
EXPMANU	0.140	(+)			0.007				0.270			
EXPPRIM	0.926				0.000				0.001			
SDGR	0.002				0.089				0.755	(+)	0.149	2.443
SDBMP	0.021				0.000				0.000			

Variable										
SDPI	0.134		0.000	−0.999	(−)	−0.001	−4.142	0.023	(−)	−2.084	−5.550
SDTP	0.086		−0.332	−1.144				0.932		
SDTT	0.058							0.121		
CIVLEG	0.034		1.773	3.340	(+)	2.828	3.756	0.000		
COMLEG	0.102		2.127	3.725	(+)	2.133	2.789	0.000		
POLITY2	0.000				(−)	−0.144	−4.539	0.000		
DURABLE	0.000							0.000		
FREE	0.985							0.125		
KKM	1.000	(−)						1.000	(−)	−2.044	−8.788
PCI	0.000	(−)	−1.119	−8.260				0.703	(+)		
EURO1900					(−)	6.226	5.693			
MEDSHARE					(+)			0.003		
SRIGHT								0.001		
CRIGHT								0.000		
RSS			40.53			14.68				
sigma			0.77			0.64					19.89
R^2			0.74			0.82					0.70
Radj^2			0.70			0.76					0.82
LogLik			26.36			28.43					0.79
AIC			−0.41			−0.68					22.09
HQ			−0.29			−0.51					−0.57
SC			−0.11			−0.22					−0.46
Chow test 1											−0.27
Chow test 2			2.27			0.70					0.45	0.77
Normality test			16.62			0.11					2.82
Hetero test			0.34			0.95					0.24

Note: The dependent variable *FDEFF* is the index of financial efficiency development over the period 1990–99. Variable description is in Appendix Table A2.1. There are 79 observations in the whole sample, 48 observations in the developing country sample and 49 observations in the La Porta sample. BMA analysis yields the posterior probabilities of inclusion (PIPs) and the sign certainty index of a relationship (Sign). No sign given means the sign of estimated relationship being uncertain. Gets analysis yields coefficients and t-values for the variables in the final model. See text for the description of PcGets output.

Table 2.8 Determinants of FDSIZE

	Whole				Developing Country				La Porta			
	BMA		Gets		BMA		Gets		BMA		Gets	
Variable	PIPs	Sign	Coeff	t-value	PIPs	Sign	Coeff	t-value	PIPs	Sign	Coeff	t-value
CONSTANT	1.000	(−)			1.000	(−)	−11.170	−4.993	1.000	(−)		
GDP90	1.000	(+)			0.809	(+)	0.356	2.073	0.825	(+)		
POP90	0.999	(+)	0.286	3.708	0.961	(+)	0.247	4.185	0.624	(+)		
ETHPOL	0.068				0.282	(+)			0.009			
ETHNIC	0.000				0.093		1.558	3.456	0.138			
RELIGION	0.000				0.808	(+)			0.000			
LANGUAGE	0.342	(+)			0.392	(+)			0.346	(+)		
EURFRAC	0.049		−0.535	−2.043	0.043				0.005			
REGEAP	0.351	(+)			0.000				0.505	(+)		
REGMENA	0.552	(+)			1.000	(+)			0.111			
REGSA	0.016		−0.568	−1.324	0.018		−1.621	−4.294	0.137			
REGSSA	0.003				0.152		−0.607	−2.369	0.003			
REGLAC	0.013				0.042				0.045			
REGWENA	0.554	(−)	−1.224	−3.319	0.105				0.640	(−)	−1.209	−2.479
LANDLOCK	0.000				0.002				0.987	(+)		
LATITUDE	0.000				0.002		0.043	4.284	0.063			
AREA	0.999	(−)	−0.267	−4.605	0.016		0.511	2.483	0.379	(−)		
MINDIST	0.008				0.269	(+)	0.012	3.817	0.594	(−)		
POP100CR	0.040				0.039		−0.388	−2.045	0.080			
RESPOINT	0.001				1.000	(+)	1.313	4.984	0.034			
TOPEN	0.987	(+)	1.353	4.065	0.076				0.616	(+)	1.971	5.253
CTRADE	0.000				0.005				0.843	(+)		
EXPMANU	0.000				0.034				0.001			
EXPPRIM	0.003				0.590	(−)			0.020			
SDGR	0.000				0.491	(−)	−0.001	−3.310	0.768	(−)		
SDBMP	0.218	(−)							0.032			

Variable	Whole sample				Developing countries				La Porta			
	PIP	Sign	Coef	t	PIP	Sign	Coef	t	PIP	Sign	Coef	t
SDPI	0.000				0.000				0.854	(−)	−0.008	−2.716
SDTP	0.000				0.000				0.824	(−)		
SDTT	0.018				0.183				0.019			
CIVLEG	0.757	(−)			0.895	(−)			0.010			
COMLEG	0.243	(+)			0.029				0.010			
POLITY2	0.000				0.012				0.000			
DURABLE	0.244	(+)	0.022	3.009	0.000				0.005			
FREE	0.004				0.249	(+)			0.002			
KKM	0.155		0.697	3.231	0.467	(+)			0.097			
PCI	0.888	(−)	−1.348	−1.921	0.008		−0.752	−4.225	0.879	(−)		
EURO1900					0.000		−2.359	−4.514				
MEDSHARE									0.015			
SRIGHT									1.000	(+)		
CRIGHT									0.001			
RSS	39.78				9.38				46.94			
sigma	0.79				0.50				1.10			
R^2	0.65				0.75				0.42			
Radj^2	0.61				0.66				0.39			
LogLik	22.15				43.18				−2.34			
AIC	−0.36				−1.14				0.25			
HQ	−0.25				−0.94				0.30			
SC	−0.08				−0.61				0.38			
Chow test 1	0.80	0.74										
Chow test 2	1.17	0.34										
Normality test	8.90	0.01			1.11	0.37			8.45	0.01		
Hetero test					0.29	0.87						

Note: Dependent variable *FDSIZE* is the index of financial size development over the period 1990–99. The variable description is in Appendix Table A2.1. There are 73 observations in the whole sample, 51 observations in developing country sample and 42 observations in La Porta sample. The BMA analysis yields the posterior probabilities of inclusion (PIPs) and the sign certainty index of a relationship (Sign). No sign given means the sign of estimated relationship being uncertain. The Gets analysis yields coefficients and *t*-values for the variables in the final model. See text for the description of PcGets output.

46 *Determinants of Financial Development*

and North African countries tend to have more efficient financial markets. Financial markets are more efficient in countries where institutional quality (captured by *KKM*) is higher. The results from two subsamples show that initial GDP and population are also important for *FDEFF*.

The determinants of financial size development (*FDSIZE*), also called financial depth, are reported in Table 2.8. The whole sample has 73 observations, the developing country sample has 51 and the La Porta sample has 42. The BMA and Gets analyses on the whole sample suggest that financial depth in a country is positively related to the initial population. The West European and North American countries – including most developed countries – witnessed a decline in financial depth. Countries with a larger land area experience relatively less financial size development. Countries with a more open trade policy are found to have better financial development in terms of size. Financial depth is also associated with a stable political system (captured by *DURABLE*) and fewer political constraints on the executive (captured by *PCI*). Most of these findings are supported by analyses based on the developing country and the La Porta samples. In addition, the analyses from the La Porta sample show that financial depth might be closely related to shareholders' rights.

We now turn to the case of bond market development. Since there are only size measures for bond market development and bond market capitalization available in the World Bank Financial Development and Financial Structure Database (2008) with incomplete data for many developing countries, the above financial development measures do not include indexes of bond market development. Appendix Table A2.8 presents the specific BMA and Gets analyses for bond market development, denoted by *FDBOND*, which is the sum of the private and public bonds share over GDP in 1990s. The analyses are based on the La Porta sample of 35 countries subject to data availability. The results show that initial GDP level (*GDP90*), language fractionalization index (*LANGUAGE*), East Asian and Pacific countries (*REGEAP*), population proportion in coastal areas[25] (*POP100CR*), terms of trade volatility (*SDTT*) and governance index (*KKM*) may influence bond market development. The results support previous findings in terms of institutions, policy and geography being important for financial development, but further study critically depends on the availability of additional data.

2.6 Conclusions

The analysis jointly applies the BMA and Gets methods to study what drives financial development using 39 institutional, policy and geographic variables. The combination of these two methods has the potential for incorporating the merits of each method and minimizing their limits, showing advantages in mitigating arbitrary choices and increasing precision in model selection. To explore the structural causes of financial development, the variables considered here are either predetermined or evolving slowly over time.

Of 39 individual variables, this research finds that the legal origin and institutional quality are significantly associated with financial development, as are the initial income and population. These findings are consistent with the literature.

The finding that the legal origins influence financial development supports the emphasis on the legal determinants of financial development of La Porta *et al.* (1998), who argued that the origins of the legal code substantially influence the treatment of creditors and shareholders, and the efficiency of contract enforcement. They document that countries with French Civil Law are said to have comparatively inefficient contract enforcement and higher corruption, and less well-developed financial systems, whilst countries with British legal origin achieve higher levels of financial development.

On the role of institutions in financial development, Beck *et al.* (2003) is a significant work among others. By applying the settler mortality hypothesis of Acemoglu *et al.* (2001) to financial development, Beck *et al.* (2003) argue that extractive colonizers in an inhospitable environment aimed to establish institutions that privileged small elite groups rather than private investors, while the settler colonizers in more favourable environments were more likely to create institutions that supported private property rights and balanced the power of the state, therefore favouring financial development.

The importance of income levels for financial development has been addressed in Levine (1997, 2003, 2005). In considering the banking sector development in transition economies, Jaffee and Levonian (2001) demonstrate that the level of GDP per capita and the saving rate have positive effects on the banking system structure as measured by bank assets, numbers, branches and employees for 23 transition economies. On the impact of differences in culture on the process of financial development, Stulz and Williamson (2003) provide evidence that culture, proxied by differences in religion and language, predicts cross-country variation in the protection and enforcement of investor rights, especially for creditor rights.

Taken as a whole, whilst this research shows the significant roles played by institutions, policy and geography, it highlights the dominant role of institutions over policy and geography in the process of financial development. The findings on the significant effects of these structural factors, which are relatively time-invariant, tend to suggest that efforts by the government to better institution quality, implement more open trade and sound macroeconomic policies and improve geographic infrastructure can stimulate financial development in the long run. An efficient and transparent institutional and legal system and a free and just society are especially important for the development of financial markets. Further research, as in Abiad and Mody (2005) and Chapter 5, is needed to explore what causes governments to undertake financial reforms aimed at financial development.

Appendix text

Here is the derivation of the posterior model probability in BMA.[26] We suppose there are many models, $\{M_1, \ldots M_K\}$ for the data D. Every model is specified by a vector of d unknown parameters $\theta_i = (\theta_{i1}, \theta_{i2}, \ldots \theta_{id})$, $i = 1, 2 \ldots K$. These models may be nested or not. Bayesians treat the unknown parameters as random variables.

Let Δ denote a quantity of interest such as a parameter. The posterior distribution of Δ given data D is derived according to

$$P(\Delta|D) = \sum_{i=1}^{K} P(\Delta|D, M_k) P(M_k|D) \tag{2.1}$$

where $P(M_k|D)$ are the posterior model probabilities, and $P(\Delta|D, M_k)$ is the posterior distribution of Δ given the data D and model M_k.

The equation contains all information needed to make inferences about Δ, indicating that the posterior distribution of Δ given data D is a weighted average of its posterior distributions given data D and a specific model. The weights are the posterior model probabilities, $P(M_k|D)$, which can be obtained by Bayes' theorem

$$P(M_k|D) = \frac{P(D|M_k)P(M_k)}{\sum_{i=1}^{K} P(D|M_i)P(M_i)} \tag{2.2}$$

where $P(M_k)$ is the prior probability of model i ($i = 1, 2 \ldots K$), and $P(D|M_i)$ is the probability of the data given M_i, also called the integrated (marginal) likelihood for model M_i or marginal (predictive) probability of the data given M_j.

To represent no prior preference for any model, each will start on an equal footing, that is $P(M_1) = P(M_2) = \cdots P(M_K) = \frac{1}{K}$. Therefore the posterior model

General Determinants of Financial Development 49

probabilities $P(M_k|D)$ can be rewritten as

$$P(M_k|D) = \frac{P(D|M_k)}{\sum_{i=1}^{K} P(D|M_i)} \tag{2.3}$$

To identify the value of $P(D|M_k)$, it is useful to compare model M_k with a baseline model. A null model (M_0) in which no independent variables are included is usually used as a baseline model.[27]

Let B_{k0} be the Bayes factor for model M_k against model M_0, that is

$$B_{k0} = \frac{P(D|M_k)}{P(D|M_0)} \tag{2.4}$$

then

$$2 \log B_{k0} = 2 \log P(D|M_k) - 2 \log P(D|M_0) \tag{2.5}$$

Using an approach developed by Raftery (1995), twice the log of the Bayesian factor, "$2 \log B_{k0}$", can be expressed as the approximation of the difference between BIC_0 and BIC_k, the values of BIC for the null model, M_0, and model, M_k, respectively

$$2 \log B_{k0} \approx BIC_0 - BIC_k \tag{2.6}$$

The fact that $BIC_0 = 0$ yields the approximation for the posterior probability $P(D|M_k)$, which is

$$P(D|M_k) \propto \exp\left(-\frac{1}{2} BIC_k\right) \tag{2.7}$$

The posterior model probabilities $P(M_k|D)$ can then be written as

$$P(M_k|D) \approx \frac{\exp\left(-\frac{1}{2} BIC_k\right)}{\sum_{i=1}^{K} \exp\left(-\frac{1}{2} BIC_i\right)} \tag{2.8}$$

Appendix tables

Table A2.1 The variables

Variable	Description	Source
Dependent variables		
FD	Index for overall financial development. The first principal component of private credit (*PRIVO*), liquidity liability (*LLY*), commercial-central bank (*BTOT*), overhead cost (*OVC*), net interest margin (*NIM*), stock market capitalization (*MCAP*), total value traded (*TVT*) and turnover ratio (*TOR*) in the 1990s.	World Bank's Financial Structure and Economic Development Database (FSED), 2008
FDBANK	Index for financial intermediary development. The first principal component of *PRIVO, LLY, BTOT, OVC* and *NIM* in the 1990s.	FSED, 2008
FDSTOCK	Index for stock market development. The first principal component of *MCAP, TVT* and *TOR* in the 1990s.	FSED, 2008
FDEFF	Index for financial efficiency development. The first principal component of *OVC, NIM, TVT* and *TOR* in the 1990s.	FSED, 2008
FDSIZE	Index for financial size development (financial depth). the first principal component of *LLY* and *MCAP* in the 1990s.	FSED, 2008
FDBOND	Index for bond market developpment, the sum of private bond and public bond share over GDP in the 1990s.	FSED, 2008
Policy variables		
TOPEN	The proportion of years that a country is open to trade during 1965–90, by the criteria in Sachs and Warner (1995). A country is considered to be open if it meets minimum criteria on four aspects of trade policy: average tariffs must be lower than 40%, quotas and licensing must cover less than 40% of total imports, the black market premium (BMP) must be less than 20%, and export taxes should be moderate.	Gallup *et al*. (1999)
CTRADE	Natural log of the Frankel-Romer measure of predisposition to external trade	Frankel and Romer (1999)
EXPMANU	Dummy for manufactured goods exporting countries Global Development Network Database in World Bank (GDN), 2002	
EXPPRIM	Dummy for fuel and non-fuel primary good exporting countries Global Development Network Database in World Bank (GDN), 2002	

SDGR	Standard deviation of annual growth of real, chainweighted GDP per capita, 1960–89	Penn World Table 6.2 (PWT62) (Heston et al., 2006)
SDPI	Standard deviation of annual inflation (PI), 1960–89	World Development Indicators (WDI), 2008
SDBMP	Standard deviation of annual black market premium (BMP), 1960–89	GDN
SDTP	Standard deviation of trading partners' GDP per capita growth (percentage weighted average by trade share)	GDN
SDTT	Standard deviation of the first log-differences of a terms of trade index for goods and services	GDN
Institutional variables		
COMLEG	The dummy for British legal origin	GDN
CIVLEG	Legal origin dummy for French, German and Scandinavian	GDN
POLITY2	Index of democracy. It is called combined polity score, the democracy score minus the autocracy score. The democracy and autocracy scores are derived from the six authority characteristics (regulation, competitiveness and openness of executive recruitment; operational independence of chief executive or executive constraints; and regulation and competition of participation). Based on these criteria, each country is assigned democracy and autocracy scores ranging from 0 to 10, accordingly, the POLITY2 ranges from –10 to 10 with higher values representing more democratic regimes, averaged over 1960–89.	PolityIV Database (Marshall and Jaggers, 2009)
DURABLE	Index of political stability based on the number of years since the last (3-point or greater) regime transition, averaged over 1960–89.	PolityIV Database (Marshall and Jaggers, 2009)
FREE	The average of indices of civil liberties and political rights over 1972–89. The basic components of the index of civil liberties are (1) freedom of expression and belief, (2) association and organizational rights, (3) rule of law and human rights, (4) personal autonomy and economic rights. Rescaled from 0 to 1, with higher values indicating better civil liberties. The basic components of the index of political rights are (1) free and fair elections; (2) those elected rule; (3) there are competitive parties or other competitive political groupings; (4) the opposition has an important role and power; (5) the entities have self-determination or an extremely high degree of autonomy. Rescaled from 0 to 1, with higher values indicating better political rights.	Freedom House (FH), www.freedomhouse.org, 2008

(continued)

Table 2.1 Continued

Variable	Description	Source
KKM	Average of six measures of institutional development: voice and accountability, political stability and absence of violence, government effectiveness, light regulatory burden, rule of law and freedom from graft.	Kaufmann et al. (2008)
PCI	Political Constraints Index is a structurally derived measure of the feasibility of policy change (the extent to which a change in the preferences of any one actor may lead to a change in government policy).	Henisz (2000), 2002 version
EURO1900	The percentage of the population that was European or European descent in 1900.	Acemoglu, et al. (2001)
MEDSHARE	The index of media owned by the government, the average of the market share of state-owned newspapers and state-owned television stations. Market share of state-owned newspapers is the market share owned by the state out of the aggregate market share of the five largest daily newspapers (by circulation). Market share of state-owned television stations is the market share owned by the state out of the aggregate market share of the five largest television stations (by viewership)	Djankov et al. (2003)
SRIGHT	An index aggregating the shareholder rights which we labelled as "anti-director rights". The index is formed by adding 1 when: (1) the country allows shareholders to mail their proxy vote to the firm, (2) shareholders are not required to deposit their shares prior to the General Shareholders' Meeting, (3) cumulative voting or proportional representation of minorities in the board of directors is allowed, (4) an oppressed minorities mechanism is in place, (5) the minimum percentage of share capital that entitles a shareholder to call for an Extraordinary Shareholders' Meeting is less than or equal to 10% (the sample median) or (6) shareholders have pre-emptive rights that can only be waived by a shareholders' vote. The index ranges from 0 to 6.	La Porta et al. (1998)
CRIGHT	An index aggregating creditor rights. The index is formed by adding 1 when: (1) the country imposes restrictions, such as creditors' consent or minimum dividends, to file for reorganization; (2) secured creditors are able to gain possession of their security once the reorganization petition has been approved (no automatic stay); (3) the debtor does not retain the administration of its property pending the resolution of the reorganization and (4) secured creditors are ranked first in the distribution of the proceeds that result from the disposition of the assets of a bankrupt firm. The index ranges from 0 to 4.	La Porta et al. (1998)

Geographic variable

Variable	Description	Source
REGEAP	Region dummy for East Asian and Pacific countries	GDN
REGMENA	Region dummy for Middle Eastern and North African countries	GDN
REGSA	Region dummy for South Asian countries	GDN
REGSSA	Region dummy for Sub-Sahara African countries	GDN
REGLAC	Region dummy for Latin American and Caribbean countries	GDN
REGWENA	Region dummy for West European and North American countries	GDN
LANDLOCK	Dummy for landlocked countries	GDN
LATUTUDE	Latitude–absolute distance from equator	GDN
AREA	Area (in log) in square kilometres from World Bank (1997), except for Taiwan and Mexico from CIA (1997), with submerged land subtracted out.	Gallup et al. (1999)
POP100CR	Proportion of the population in 1994 within 100 km of the coastline or navigable to the ocean river.	Gallup et al. (1999)
MINDIST	The log of minimum distance from three capital-goods-supplying centres plus one.	Jon Haveman's International trade data. www.eiit.org
RESPOINT	Dummy for point source exporting countries.	Isham et al. (2002)

Other variables

Variable	Description	Source
GDP90	Log of real GDP per capita (chain) in 1990	PWT62
POP90	Log of total population in 1990	PWT62
ETHPOL	Index of ethnic polarization	Reynal-Querol and Montalvo (2005)
ETHNIC	Index of ethnic fractionalization	Alesina et al. (2003)
RELIGION	Index of religious fractionalization	Alesina et al. (2003)
LANGUAGE	Index of language fractionalization	Alesina et al. (2003)
ERUFRAC	Index of the "first" language variables, corresponding to the fraction of the population speaking one of the major languages of Western Europe: English, French, German, Portuguese or Spanish.	Hall and Jones (1999)
INCLOW	Low income countries	GDN
INCMID	Upper-middle- and lower-middle income countries	GDN
INCHIGH	High-income OECD and non-OECD countries	GDN

Table A2.2 Descriptive statistics

	FD	LANDLOCK	LATITUDE	AREA	MINDIST	POP100CR	RESPOINT
Geography							
FD	1.000						
LANDLOCK	−0.163	1.000					
LATITUDE	0.536	−0.057	1.000				
AREA	−0.098	0.001	−0.008	1.000			
MINDIST	−0.514	0.119	−0.429	−0.053	1.000		
POP100CR	0.378	−0.508	0.252	−0.455	−0.293	1.000	
RESPOINT	−0.237	0.084	−0.255	−0.122	0.242	−0.053	1.000

	FD	TOPEN	CTRADE	EXPMANU	EXPPRIM	SDGR	SDBMP	SDPI	SDTP	SDTT
Institution										
FD	1.000									
TOPEN	0.664	1.000								
CTRADE	0.242	0.249	1.000							
EXPMANU	0.447	0.409	0.049	1.000						
EXPPRIM	−0.463	−0.367	−0.150	−0.274	1.000					
SDGR	−0.322	−0.259	0.353	−0.288	0.403	1.000				
SDBMP	−0.142	0.041	−0.154	−0.084	0.018	0.044	1.000			
SDPI	−0.086	0.076	−0.116	−0.073	0.237	0.000	0.096	1.000		
SDTP	−0.112	−0.209	−0.076	−0.196	0.265	0.147	0.116	0.092	1.000	
SDTT	−0.411	−0.403	−0.024	−0.186	0.395	0.437	0.184	0.005	0.128	1.000

	FD	CIVLEG	COMLEG	POLITY2	DURABLE	FREE	KKM	PCI
Policy								
FD	1.000							
CIVLEG	−0.071	1.000						
COMLEG	0.037	−0.968	1.000					
POLITY2	0.332	−0.281	0.324	1.000				
DURABLE	0.455	−0.143	0.147	0.532	1.000			
FREE	−0.374	0.015	−0.074	−0.710	−0.563	1.000		
KKM	0.675	0.100	−0.072	0.547	0.561	−0.714	1.000	
PCI	0.314	0.048	−0.006	0.701	0.453	−0.885	0.665	1.000

	FD	GDP90	POP90	ETHPOL	ETHNIC	RELIGION	LANGUAGE	EURFRAC
Others								
FD	1.000							
GDP90	0.627	1.000						
OPO90	0.070	−0.210	1.000					
ETHPOL	−0.169	−0.282	−0.073	1.000				
ETHNIC	−0.358	−0.499	0.063	0.660	1.000			
RELIGION	0.151	0.036	0.052	0.148	0.256	1.000		
LANGUAGE	−0.161	−0.473	0.149	0.266	0.631	0.307	1.000	
EURFRAC	−0.082	0.283	−0.167	0.251	0.012	0.184	−0.397	1.000

Table A2.3 The list of countries in the full sample

East Asia & Pacific		Middle East & North Africa		South Asia	
AUS	Australia	BHR	Bahrain	BGD	Bangladesh
CHN	China	DZA	Algeria	IND	India
FJI	Fiji	EGY	Egypt, Arab Rep.	LKA	Sri Lanka
HKG	Hong Kong, China	GRC	Greece	NPL	Nepal
IDN	Indonesia	IRN	Iran, Islamic Rep.	PAK	Pakistan
JPN	Japan	ISR	Israel		
KOR	Korea, Rep.	JOR	Jordan		
MAC	Macao	KWT	Kuwait		
MNG	Mongolia	LBN	Lebanon		
MYS	Malaysia	MAR	Morocco		
NZL	New Zealand	MLT	Malta		
PHL	Philippines	OMN	Oman		
PNG	Papua New Guinea	PRT	Portugal		
SGP	Singapore	QAT	Qatar		
THA	Thailand	SAU	Saudi Arabia		
TWN	Taiwan, China	TUN	Tunisia		
VNM	Vietnam				

Sub-Saharan Africa		Latin America & Caribbean		Western Europe & North America	
BDI	Burundi	ARG	Argentina	AUT	Austria
BEN	Benin	BOL	Bolivia	BEL	Belgium
BFA	Burkina Faso	BRA	Brazil	CAN	Canada
BWA	Botswana	BRB	Barbados	CHE	Switzerland
CIV	Cote d'Ivoire	CHL	Chile	CYP	Cyprus
CMR	Cameroon	COL	Colombia	DEU	Germany
ETH	Ethiopia	CRI	Costa Rica	DNK	Denmark
GHA	Ghana	DOM	Dominican Rep.	ESP	Spain
KEN	Kenya	ECU	Ecuador	FIN	Finland
MDG	Madagascar	GTM	Guatemala	FRA	France
MLI	Mali	GUY	Guyana	GBR	United Kingdom
MOZ	Mozambique	HND	Honduras	IRL	Ireland
MRT	Mauritania	HTI	Haiti	ISL	Iceland
MUS	Mauritius	JAM	Jamaica	ITA	Italy
MWI	Malawi	MEX	Mexico	LUX	Luxembourg
NAM	Namibia	NIC	Nicaragua	NLD	Netherlands
NGA	Nigeria	PAN	Panama	NOR	Norway
RWA	Rwanda	PER	Peru	SWE	Sweden
SDN	Sudan	PRY	Paraguay	USA	United States
SEN	Senegal	SLV	El Salvador		
SLE	Sierra Leone	TTO	Trinidad and Tobago		
SWZ	Swaziland	URY	Uruguay		
TGO	Togo	VEN	Venezuela		
UGA	Uganda				
ZAF	South Africa				
ZMB	Zambia				
ZWE	Zimbabwe				

Table A2.4 The eigenvalue, proportion and eigenvector of each first principal component

Measure	Eigenvalue	Proportion	LLY	PRIVO	BTOT	OVC	NIM	MCAP	TVT	TOR
FD	3.922	0.490	0.411	0.454	0.278	−0.357	−0.368	0.364	0.357	0.157
FDBANK	3.063	0.613	0.479	0.479	0.357	−0.437	−0.471			
FDSTOCK	1.986	0.662						0.535	0.676	0.506
FDEFF	2.160	0.540				0.546	0.561		−0.467	−0.411
FDSIZE	1.612	0.806	0.707					0.707		

Notes: The financial development measures are described in the text. The first principal component is the linear combination of the measures selected. The eigenvalues are the variances of the (first) principal components. The eigenvectors give the coefficients of the standardised variables.
LLY = the ratio of liquid liabilities of financial system (currency plus demand and interest-bearing liabilities of banks and non-banks) to GDP;
$PRIVO$ = the ratio of credits issued to private sector by banks and other financial intermediaries to GDP;
OVC = the ratio of overhead costs to total assets of the banks;
NIM = the bank interest income minus interest expenses over total assets;
$MCAP$ = the ratio of the value of domestic shares traded on domestic exchange to GDP;
TVT = the ratio of the value of domestic shares traded on domestic exchange to GDP;
TOR = the ratio of the value of domestic shares traded or. domestic exchange to total value of listed domestic shares

Table A2.5 Imputation

Variables	Variables used to impute the missing data								
ETHPOL	REGEAP	REGMENA	REGSA	REGLAC	REGSSA	REGWENA	RELIGION		
ETHNIC	REGEAP	REGMENA	REGSA	REGLAC	REGSSA	REGWENA	RELIGION		
LANGUAGE	REGEAP	REGMENA	REGSA	REGLAC	REGSSA	REGWENA	RELIGION		
EURFRAC	REGEAP	REGMENA	REGSA	REGLAC	REGSSA	REGWENA	RELIGION		
CTRADE	REGEAP	REGMENA	REGSA	REGLAC	REGSSA	REGWENA	INCLOW	INCMID	INCHIGH
TOPEN	REGEAP	REGMENA	REGSA	REGLAC	REGSSA	REGWENA	INCLOW	INCMID	INCHIGH
AREA	REGEAP	REGMENA	REGSA	REGLAC	REGSSA	REGWENA	LANDLOCK	LATITUDE	
MINDIST	REGEAP	REGMENA	REGSA	REGLAC	REGSSA	REGWENA	LANDLOCK	LATITUDE	
POP100CR	REGEAP	REGMENA	REGSA	REGLAC	REGSSA	REGWENA	LANDLOCK	LATITUDE	
POP90	REGEAP	REGMENA	REGSA	REGLAC	REGSSA	REGWENA	LANDLOCK		
RESPOINT	REGEAP	REGMENA	REGSA	REGLAC	REGSSA	REGWENA	LANDLOCK	LATITUDE	
POLITY2	CIVLEG	COMLEG	LATITUDE						
DURABLE	CIVLEG	COMLEG	LATITUDE						
FREE	CIVLEG	COMLEG	LATITUDE						
KKM	CIVLEG	COMLEG	LATITUDE						
PCI	CIVLEG	COMLEG	LATITUDE						
EURO1900	CIVLEG	COMLEG	LATITUDE	REGEAP	REGMENA	REGSA	REGWENA		
SRIGHT	CIVLEG	COMLEG	LATITUDE						
CRIGHT	CIVLEG	COMLEG	LATITUDE						
MEDSHARE	CIVLEG	COMLEG	LATITUDE						
GDP90	INCLOW	INCMID	INCHIGH	REGEAP	REGMENA	REGSA	REGLAC	REGWENA	LATITUDE
SDGR	INCLOW	INCMID	INCHIGH	REGEAP	REGMENA	REGSA	REGLAC	REGWENA	LATITUDE
SGBMP	INCLOW	INCMID	INCHIGH	CIVLEG	COMLEG	LATITUDE			
SDP1	INCLOW	INCMID	INCHIGH	CIVLEG	COMLEG	LATITUDE			
SDTP	INCLOW	INCMID	INCHIGH	REGEAP	REGMENA	REGSA	REGLAC	REGWENA	LATITUDE
SDTT	INCLOW	INCMID	INCHIGH	REGEAP	REGMENA	REGSA	REGLAC	REGWENA	LATITUDE

Table A2.6 Setting for PcGets

expert significance:	0.075	0.075	0.75	0.075	0.01	0.005		
expert presearch:	0.75	1	0.5	0.075	0.075	0.05	0.05	1
expert block search:	1	1	1	1	1	1	1	1
expert choose specific:		"HQ"						
expert split sample:	0.075	0.75	0.2	0.4	0.4			
expert outlier dection:		2.56						
expert tests:	1	1	0	1	0	0	1	
expert test options:	0.5	0.9	12	1	4	1	4	
set detect outliers:	"1"							
set0lagorder:	"0"							
set0topdown:	"1"							
set0bottomup:	"1"							
setsplitsample:	"1"							
setstrategy:	"expert",	1						
setreporting:	"0"							
estimate:	"Gets",	1	1	n	1			

Note: A change has been made to the "liberal strategy" default setting by increasing the F pre-search testing (top-down) at step 1 from 0.75 to 1. "n" denotes the sample size.

Table A2.7 Determinants of *FD* by Gets

	Full				Developing Country				La Porta			
	GUM		Final Model		GUM		Final Model		GUM		Final Model	
Variable	Coeff	t-value	Coeff	t-value	Coeff	t-value	Coeff	t-value	Coeff	t-value	Coeff	t-value
CONSTANT	−8.112	−1.338	−10.563	−4.074	−16.154	−1.151	−15.723	−5.932	0.000	0.000		
GDP90	1.326	2.660	1.391	4.403	2.250	2.823	2.049	7.192	−0.878	−0.316		
POP90	0.566	2.549	0.705	5.856	0.768	1.816	0.248	2.855	1.044	1.733	1.314	8.610
ETHPOL	0.497	0.511			−1.290	−0.671			2.592	0.672	3.131	4.652
ETHNIC	−0.774	−0.557			0.282	0.137			0.111	0.032		
RELIGION	−0.214	−0.188			−0.386	−0.156			2.183	0.400		
LANGUAGE	1.132	1.138			2.920	1.847	1.487	2.941	1.469	0.492		
EURFRAC	−0.702	−0.940	−1.287	−3.694	2.010	0.797			−4.480	−2.036	−3.988	−6.216
REGEAP	0.938	0.659			1.486	0.334			−4.249	−0.841	−4.224	−3.847
REGMENA	0.798	0.600			5.417	1.011	3.353	7.548	−0.477	−0.104		
REGSA	0.311	0.227			2.864	0.457			−4.670	−0.853	−3.000	−4.524
REGSSA	−0.275	−0.178			1.664	0.309			−1.473	−0.193		
REGLAC	0.029	0.022			0.275	0.079			3.615	1.283	2.435	3.317
REGWENA	−0.388	−0.262							−9.044	−1.455	−7.789	−5.614
LANDLOCK	−0.266	−0.325			1.098	0.772	2.585	1.188	2.562	3.979		
LATITUDE	−0.021	−0.805	−0.041	−2.948	−0.046	−1.241			0.071	0.644		
AREA	−0.421	−2.383	−0.417	−4.188	−0.246	−0.725			−0.260	−0.564	−0.416	−4.095
MINDIST	−0.036	−0.258			−0.272	−0.183			−0.232	−0.508		
POP100CR	−0.010	−0.824			0.010	0.726			0.015	0.471	0.015	2.592
RESPOINT	−0.269	−0.500			−0.774	−0.916	3.353	7.548	−3.148	−1.723	−2.960	−4.633
TOPEN	0.608	0.712			2.046	1.220	1.990	5.192	3.184	1.237	1.854	3.512
CTRADE	0.013	0.640			0.036	1.495			0.046	0.487	0.034	2.421
EXPMANU	−0.097	−0.198			−1.975	−0.349			0.848	0.958	1.246	4.264
EXPPRIM	−0.378	−0.792			0.362	0.478			1.844	1.164	1.416	2.597

SDGR	-0.026				-0.126	-0.636			-0.794	-1.154	-0.571	-3.875
SDBMP	0.000				-0.001	-1.315			0.004	1.485	0.004	4.876
SDPI	0.001				0.001	1.053			-0.031	-1.513	-0.035	-5.076
SDTP	0.120				-0.435	-0.519	0.001	2.193	-2.270	-0.825	-1.390	-2.263
SDTT	-0.008	-0.024	-3.270		-0.015	-0.720			0.033	0.827	0.036	3.222
CIVLEG	-2.353	-0.927	-3.396		-6.899	-1.458	-4.562	-5.239	10.563	0.332		
COMLEG	-1.885	-1.037			-5.840	-1.083	-3.445	-3.879	12.554	0.390	1.687	4.452
POLITY2	0.051	0.927			0.151	1.528	0.164	4.382	0.083	0.326		
DURABLE	0.014	0.903			-0.025	-0.781			0.010	0.248		
FREE	0.001	0.004			0.168	0.596			-0.542	-0.424	-0.453	-3.033
KKM	1.191	1.974	1.846	5.064	0.099	0.119			3.425	1.245	4.849	9.156
PCI	-4.827	-2.095	-5.363	-5.184	-6.769	-1.870	-5.391	-4.026	-13.777	-1.472	-13.547	-7.002
EURO1900					3.579	0.633						
MEDSHARE									0.627	0.152		
SRIGHT									-0.282	-0.320		
CRIGHT									-0.413	-1.098	-0.374	-3.169
RSS	26.44				51.11	5.37						
sigma	0.97				0.97	0.82			17.06		3.78	
R^2	0.90				0.80	0.96			0.73		0.50	
Radj^2	0.77				0.77	0.77			0.86		0.98	
LogLik	28.28				7.20	46.26			0.82		0.94	
AIC	0.24				0.09	-0.47			20.84		47.21	
HQ	0.72				0.22	0.08			-0.40		-1.11	
SC	1.46				0.42	0.99			-0.22		-0.73	
Chow test 1	0.00				0.00	0.00			0.08		-0.05	
Chow test 2	1.34	0.28	0.66		7.45	0.39	1.35	0.28	0.00			
Normality test	0.17	0.92	8.46		1.77	0.41	1.76	0.41	0.00			
Hetero test									2.59	0.27	1.35	0.51

Note: The dependent variable *FD* is the index of overall financial development over the period 1990–99. The variable description is in Appendix Table A2.1. The Gets analysis yields coefficients and *t*-values for the variables in the final model. There are 64 observations in the whole sample, 44 observations in the developing country sample and 40 observations in the La Porta sample.

62 Determinants of Financial Development

Table A2.8 Determinants of *FDBOND*

	La Porta Sample			
	BMA		Gets	
Variable	PIPs	Sign	Coeff	t-value
CONSTANT	1.000	(−)		
GDP90	0.105			
POP90	0.915	(−)		
ETHPOL	0.916	(−)		
ETHNIC	0.951	(−)		
RELIGION	0.251			
LANGUAGE	0.979	(+)		
EURFRAC	0.920	(+)		
REGEAP	0.859	(+)		
REGMENA	0.829	(+)		
REGSA	0.908	(−)		
REGSSA	0.317	(−)		
REGLAC	0.874	(+)		
REGWENA	0.828	(+)		
LANDLOCK	0.842	(−)		
LATITUDE	0.084			
AREA	0.731	(−)		
MINDIST	0.233			
POP100CR	0.326	(+)		
RESPOINT	0.606	(+)		
TOPEN	0.142			
CTRADE	0.848	(−)	0.0164	3.812
EXPMANU	0.944	(−)		
EXPPRIM	0.938	(−)		
SDGR	0.956	(+)		
SDBMP	0.173			
SDPI	0.847	(+)		
SDTP	0.153			
SDTT	0.311			
CIVLEG	0.465	(+)		
COMLEG	0.449	(−)		
POLITY2	0.944	(+)		
DURABLE	0.877	(+)		
FREE	0.124			
KKM	0.825	(−)		
PCI	0.850	(+)		
EURO1900				
MEDSHARE	0.267			
SRIGHT	0.197		0.0751	2.717
CRIGHT	0.838	(+)		

(continued)

Table A2.8 Continued

| | La Porta Sample | | | |
| | BMA | | Gets | |
Variable	PIPs	Sign	Coeff	t-value
RSS				6.06
sigma				0.43
R^2				−0.08
Radj^2				−0.11
LogLik				30.68
AIC				−1.64
HQ				−1.61
SC				−1.55
Chow test 1				
Chow test 2				
Normality test				
Hetero test				

Note: The dependent variable *FDBOND* is the index of bond market development over the period 1990–99. The variable description is in Appendix Table A2.1. This study is based on La Porta sample with 35 countries. The BMA analysis yields posterior probabilities of inclusion (PIPs), the total posterior model probabilities (PMPs) for all models including a given variable, and the sign certainty index of a relationship (Sign). No sign given means the sign of estimated relationship being uncertain. The Gets analysis yields coefficients and *t*-values for the variables in the final model.

3
Private Investment and Financial Development

3.1 Introduction

In recent decades there has been a large body of literature studying the substantial roles that investment and financial development play in long-run economic growth (Levine and Renelt, 1992; King and Levine, 1993 among others). This chapter aims to provide an exhaustive analysis of the existence of and directions of causality between these two important aspects of economic activities, namely aggregate private investment and financial development. By exploiting the time series variation in both private investment and financial development, and allowing for global interdependence and heterogeneity across countries, this chapter suggests positive causal effects going in both directions.

As is well known, in the absence of asymmetric information, financial markets can function efficiently in the sense that, for any investment project, the financial contract provides the borrowers and investors with expected payments determined by the prevailing economy-wide interest rate. However, in reality, entrepreneurs are always much better informed than investors as to the outcome of investment projects and their actions, calling for costly state verification conducted by financial intermediaries (Townsend, 1979),[28] and the corresponding contracting problem between financial intermediaries and entrepreneurs (Diamond, 1984; Gale and Hellwig, 1985; Williamson, 1986, 1987 and Bernanke and Gertler, 1989). Does entrepreneurs' investment behaviour exert any effect on the expansion of financial systems or the reduction of agency costs? Does the increase in private investment as a whole contribute to financial development? On the other hand, another natural question could be whether more efficient financial markets encourage entrepreneurs' investment behaviour, or whether financial development brings about a surge of private investment.

Economic theory in general predicts that private investment and financial intermediary development contribute in a significant way to each other. On the one hand, an increase in private investment constitutes rising demand for external finance, enlarging the extent of financial intermediation by directly encouraging financial intermediaries to persuade savers to switch their holdings of unproductive tangible assets to bank deposits. Levine and Renelt (1992) suggest that more investment raises the rate of economic growth, which could stimulate financial development (Greenwood and Smith, 1997). On the other hand, the endogenous finance-growth models (for example Diamond, 1984; Diamond and Dybvig, 1983; Greenwood and Jovanovic, 1990; Bencivenga and Smith, 1991 and Greenwood and Smith, 1997) suggest that financial markets have an important role in channelling investment capital to its highest valued use. Financial intermediaries tend to induce a portfolio allocation in favour of productive investment by offering liquidity to savers, easing liquidity risks, reducing resource mobilization costs and exerting corporate control. It seems natural to wonder if what is possible in theory is consistent with what has happened in reality.

The causes of financial development have become an increasingly significant research area in recent years.[29] Following the renowned Solow-Swan growth model, much research has been undertaken to examine the long-run determinants of economic growth. Levine and Renelt (1992) emphasize the critical role of investment in growth, leading to investment being included in most growth regressions. However, there has been little work on the role of investment in the determination of financial development.

Much work has been done to investigate the determinants of investment since the 1990s.[30] Following the influential work of King and Levine (1993), who find a positive effect of financial development on various aspects of economic activity, several empirical studies provide evidence in support of a positive impact of financial development on capital formation in the private sector.[31] However, existing research in general assumes error independence across countries, which is a highly restrictive assumption to make, particularly in the context of globalization.

This background has motivated research into the interactions between aggregate private investment and financial development in this chapter. The econometric analysis is based on a dataset for 43 developing countries over the period 1970–98. Since commercial banks dominate the

66 *Determinants of Financial Development*

financial sector and stock markets play only very minor roles in most developing countries, this research focuses on the level of financial intermediary development, for which a new index is constructed by using principal component analysis based on three banking development indicators[32] widely used in the literature. This research has become more important as since the 1970s many developing countries have sought to stimulate economic growth by choosing to encourage private investment, while abandoning import-substitution policies led by the public sector.

It is worth noting that this analysis focuses on the period when, after the collapse of the Bretton Woods system, the world economy has experienced "a new and deeper version of globalization" following "a gradual liberalization of trade and capital flows" (Crafts, 2000). The increase in global trade and financial integration[33] has been found to induce closer interdependence in the global economy through its implications for the properties of business cycle fluctuations. Imbs (2003), using data for a group of developed and developing countries over 1983–98, finds that the intensity of financial linkages and the volume of intra-industry trade have a positive impact on cross-country business cycle co-movement. Frankel and Rose (1998) show that trading partners have a higher degree of business cycle co-movement. Kim *et al.* (2003) observe a high degree of business cycle co-movement for a set of Asian emerging market countries over 1960–96.

The phenomenon of business cycle co-movement has often been explained by using a common factor analysis in which macroeconomic variables such as aggregate output, consumption and investment are decomposed into common observed global shocks (like sharp fluctuations of oil prices), common unobserved global shocks (like technological shocks), specific regional shocks and country shocks (Gregory *et al.*, 1997; Kose *et al.*, 2003 and Bai and Ng, 2004). It is these shocks that lead to a closer real and financial interdependence across countries.

The 1990s witnessed growing research on the stochastic properties of panel datasets where the time dimension and cross section dimension are relatively large, and, especially, the issue of cross section error dependence has received a great deal of attention in recent years. The application of unit root and cointegration tests to panels is motivated by the possible increase of statistical power through pooling information across units. However, the power of tests is increased only when the cross section units are independent, which is an assumption that may be hard to justify given the rising degree of financial market integration and business cycle synchronization. This research attempts to explore this issue by fully taking into account the effects of global shocks causing cross section dependence across countries.

The analysis in this chapter includes two steps. The first step is an analysis on data for five-year averages, which is commonly used in the literature. It applies the system GMM estimation method due to Arellano and Bover (1995) and Blundell and Bond (1998) allowing for possible correlations between regressors, and both individual effects and global shocks. It then moves on to the second step, an analysis using methods on pooled annual data assuming a common factor structure in the error term from Bai and Ng (2004). Before proceeding to estimation, the time series properties of the panel dataset are carefully examined. The so-called "second-generation tests" are applied, which allow for cross section dependence, including a panel unit root test of Bai and Ng (2004) and a panel cointegration test of Pedroni (2004) on defactored data. The models are then estimated by the Pesaran (2006) Common Correlated Effect approach.

The analysis on averaged data produces significant findings of positive causal effects going in both directions, and indicates a high degree of persistence exists in the averaged data of financial development and private investment. The annual data study suggests that the series of both private investment and financial development are integrated, and two-way positive long-run causal effects exist in the cointegrated system. The findings of this chapter support the view that a private investment boom typically follows further financial development, while the demand for external finance is reflected in the subsequent level of financial development. This has significant policy implications for the development of financial markets and the conduct of macroeconomic policies in developing countries in a global economy.

The remainder of the chapter proceeds in Section 3.2 to describe the data. Section 3.3 analyses this link using system GMM estimation on data for five-year averages. Section 3.4 employs the common factor approach to examine this link with annual data, including panel unit root testing panel cointegration testing and estimation. Section 3.5 concludes.

3.2 The data

This section outlines the measures and data for private investment and financial development. Appendix Table A3.1 summarizes the variable description and sources.

68 *Determinants of Financial Development*

The measure of private investment, denoted by *PI*, is the ratio of nominal private investment to nominal GDP. The data are taken from the World Bank Global Development Network Database (2002).[34]

The measure of financial development, denoted by *FD*. Since commercial banks dominate the financial sector and stock markets play very minor roles in most developing countries, this research focuses on the level of financial intermediary development, for which a new index is constructed by using principal component analysis[35] based on three banking development indicators widely used in the literature.

The principal component analysis is based on the following three popular banking development indicators:[36]

The first measure, Liquid Liabilities (*LLY*), is one of the major indicators used to measure the size, relative to the economy, of financial intermediaries including three types of financial institutions: the central bank, deposit money banks and other financial institutions. It is calculated by the ratio of liquid liabilities of banks and non-bank financial intermediaries (currency plus demand and interest-bearing liabilities) over GDP.

The second indicator, Private Credit (*PRIVO*), is defined as credit issued to the private sector by banks and other financial intermediaries divided by GDP. This excludes the credit issued to government, government agencies and public enterprises, as well as the credit issued by the monetary authority and development banks. It is a general indicator of financial intermediary activities provided to the private sector.

The third, Commercial-Central Bank (*BTOT*), is the ratio of commercial bank assets to the sum of commercial bank and central bank assets. It reflects the advantage of financial intermediaries in dealing with lending, monitoring and mobilizing saving and facilitating risk management relative to the central bank.

Data on these financial development indicators are obtained from the World Bank's Financial Structure and Financial Development Database (2008). *FD* is the first principal component of these three indicators above and accounts for 74% of their variation. The weights resulting from principal component analysis over the period 1990–98 are 0.60 for Liquid Liabilities, 0.63 for Private Credit and 0.49 for Commercial-Central Bank.[37] Since these indicators are used to measure the size of financial intermediary development,[38] the composite index, *FD*, mainly captures the depth of bank-based intermediation.

Appendix Table A3.2 presents descriptive statistics for private investment, the measure of financial development, real GDP and trade openness. The panel dataset contains 43 developing countries over the period 1970–98. The countries in the full sample are listed in Appendix Table A3.3. The transition economies are omitted. We also exclude countries with fewer than 20 observations over 1970–98.

3.3 Analysis on data for five-year averages

To examine the relationship between private investment and financial development, this chapter conducts panel data estimation for 43 developing countries over 1970–98, based on averaged data over non-overlapping, five-year periods in this section, and annual data in Section 3.4. Panel data estimation tends to produce more convincing findings than cross section analysis and classical time series analysis since it exploits both the cross section and time dimensions of the data.[39] It allows us to control for unobserved country-specific effects and omitted variables bias, and look at both long-run and short-run effects.

This section mainly focuses on the system GMM method proposed by Arellano and Bover (1995) and Blundell and Bond (1998), using averaged data (with a maximum of six observations per country). As widely used in the growth literature (Islam, 1995; Caselli *et al.*, 1996; Levine *et al.*, 2000), averaging data over fixed intervals has the potential for eliminating business cycle fluctuations and makes it easier to capture the relationships of interest. Section 3.3.1 briefly describes the system GMM approach, and section 3.3.2 presents the empirical results.

3.3.1 Methodology: System GMM

The following AR(1) model has been found appropriate for this application:[40]

$$FD_{it} = \alpha_{11} FD_{i,t-1} + PI_{i,t-1}\beta_{11} + \eta_{i1} + \phi_{1t} + v_{it1} \quad (3.1)$$

$$PI_{it} = \alpha_{12} PI_{i,t-1} + FD_{i,t-1}\beta_{12} + \eta_{i2} + \phi_{2t} + v_{it2} \quad (3.2)$$

$$i = 1, 2, \ldots, 43 \text{ and } t = 2, \ldots, 6$$

For the sake of convenience, denote by y the dependent variable (either *FD* or *PI*) and by x the explanatory variables other than the lagged dependent variable:

$$y_{it} = \alpha y_{i,t-1} + x'_{i,t-1}\beta + \eta_i + \phi_t + v_{it} \quad (3.3)$$

$$i = 1, 2, \ldots, 43 \text{ and } t = 2, \ldots, 6$$

where η_i is an unobserved country-specific time-invariant effect not captured by $x_{i,\,t-1}$, and can be regarded as capturing the combined effects of all time-invariant omitted variables.

ϕ_t captures the global shocks. Recently a large body of literature has indicated that the existence of common factors, either global, cyclical or seasonal effects, has the potential for causing co-movements of variables in the world economy. Since common factors are likely to be partially cancelled out when the data are averaged, for simplicity this section considers only common time effects or a single global shock having an identical effect on each cross section unit. Section 3.4 explores the effects of common factors in more depth.

v_{it} is the transitory disturbance term, assumed to satisfy sequential moment conditions of the form

$$E(v_{it}|\, y_i^{t-1},\, x_i^{t-1},\, \eta_i, \phi_t) = 0 \tag{3.4}$$

where $y_i^{t-1} = (y_{i1}, y_{i2} \ldots, y_{i,t-1})'$, $x_i^{t-1} = (x_{i1}, x_{i2} \ldots, x_{i,t-1})'$.

This assumption implies that (1) the transient errors are serially uncorrelated; (2) xs are predetermined variables with respect to the time-varying errors in the sense that $x_{i,\,t-1}$ may be correlated with $v_{i,\,t-1}$ and earlier shocks, but is uncorrelated with $v_{i\,t}$ and subsequent shocks; (3) the individual effects are uncorrelated with the idiosyncratic shocks, but correlations between individual effects and lagged y and lagged x are not ruled out and (4) the global shocks are uncorrelated with the idiosyncratic shocks, while correlations between global shocks and lagged y and lagged x are possible.

The assumption of the explanatory variables xs being predetermined rules out a potential endogeneity bias, but allows for feedbacks from the past realizations of y to current xs. This assumption is believed to be appropriate given that financial development is potentially both a consequence and an origin of private investment, and vice versa.[41]

For the stability of the estimated model, the autoregressive coefficient is assumed to lie inside the unit circle, $|\alpha| < 1$.

The coefficient β reflects the existence and direction of Granger causality going from lagged x to y. According to work by Chamberlain (1984) and Holtz-Eakin *et al.* (1988) on Granger non-causality tests in the general setting of dynamic panel data estimation, the non-causality hypothesis can be tested by checking whether the coefficients of the lagged values of the independent variables are zero or the coefficients on the lagged difference of independent variables in the transformed equations are zero, that is $\beta = 0$. Given that the model is stable, a point estimate for the long-run effect can be calculated as follows:

$$\beta_{LR} = \frac{\beta}{(1-\alpha)}$$

The standard error for the long-run effect can be approximated by using the delta method (for example Papke and Wooldridge, 2005).

This analysis employs the system GMM method, which is proposed by Arellano and Bover (1995) and Blundell and Bond (1998) to improve upon the Arellano and Bond (1991) first-differenced GMM method, which may be plagued with weak instrument problems. There have been a number of methods proposed to estimate dynamic panel data models with a short time dimension, in which first-differencing is used to eliminate the individual effects. Below is Equation (3.3) in first differences:

$$\Delta y_{it} = \alpha \Delta y_{i,t-1} + \Delta x'_{i,t-1} \beta + \Delta \phi_t + \Delta v_{it} \qquad (3.5)$$

$$i = 1, 2, \ldots, 43 \text{ and } t = 3, \ldots, 6$$

where $\Delta y_{it} = y_{it} - y_{i,t-1}$, $\Delta x_{i,t-1} = x_{i,t-1} - x_{i,t-2}$, $\Delta \phi_t = \phi_t - \phi_{t-1}$ and $\Delta v_{it} = v_{it} - v_{i,t-1}$.

The sequential moment conditions above imply that all lagged values of y_{it} and x_{it} dated from $t - 2$ and earlier are suitable instruments for the differenced values of the original regressors, $\Delta y_{i,t-1}$ and $\Delta x_{i,t-1}$. While the first-differenced 2SLS estimator taken from Anderson and Hsiao (1981, 1982) uses y_{it-2} and x_{it-2}, the first-differenced GMM estimator uses all lagged values of y_{it} and x_{it} dated from $t - 2$ and earlier. The moment conditions for errors in differences on which the first-differenced GMM estimator is based can be written as:

$$E\left[\begin{pmatrix} y_i^{t-2} \\ x_i^{t-2} \end{pmatrix} (\Delta y_{it} - \alpha \Delta y_{i,t-1} - \Delta x'_{i,t-1}\beta - \Delta \phi_t)\right] = 0 \qquad (3.6)$$

$$t = 3, \ldots, 6$$

where $y_i^{t-2} = (y_{i1}, y_{i2} \ldots, y_{i,t-2})'$ and $x_i^{t-2} = (x_{i1}, x_{i2} \ldots, x_{i,t-2})'$.

Blundell and Bond (1998) argue that in the standard AR(1) model when the time series becomes highly persistent in the sense that "the value of the autoregressive parameter approaches unity or the variance of the individual effects increases relative to the variance of the disturbances", the lagged values of the series may be weak instruments for first differences. The first-differenced GMM estimator employing these weak instruments has been found to have poor finite sample properties in terms of bias and imprecision.

To tackle the weak instruments problem, Arellano and Bover (1995) and Blundell and Bond (1998) develop a "system GMM" estimator[42] by considering a mean stationarity assumption on initial conditions in the sense that the mean of the distribution of the initial observations coincides with the mean of the steady-state distribution of the process. For the multivariate autoregressive model, Blundell and Bond (2000) show that a sufficient condition for the additional moment conditions to be valid is the joint mean stationarity of the series.

For this context the additional mean stationarity condition of (y_{it}, x_{it}) enables the lagged first differences of the series (y_{it}, x_{it}) dated t-1 as instruments for the untransformed equations in levels. In addition to the moments for errors in differences described before, the system GMM estimator, denoted by SYS-GMM, is also based on the additional moments for errors in levels as follows:

$$E\left[\begin{pmatrix}\Delta y_{i,t-1} \\ \Delta x_{i,t-1}\end{pmatrix}(y_{it} - \alpha y_{i,t-1} - x'_{i,t-1}\beta - \phi_t)\right] = 0 \qquad (3.7)$$

$$t = 3, \ldots, 6$$

As suggested by Blundell and Bond (1998), combining the first-differenced equations using suitably lagged levels as instruments, with levels equations using suitably lagged first differences as instruments, the SYS-GMM estimator is expected to have much smaller finite sample bias and greater precision in the presence of persistent data.

Apart from the orthogonality conditions (3.6) and (3.7) stated above, the SYS-GMM estimator also makes use of the following moments for the period-specific constants due to the existence of global shocks:

$$E(\Delta y_{it} - \alpha \Delta y_{i,t-1} - \Delta x'_{i,t-1}\beta - \Delta \phi_t) = 0 \qquad (3.8)$$

$$t = 3, \ldots, 6$$

To avoid the possible over-fitting bias associated with using the full Arellano and Bond (1991) instrument set, this analysis uses restricted instrument sets suggested by Bowsher (2002), who proposes selectively reducing the number of moment conditions for each first-differenced equation. More specifically, we use only lagged values of y_{it} and x_{it} from $t-2$ to $t-4$ as instruments. Accordingly, for SYS-GMM estimators the number of orthogonality conditions reduces to 31 in total, so that there are 24 over-identifying restrictions. Another way to avoid the possible over-fitting bias is the introduction of the two additional versions of SYS-GMM discussed below.

3.3.2 Empirical results

This section presents the SYS-GMM estimates for Equations (3.1) and (3.2). Two additional versions of SYS-GMM are also considered in order to circumvent over-fitting and the possibility that the mean stationarity assumptions may be incorrect. While SYS-GMM-1 uses only $\Delta y_{i,t-1}$ as instruments in levels, SYS-GMM-2 uses only $\Delta x_{i,t-1}$ in the same way. The OLS and within group estimates are also reported. Conventional wisdom has revealed that, although both of them are inconsistent for short panels, the OLS and within group (WG) estimates of the first-order autoregressive parameter act as two extremes of the interval in which a consistent estimate of this parameter is expected to lie.[43]

Three specification tests are conducted to address the consistency of SYS-GMM estimator, which mainly depends on the validity of the instruments. The first is a Serial Correlation test, which tests the null hypothesis of no first-order serial correlation and no second-order serial correlation in the residuals in the first-differenced equation. The second is a Sargan test of over-identifying restrictions, which is used to examine the overall validity of the instruments by comparing the moment conditions with their sample analogue. A finite sample correction is made to the two-step covariance matrix using the method of Windmeijer (2005). The third is a difference Sargan test, denoted by Diff-Sargan, proposed by Blundell and Bond (1998), which examines the null hypothesis of mean stationarity for the SYS-GMM estimator. This statistic, called an incremental Sargan test statistic, is the difference between the Sargan statistics for first-differenced GMM and SYS-GMM. It would be asymptotically distributed as a χ^2 with k degrees of freedom, where k is the number of additional moment conditions.

Table 3.1 presents the results for causality going from private investment to financial development. The OLS level and WG estimates for the lagged dependent variable form an interval in which the system GMM estimates fall. The specification tests for the three versions of SYS-GMM used indicate that we can reject the null that the error term in first differences exhibits no first-order serial correlation and cannot reject the hypothesis that there is no second-order serial correlation. The Sargan tests in three models do not signal that the instruments are invalid. The difference Sargan for SYS-GMM cannot reject the null of the additional moment conditions being valid. These results indicate that every model

Table 3.1 Does private investment cause financial development? 1970–98 (five-year-average data)

Dependent variable: FD_{it}	OLS	WG	SYS-GMM	SYS-GMM-1	SYS-GMM-2
$FD_{i,t-1}$	0.880	0.597	0.806	0.741	0.578
	[16.46]***	[8.32]***	[8.87]***	[6.87]***	[2.82]***
$PI_{i,t-1}$	2.785	5.091	5.286	6.745	3.779
	[5.08]***	[5.62]***	[4.27]***	[4.58]***	[2.21]**
M1 (p-value)			0.00	0.00	0.05
M2 (p-value)			0.89	0.92	0.69
Sargan (p-value)			0.36	0.24	0.44
Diff-Sargan (p-value)			0.87	0.76	1.00
Granger Causality (p-value)	0.00	0.00	0.00	0.00	0.03
LR effect point estimate	23.21	12.63	27.22	26.02	8.96
(Standard error)	[9.70]**	[2.84]***	[12.53]**	[9.04]***	[7.61]
Observations	212	212	212	212	212

Notes: 43 developing countries. Robust t statistics in brackets below point estimates.
*, **, *** significant at 10%, 5% and 1%, respectively. The system GMM results are two-step estimates with heteroscedasticity-consistent standard errors and test statistics; the standard errors are based on finite sample adjustment of Windmeijer (2005). The M1 and M2 test the null of no first-order and no second-order serial correlation in first-differenced residuals. The Sargan tests the over-identifying restrictions for GMM estimators, asymptotically X^2. The Diff-Sargan tests the null of mean stationarity for system GMM estimators in which SYS-GMM uses standard moment conditions, while SYS-GMM-1 only uses lagged first-differences of FD dated $t-1$ as instruments in levels and SYS-GMM-2 uses only lagged first-differences of PI dated $t-1$ as instruments in levels. The Granger causality test is used to examine the null hypothesis that private investment doesn't cause financial development. LR measures the long-run effect of private investment on financial development. Its standard error is approximated using the delta method.

from column 3 to column 5 is well specified and the SYS-GMM estimator is indeed preferable to the first-differenced GMM estimator for this context. SYS-GMM estimates provide strong evidence for the positive impact of private investment on financial development. This result is supported by the Granger non-causality test, which clearly rejects the null hypothesis, suggesting that there is a causal effect going from private investment to financial development. The Long-Run (LR) effect estimate of SYS-GMM indicates that this effect tends to persist into the long run. The SYS-GMM-1 estimates further confirm the findings, while SYS-GMM-2 estimates support the short-run effect only, not the long-run effect. Moreover, SYS-GMM and SYS-GMM-1 estimates indicate that a high degree of persistence exists in the averaged data.

Table 3.2 Does financial development cause private investment? 1970–98 (five-year-average data)

Dependent variable: PI_{it}	OLS	WG	SYS-GMM	SYS-GMM-1	SYS-GMM-2
$PI_{i,t-1}$	0.744	0.232	0.521	0.490	0.424
	[14.04]***	[3.12]***	[4.27]***	[3.75]***	[3.00]***
$FD_{i,t-1}$	0.008	0.010	0.015	−0.008	0.022
	[2.09]**	[1.67]*	[2.32]**	[0.85]	[2.11]**
M1 (p-value)			0.00	0.01	0.01
M2 (p-value)			0.34	0.51	0.26
Sargan (p-value)			0.50	0.40	0.31
Diff-Sargan (p-value)			0.83	0.75	0.48
Granger Causality (p-value)	0.04	0.10	0.03	0.40	0.04
LR effect point estimate	0.03	0.01	0.03	−0.02	0.04
(Standard error)	[0.01]**	[0.01]*	[0.01]**	[0.02]	[0.01]**
Observations	198	198	198	198	198

Notes: 43 developing countries. The Granger causality test is used to examine the null hypothesis that financial development doesn't cause private investment. See Table 3.1 for more notes.

In Table 3.2 we turn to whether financial development Granger causes private investment. The specification tests indicate that the models associated with the three types of SYS-GMM are well specified. More specifically, we can reject no first-order serial correlation but cannot the hypothesis that there is no second-order serial correlation. Sargan tests and difference Sargan tests suggest that neither the instruments and mean stationarity conditions are invalid. Both SYS-GMM and SYS-GMM-2 show a positive causal effect going from financial development to private investment, not only in the short run but also in the long run.

Both SYS-GMM-1 in Table 3.1 and SYS-GMM-2 in Table 3.2 produce consistent findings with their counterparts, respectively. However, using the lagged first differences of *PI* dated *t*–1 as instruments in levels, SYS-GMM-2 in Table 2.1 and SYS-GMM-1 in Table 3.2 do not confirm the findings by their respective SYS-GMMs, especially the latter, perhaps suggesting that the moment conditions using lagged first differences of *PI* dated *t*–1 may not contain much information.

The SYS-GMM-1 and SYS-GMM-2 above potentially serve as the robustness tests to the SYS-GMM in the two tables. In addition, a set of experiments are conducted to test whether the above findings are robust to various model specifications. We first consider including GDP per capita in logs and trade openness separately as additional regressors, with the results reported on Appendix Tables A3.4 and A3.5, respectively. Second, we introduce the second lags of dependent and independent variables into the related models and report the results in Appendix Table A3.6.

In part A of Appendix Table A3.4, with *GDP* in log every model is still well specified. Both SYS-GMM and SYS-GMM-1 estimates indicate the positive short-run and long-run effects of private investment on financial development. SYS-GMM-1 estimates also show a positive effect of *GDP* in log on financial development. SYS-GMM-2 estimates find that both *PI* and *LGDP* in log are significantly positively associated with *FD* in the short run, but not in the long run. In part A of Appendix Table A3.4, with *GDP* in log in the models SYS-GMM and SYS-GMM-2 estimates suggest that *GDP* in log enters the models significantly while *FD* is no longer significant. *GDP* in log seems to pick up the short-run effects of financial development on private investment.

In part A of Appendix Table A3.5, when trade openness (*OPENC*) is included the SYS-GMM estimates continue to show a positive effect of private investment on financial development, not only in the short run but also in the long run. The model for SYS-GMM-1 is not well specified. The SYS-GMM-2 estimates find that both *PI* and *OPENC* have been found to exert significantly positive effects on financial development in the short run, but not in the long run. In part B of Appendix Table A3.5, SYS-GMM estimates suggest that the inclusion of *OPENC* doesn't change the significantly positive effect of financial development on private investment, in either the short run or the long run.

In Appendix Table A3.6 we investigate the causality with AR(2) models. Models for SYS-GMM and SYS-GMM-1 in both parts A and B of Appendix Tables A3.6 and A3.6 are well specified, as supported by the specification tests. Both SYS-GMM and SYS-GMM-1 estimates in part A of Appendix Table A3.6 continue to support the first lag of *PI* to enter the models significantly; in addition the second lag of *PI* is also observed to be significantly associated with financial development. The second lag of *FD* has been found to be insignificant in the models. The SYS-GMM estimates in part B of Appendix Table A3.6 show that the first lag of *PI* remains significantly positive; however, the second lag of *FD* and *PI* is insignificant.

At least the robustness tests suggest that the inclusion of trade openness in the models doesn't affect the pattern of the findings in Tables 3.1

and 3.2, and nor does the inclusion of the second lags of dependent and independent variables in the models.

In summary, by using the SYS-GMM estimation method on averaged data over 1970–1998 and controlling for the possibility of endogeneity and omitted variable biases, this analysis finds that the positively significant causation exists in both directions between private investment and financial development for 43 developing countries. It also indicates a high degree of persistence in the averaged data. The findings are robust to various estimation methods and model specifications.

However, it is worth noting that the asymptotic properties of the SYS-GMM estimator depend on having a large number of cross section units. Concerns remain regarding the finite sample bias for this context. The findings still await further confirmation from the analysis on pooled annual data which will be undertaken in Section 3.4.

3.4 Analysis on annual data

Using averaged data has a number of advantages, as well documented in the literature, but its limitations are also notable. Averaging data over fixed intervals (typically over five or ten years) arbitrarily modifies the time series dimension so that information loss is inevitable. Although averaging data has the potential for removing business cycle fluctuations, it is not guaranteed that such fluctuations are eliminated effectively given the varied length of business cycles across countries and over time. Moreover, methods like GMM – imposing homogeneity over all slope coefficients – fail to capture potential cross sectional heterogeneity in the parameters.

This section moves on to explore the link between private investment and financial development by using pooled annual data. In principle, annual data can be more informative than averaged data in examining the relevant effect. By explicitly looking at the yearly time series variation, one can explore the existence of heterogeneity across countries adequately and estimate the parameters of interest more precisely.

As widely pointed out, assuming cross section error independence fails to reflect a reality in which financial market integration and business cycle synchronization are key features of a global economy. The analysis in this section attempts to study the causality between private investment and financial development in a world where the existence of global shocks causes cross section dependence across countries.

The remainder of this section proceeds as follows. Subsection 3.4.1 sets out the common factor approach of Bai and Ng (2004). Subsection 3.4.2

contrasts the panel unit root test of Bai and Ng (2004) with the Maddala and Wu (1999) Fisher test, which is associated with the assumption of cross section independence. Subsection 3.4.3 conducts the panel cointegration test of Pedroni (1999, 2004) on observed data and defactored data. Subsection 3.4.4 adopts the Pesaran (2006) Common Correlated Effect approach to estimate the models.

3.4.1 Methodology: Common factor approach

Assuming the interactions between financial development (FD) and private investment over GDP (PI) are represented by the unrestricted autoregressive distributed lag ARDL(p, p) systems:

$$FD_{it} = \sum_{j=1}^{p} \alpha_{1ij} FD_{i,t-j} + \sum_{j=1}^{p} \beta_{1ij} PI_{i,t-j} + \theta_{1i}t + \lambda_{1i}'f_{1t} + v_{1it} \quad (3.9)$$

$$PI_{it} = \sum_{j=1}^{p} \alpha_{2ij} PI_{i,t-j} + \sum_{j=1}^{p} \beta_{2ij} FD_{i,t-j} + \theta_{1i}t + \lambda_{2i}'f_{2t} + v_{2it} \quad (3.10)$$

$i = 1, 2, \ldots, 43$ and $t = 2, \ldots, 29$

For the sake of simplicity, denoting by y the dependent variable (either FD or PI) and by xs the explanatory variables other than the lagged dependent variable, we have

$$y_{it} = \sum_{j=1}^{p} \alpha_{ij} y_{i,t-j} + \sum_{j=1}^{p} \beta_{ij} x_{i,t-j} + \theta_{1i}t + \lambda_i'f_t + v_{it} \quad (3.11)$$

$i = 1, 2, \ldots, 43$ and $t = 2, \ldots, 29$

where f_t is a $(r \times 1)$ vector of unobserved common factors, and λ_i is a factor loading vector, such that $\lambda_i'f_t = \lambda_{i1}'f_{t1} + \lambda_{i2}'f_{t2} \cdots + \lambda_{ir}'f_{tr}$ (here r is the number of common factors). The common factors could be a global trend component, a global cyclical component, common technological shocks or macroeconomic shocks that cause cross section dependence. v_{it} are errors assumed to be serially uncorrelated and independently distributed across countries. We allow for richer dynamics in the representations to control for business cycle influences, while the current value of x, x_{it}, is excluded to avoid a potential endogeneity problem.

The above representations with a factor structure are believed to be very general. Bai (2009) points out that the interactive effects model including the interaction between factors, f_t, and factor loadings, λ_i, is more general than an additive effects model, the traditional one-way or two-way fixed effects model.[44]

Since the common factors are unobservable, standard regression methods are not applicable for an equation like (3.11). Estimation of models with a common factor structure is still at its early stage of development. Pesaran (2006) estimates this type of model directly by proxying the common factors with weighted cross section averages (Subsection 3.4.4 discusses this in detail). In spite of its convenience in not involving estimation of common factors, the Pesaran (2006) approach is confined to the single factor case. Among others, Bai and Ng (2004) and Moon and Perron (2004) seek to estimate the common factors. Their approaches have advantages in accommodating multiple common factors that may coexist in the economy, effectively contributing to panel unit root testing, panel cointegration testing and estimation of models in a more general setting. Below is a brief description of common factor analysis resulting from Bai and Ng (2004).

To overcome possible cross section dependence in panel unit root testing, Bai and Ng (2004) propose a PANIC approach – Panel Analysis of Non-stationarity in Idiosyncratic and Common Components. Essentially they assume the DGP of a series z_{it} (which could be y_{it} or x_{it} for this case) has a common factor structure in the sense that the series is the sum of an unobserved deterministic component (d_{it}), an unobserved common component $(\lambda_i' f_t)$ and an idiosyncratic component (e_{it}) as follows:

$$z_{it} = d_{it} + \lambda_i' f_t + e_{it} \tag{3.12}$$

where f_t is a vector of unobserved common factors and λ_i is the factor loading vector as defined before. The common and idiosyncratic components could be stationary or non-stationary and are allowed to be integrated of different orders. The common factor (f_t) and the idiosyncratic component (e_{it}) can be expressed as:

$$f_{kt} = \alpha_k f_{k,t-1} + v_{it} \tag{3.13}$$

$$e_{it} = \rho_i e_{i,t-1} + \varepsilon_{it} \tag{3.14}$$

The factor k is stationary if $\alpha_k < 1$ while the idiosyncratic component (e_{it}) is stationary if $\rho_i < 1$. When the idiosyncratic component (e_{it}) is stationary, conventional wisdom suggests that the factors can be estimated by using principal component (PC) analysis. As a crucial step Bai and Ng (2004) propose applying a principal components analysis on the differenced data (when a linear trend is not allowed) or differenced and demeaned data (when a linear trend is allowed) to estimate the factors for the case where e_{it} is integrated of order one.

To estimate the factors, the following two steps should be taken.

The first step is to estimate the number of common factors, and this is discussed by Bai and Ng (2002) and Moon and Perron (2004). Bai and Ng (2002) suggest using a principal component analysis on the observed data to calculate the number of factors.[45] For any arbitrary k ($k < \min\{N, T\}$), the estimates of λ^k and f^k are derived by solving the following minimization problem ($d_{it} = 0$ is assumed for simplicity):

$$V(k) = \min_{\Lambda^k, f^k} (NT)^{-1} \sum_{i=1}^{N} \sum_{j=1}^{T} (z_{it} - \lambda_i^{k'} f_t^k)^2 \qquad (3.15)$$

$$\text{s.t.} \quad \frac{\Lambda^{k'} \Lambda^k}{N} = I_k \text{ or } \frac{f^{k'} f^k}{T} = I_k$$

where $f_t = (f_{t1}, f_{t2}, f_{t3}, ... f_{tr})'$, $\lambda_i = (\lambda_{i1}, \lambda_{i2}, \lambda_{i3} ... \lambda_{ir})'$, $\Lambda_i = (\lambda_1, \lambda_2, \lambda_3 ... \lambda_N)'$ and f is the $(T \times r)$ matrix of common components. Typically when $T < N$, the normalization that $\frac{f^{k'} f^k}{T} = I_k$ is used.[46] The estimated factor matrix, denoted by $\tilde{f}^k$, can be expressed as $\sqrt{T}$ times the eigenvectors corresponding to the k largest eigenvalues of the $T \times T$ matrix zz'. Given $\tilde{f}^k$, the estimated factor loading matrix, denoted by $\tilde{\Lambda}^k$, can be computed by $\frac{z' \tilde{f}^k}{T}$.

Given $\tilde{f}^k$ and $\tilde{\Lambda}^k$, Bai and Ng (2002) propose to determine the number of factors by minimizing one of the following criterion functions:

$$PC(k) = V(k, \tilde{f}^k) + kg(N, T) \qquad (3.16)$$

$$IC(k) = \ln[V(k, \tilde{f}^k)] + kg(N, T) \qquad (3.17)$$

where $V(k, \tilde{f}^k) = (NT)^{-1} \sum_{i=1}^{N} \sum_{j=1}^{T} (\varepsilon_i' \varepsilon_i)$ is a measure of fit, and $g(N, T)$ is a penalty function that depends on the size of panel. The criterion functions capture a trade-off between measures of fit and a penalty function. When the number of factors increases, the fit must improve, but the penalty goes up. Bai and Ng (2002) provide three criterion functions for $PC(k)$ and $IC(k)$, respectively. In general, $IC(k)$ is easier to use since it does not involve the estimation of a penalty function which requires the choice of a bounded integer (kmax).

The integer minimizing a criterion function is the estimated number of factors.

The second step is to estimate the common and idiosyncratic components once the true number of factors, denoted by r, has been worked out. Let Z_{it} be the differenced data (without a linear trend) or differenced and demeaned data (with a linear trend) of observed data z_{it}.[47] The principal component estimator of the factor matrix f, denoted by $\widehat{f}$, is $\sqrt{T-1}$ times the eigenvectors corresponding to the r largest eigenvalues of the $(T-1) \times (T-1)$ matrix ZZ'. Given $\widehat{f}$, the estimated factor loading matrix, denoted by $\widehat{\Lambda}$, can be computed by $\frac{Z'\widehat{f}}{T-1}$.

The approach above yields r estimated common factors $\widehat{f}_t$ and associated factor loadings $\widehat{\lambda}_i$. The estimated idiosyncratic component takes the form of

$$\widehat{e}_{it} = Z_{it} - \widehat{\lambda}_i'\widehat{f}_t \tag{3.18}$$

To remove the effect of possible over-differencing, Bai and Ng (2004) propose to re-cumulate the estimated common factors, $\widehat{f}_t$, and estimated idiosyncratic component, $\widehat{e}_{it}$, yielding

$$\widehat{F}_t = \sum_{s=2}^{t} \widehat{f}_s \tag{3.19}$$

$$\widehat{E}_{it} = \sum_{s=2}^{t} \widehat{e}_{is} \tag{3.20}$$

$$t = 2, \ldots T$$

The resulting idiosyncratic component, $\widehat{E}_{it}$, is in fact the defactored data corresponding to the observed data z_{it}.

3.4.2 Panel unit root tests

Over recent decades a number of panel unit root testing procedures have been proposed in the literature to increase the power of univariate unit root tests, such as Im *et al.* (2003), Levine *et al.* (2002) and Maddala and Wu (1999). Associated with the unrealistic assumption of cross section independence, these testing procedures are often classified as the first generation of panel unit root tests. Since the influential work by Banerjee *et al.* (2004), testing for unit roots in heterogeneous panels under the assumption of cross section dependence has attracted a great deal of attention. The testing procedures proposed by Pesaran (2007), Moon and Perron (2004) and Bai and Ng (2004) are among the second generation of panel unit root tests.

82 Determinants of Financial Development

With the common factor structure presented earlier, Bai and Ng (2004) note that the non-stationarity of series with a factor structure originates from the non-stationarity of either the common component or idiosyncratic component or both. Bai and Ng (2004) test for unit roots for the common component and idiosyncratic component, $\widehat{E}_{it}$, separately. For the idiosyncratic component, Bai and Ng (2004) propose testing the following ADF equation by using the (defactored) estimated idiosyncratic component, $\widehat{E}_{it}$, with no deterministic term:

$$\Delta \widehat{E}_{it} = d_{i0}\widehat{E}_{it} + d_{i1}\Delta \widehat{E}_{it-1} \ldots + d_{ip}\Delta \widehat{E}_{it-p} + \mu_{it} \tag{3.21}$$

They propose to use the Fisher P-test as suggested by Maddala and Wu (1999) on the above ADF equation.

For the non-stationarity of the common factors, Bai and Ng (2004) distinguish two cases. When there is only one common factor, a standard ADF test with an intercept is suggested:

$$\Delta \widehat{F}_t = D_t + \theta_0 \Delta \widehat{F}_{t-1} + \sum_{j=1}^{p} \theta_j \Delta \widehat{F}_{t-j} + v_{it} \tag{3.22}$$

When there is more than one common factor, Bai and Ng (2004) propose an interactive procedure, analogous to the Johansen trace test for cointegration.

Appendix Figure AF3.1 displays the time series plots of *FD* and *PI* for 43 countries over 1970–98. The data for *FD* and *PI* are standardized to control for common trends. More specifically, taking deviations from year-specific means removes the common components, common technological shocks or macro shocks, which have common effects across countries. The development process of *FD* was in general more gradual and growing without bounds while the development process of *PI* was more volatile and subject to bounds, in particular, *PI* experienced increases in the 1970s, late 1980s and early 1990s, but fell in the early 1980s.

Appendix Table A3.7 reports the values of information criterion $IC_{p1}(k)$ (Bai and Ng, 2002) for the series of *FD* and *PI*.[48] When $r = 1$, the $IC_{p1}(k)$ values for both *FD* and *PI* are minimized, clearly suggesting that there is only one common factor for *FD* and *PI*, respectively. The time series of the common factors for *FD* and *PI* are presented in Appendix Figure AF3.2.

Table 3.3 contrasts the panel unit root test proposed by Maddala and Wu (1999) and Bai and Ng (2004). The former is related to the assumption of cross section independence while the latter is defined under the

Table 3.3 Unit root tests in heterogeneous panels

	Maddala and Wu (1999) Fisher test	
	Without trend	With trend
FD	65.143	71.679
	[0.95]	[0.87]
PI	97.754	94.101
	[0.18]	[0.26]

	Bai and Ng (2004) test			
	FD		PI	
	Without trend	With trend	Without trend	With trend
Common Components (ADF)	−2.713 [0.07]*	−3.099 [0.11]	−1.981 [0.29]	−2.202 [0.49]
Idiosyncratic Components (P test)	214.555 [0.00]***	199.876 [0.00]***	79.206 [0.68]	55.067 [1.00]
Unit Root	no	yes	yes	yes

Note: The upper panel presents the results of Maddala and Wu (1999) Fisher test on the observed data under the null hypothesis of a unit root. The lower panel reports the Bai and Ng (2004) test, which decomposes the errors and conducts the unit root tests for the common components (ADF test) and idiosyncratic components (Maddala and Wu (1999) Fisher test) separately. *P*-values are in brackets.

assumption of cross section dependence. The Maddala and Wu (1999) Fisher test, which does not require a balanced panel, indicates the series of *FD* and *PI* may be I(1) processes no matter whether a trend is allowed.[49] Controlling for the common factor, the Bai and Ng (2004) approach suggests that the series for *FD* and *PI* are I(1) variables when we allow for a trend.

Since *PI* is the ratio of nominal private investment to nominal GDP, the evolution of *PI* is bounded between 0 and 1. The above finding on the *PI* series being an I(1) process, even though it is constrained within the interval between 0 and 1, is consistent with the finding in Section 3.3 on the averaged *PI* series being highly persistent. However, given that the *PI* series is bounded and the low power of these tests, more sophisticated testing methods may be called for.

84 *Determinants of Financial Development*

3.4.3 Panel cointegration tests

When both *FD* and *PI* are integrated, cointegration between the two variables is possible. This section uses panel cointegration techniques to investigate the existence of a long-run relationship between them. Banerjee *et al.* (2004) point out that "cointegration across units and within each unit may not be easily differentiatied due to the presence of cross section cointegration". The analysis of panel cointegration allowing for cross section dependence is still in its infancy. Motivated by Gengenbach *et al.* (2005), who suggest the use of defactored data, $\widehat{E}_{it}$, in panel cointegration testing to control for cross section dependence, this section contrasts the Pedroni (1999, 2004) residual-based panel cointegration tests using observed data and defactored data.

The Pedroni (2004) test, widely used in empirical research in recent years, assumes cross section independence of panel units but allows for some heterogeneity in the cointegrating relationships. He proposes two classes of statistics based on individual OLS residuals of the single cointegration regression below to test the null hypothesis of no cointegration:

$$y_{it} = \alpha_i + x'_{i,t}\delta_{it} + u_{it} \qquad (3.23)$$

One class is the "panel" statistics,[50] which are constructed by taking the ratio of the sum of the numerators and the sum of the denominators of individual unit root statistics across the within dimension of the panel with a homogeneity restriction, and the other is the "group mean" statistics,[51] which are based on the averages of individual unit root statistics along the between dimension of the panel allowing for heterogeneity.

Pedroni (2004) shows that the ADF-based tests perform better when the sample size is small. Table 3.4 reports the group and panel ADF statistics of Pedroni (1999, 2004) using observed data and defactored data, both with and without a deterministic trend. The result associated with using observed data shows, when common factors are allowed, that the presence of cross section dependence might render the Pedroni test unable to detect the cointegration relationship in question. However, when common factors are extracted, the null of no cointegration can always be rejected clearly, no matter whether we allow for a trend.[52] This table indicates that a stationary long-run relationship exists between financial development and private investment, and highlights allowing for cross section dependence as an important source of information for this analysis.

Table 3.4 Panel cointegration tests between FD and PI

	Observed data		Defactored data	
	Without trend	With trend	Without trend	With trend
Panel ADF	1.749	1.039	−3.956	−6.311
Group ADF	2.661	1.360	−3.822	−5.855

Note: This table reports the Pedroni (1999, 2004) cointegration test. The number of lag truncations used in the calculation of the Pedroni statistics is four. These are one-sided tests with an critical value of −1.64. Under the null hypothesis of no cointegration, the test statistic is asymptotically distributed as a standard normal.

Given the low power of these tests, this chapter still reports two estimates of the long-run relationship between FD and PI. One should soon realize that the long-run coefficients in Table 3.5 and Table 3.6 are very similar after normalizing the coefficients.

3.4.4 Estimation on annual data

Study of the estimation of large cross section and time series panel datasets with a common factor structure has been fairly scarce. This section undertakes the Pesaran (2006) common correlated effects approach for the estimation of heterogeneous panels with common factors. Section 3.4.4.1 sets out the estimation methods associated with both cross section error independence and cross section error dependence. Section 3.4.4.2 presents the empirical evidence.

3.4.4.1 Estimation methods

Given that the series of FD and PI appear to be cointegrated, there must be a vector error correction representation, as shown by Engle and Granger (1987), governing the co-movements of the series of FD and PI over time. The corresponding error correction equation to Equation (3.11) is as follows:

$$\Delta FD_{it} = \alpha_{1i} \left(FD_{i,t-1} - \frac{\beta_{1i}}{\alpha_{1i}} PI_{it} \right) - \sum_{j=1}^{p-1} \left[\left(\sum_{m=j+1}^{p} \alpha_{1im} \right) \Delta FD_{i,t-j} \right]$$
$$- \sum_{j=0}^{q-1} \left[\left(\sum_{m=j+1}^{q} \beta_{1im} \right) \Delta PI_{i,t-j} \right] + \theta_{1i} t + \lambda_i' f_t + v_{1it} \quad (3.24)$$

$$\Delta PI_{it} = \alpha_{2i}\left(PI_{i,t-1} - \frac{\beta_{2i}}{\alpha_{2i}}FD_{it}\right) - \sum_{j=1}^{p-1}\left[\left(\sum_{m=j+1}^{p}\alpha_{2im}\right)\Delta PI_{i,t-j}\right]$$

$$- \sum_{j=0}^{q-1}\left[\left(\sum_{m=j+1}^{q}\beta_{2im}\right)\Delta FD_{i,t-j}\right] + \theta_{2i}t + \lambda'_i f_t + v_{2it} \quad (3.25)$$

$$i = 1, 2, \ldots, 43 \text{ and } t = p+1, \ldots, 29$$

where

$$\alpha_{1i} = \sum_{j=1}^{p}\alpha_{1ij} - 1$$

$$\alpha_{2i} = \sum_{j=1}^{p}\alpha_{2ij} - 1$$

$$\beta_{1i} = \sum_{j=0}^{q}\beta_{1ij}$$

$$\beta_{2i} = \sum_{j=0}^{q}\beta_{2ij}$$

In Equations (3.24) and (3.25), α_{1i} and α_{2i} are the coefficients for the speeds of adjustment. $-\frac{\beta_{1i}}{\alpha_{1i}}$ and $-\frac{\beta_{2i}}{\alpha_{2i}}$ are the long-run coefficients for PI_{it} and FD_{it}, respectively. $\sum_{m=j+1}^{p}\alpha_{1im}$ and $\sum_{m=j+1}^{q}\beta_{1im}$ are the short-run coefficients for $\Delta FD_{i,t-j}$ and $\Delta PI_{i,t-j}$ in Equation (3.24), respectively, whereas $\sum_{m=j+1}^{p}\alpha_{1im}$ and $\sum_{m=j+1}^{q}\beta_{1im}$ are, respectively, the short-run coefficients for $\Delta PI_{i,t-j}$ and $\Delta FD_{i,t-j}$ in Equation (3.25).

For identification, the following equation should hold:

$$\frac{\beta_{1i}}{\alpha_{1i}} = 1 \bigg/ \left(\frac{\beta_{2i}}{\alpha_{2i}}\right)$$

In the absence of common factors, the within groups (WG) approach, mean group (MG) approach of Pesaran and Smith (1995) and pooled mean group (PMG) approach of Pesaran et al. (1999) are especially suited to the analysis of panels with large time and large cross section dimensions. The consistency of the WG estimator for the dynamic homogeneous model is approximately justified when T is large, as $N \to \infty$ (Nickell, 1981). In comparison to the WG method, which allows only the intercept to vary across countries but imposes homogeneity on all slope coefficients, the MG and PMG approaches allow for considerable heterogeneity across countries. The MG approach applies an OLS regression for each country to obtain individual slope coefficients, and then averages the country-specific coefficients to derive a long-run parameter for the panel.[53] For small samples, the MG estimator is likely to be inefficient although it is still consistent.

Unlike the MG approach, which imposes no restriction on slope coefficients, the PMG approach imposes cross section homogeneity restrictions only on the long-run coefficient, but allows short-run coefficients, the speeds of adjustment and the error variances to vary across countries. The restriction of long-run homogeneity can be tested via a Hausman test. Under the null hypothesis of long-run homogeneity, the PMG estimators are consistent and more efficient than the MG estimators. Moreover, Pesaran *et al.* (1999) show that the PMG estimators are consistent and asymptotically normal irrespective of whether the underlying regressors are I(1) or I(0).

The PMG approach requires that the coefficients for long-run effects are common across countries, that is,

$$\alpha_{1i} = \sum_{j=1}^{p} \alpha_{1j} - 1$$

$$\alpha_{2i} = \sum_{j=1}^{p} \alpha_{2j} - 1$$

$$\beta_{1i} = \sum_{j=0}^{q} \beta_{1j}$$

$$\beta_{2i} = \sum_{j=0}^{q} \beta_{2j}$$

When common factors are allowed, Pesaran (2006) suggests the use of the (weighted) cross-sectional averages of the dependent variable and individual specific regressors to proxy the common factors. More specifically, he proposes augmenting the observed regressors with the (weighted) cross-sectional averages of the dependent variable and the individual specific regressors such that as the number of cross section

88 Determinants of Financial Development

units goes to infinity, the effects of unobserved common factors can be eliminated.

Pesaran (2006) proposes two common correlated effect (CCE) approaches for large heterogeneous panels whose errors contain unobserved common factors. One is the common correlated effect pooled (CCEP) estimator, a generalization of the within groups estimator that allows for the possibility of cross section correlation, and the other is the common correlated effects mean group (CCEMG) estimator, a generalization of the mean group estimator of Pesaran and Smith (1995) which is adapted for the possibility of cross section correlation. The CCEP estimator is the within groups estimator with the (weighted) cross-sectional averages of the dependent variable and the individual specific regressors included in the model. The CCEMG approach uses OLS to estimate an auxiliary regression for each country in which the (weighted) cross sectional averages of the dependent variable and the individual specific regressors are added, and then the coefficients and standard errors are computed as usual.

The Pesaran (2006) approach exhibits considerable advantages. It does not involve estimation of unobserved common factors and factor loadings. It allows unobserved common factors to be possibly correlated with exogenous regressors and exert differential impacts on individual units. It permits unit root processes amongst the observed and unobserved common effects. The proposed estimator is still consistent, although it is no longer efficient, when the idiosyncratic components are not serially uncorrelated.

In this context, the cross section means of ΔFD_{it}, $FD_{i,t-1}$, ΔPI_{it} and $PI_{i,t-1}$ are considered.[54] The models are augmented with the interactions between regional dummies and cross sectional means of these variables, and time dummies. The CCEP and CCEMG estimators have been shown to be asymptotically unbiased and consistent as $N \rightarrow \infty$ and $T \rightarrow \infty$, and to have generally satisfactory finite sample properties. More importantly, the CCEP and CCEMG estimators hold for any number of unobserved common factors as long as the number is fixed, which is especially attractive.

A common correlated effects pooled mean group (CCEPMG) estimator is introduced in this study, which is a generalization of the pooled mean group estimator of Pesaran *et al.* (1999) which also allows for the possibility of cross section correlation. The restriction of long-run homogeneity can also be tested via a Hausman test. Under the null hypothesis of long-run homogeneity, the CCEPMG estimators are expected to be consistent and more efficient than the CCEMG estimators.

3.4.4.2 Estimation results

Table 3.5 examines whether private investment causes financial development for 43 developing countries over 1970–98, while Table 3.6 studies causality in the reverse direction. Tables 3.5 and 3.6 contrast the CCEP, CCEMG and CCEPMG estimates with their counterparts, the WG, MG and PMG estimates.[55] The first group of estimates is associated with the assumption of errors being cross sectionally dependent, while the latter group assumes cross section error independence. An autoregressive distributed lag ARDL(3, 3) system has been adopted for this analysis.[56]

We look first at the case of cross section error dependence. The coefficients corresponding to the speeds of adjustment in the two tables are significantly different from zero, suggesting that two-way Granger causalities exist between them.

Imposing homogeneity on all slope coefficients except for the intercept, the CCEP estimates in the two tables suggest that there are positive long-run effects going in two directions. When heterogeneity is sought, the CCEMG and CCEPMG are called for. The CCEMG estimates find that the long-run effects are less precisely estimated for both directions. This is of no surprise – the long-run effects become much harder to capture when full heterogeneity is allowed. Nevertheless, it does imply that heterogeneity is especially prominent in this context. Moving from the CCEMG (no restriction, but potentially inefficient) to CCEPMG (a common long-run effect required) changes the results significantly: in particular, imposing long-run homogeneity reduces the standard errors and the speeds of adjustment. The restriction cannot be rejected at a conventional level by a Hausman test. The CCEPMG estimates provide evidence in support of significant long-run effects in both directions.

The long-run coefficients in Tables 3.5 and 3.6 are actually quite similar. For example, the CCPMG and CCEMP estimates of the long-run coefficients for FD in Table 3.6 are 0.008 and 0.028, respectively, while their counterparts in Table 3.5 are 0.043 (1/23.055) and 0.040 (1/25.220). This result suggests that it is very likely for a single long-run relationship to exist in this context.

Comparing the above case with the case of cross section error independence is worthwhile. As its counterpart associated with cross section error dependence, the WG estimates (restrictions on all slope coefficients except for the intercept) show positive long-run effects in both directions. Allowing for heterogeneity, but no error dependence, across countries, the MG approach finds no evidence in support of significant long-run effects in both directions. Supported by the Hausman tests in

Table 3.5 Does private investment cause financial development? 1970–98 (Annual data)

Dependent variable: FD_{it}	Cross section dependence				Cross section independence			
	CCEP	CCEPMG	CCEMG	Hausman	WG	PMG	MG	Hausman
Speed of adjustment	−0.073 [0.02]***	−0.090 [0.02]***	−0.335 [0.06]***		−0.070 [0.02]***	−0.077 [0.01]***	−0.142 [0.02]***	
Long-run coefficient $PI_{i,t-1}$	12.398 [3.51]***	23.055 [2.15]***	25.220 [19.18]	0.91	12.256 [3.96]***	10.098 [1.33]***	12.085 [7.71]	0.79
Short-run coefficients								
$\Delta PI_{i,t=1}$	−0.250 [0.18]	−1.154 [0.31]***	−0.764 [0.38]**		−0.244 [0.18]	−0.206 [0.18]	−0.152 [0.26]	
$\Delta PI_{i,t=2}$	−0.275 [0.22]	−0.513 [0.24]***	−0.229 [0.25]		−0.269 [0.22]	0.001 [0.16]	0.028 [0.19]	
Observations	987	987	987		987	987	987	
No. of countries	43	43	43		43	43	43	

Notes: This table presents the Pesaran (2006) CCEP and CCEMG estimates, and CCEPMG estimates defined in the text under the assumption of cross section dependence, and their counterparts associated with the assumption of cross section error independence including the within group estimates (WG), Pesaran and Smith (1995) mean group (MG) and Pesaran et al. (1999) pooled mean group (PMG) estimates. The PMG and CCEPMG approaches use the long-run coefficients of MG and CCEMG estimates, respectively, as initial values, and the Newton-Raphson algoithm. The Hausman test (p-values reported) is used to examine the null hypothesis of no difference between the MG and PMG estimators, and between CCEMG and CCEPMG estimators. The asymptotic standard errors are reported in brackets. For WG and CCEP estimates the standard errors are corrected for possible heteroscedasticity in cross sectional error variances.

*, **, *** significant at 10%, 5% and 1%, respectively.

Table 3.6 Does financial development cause private investment? 1970–98 (Annual data)

Dependent variable: PI_{it}	Cross section dependence				Cross section independence			
	CCEP	CCEPMG	CCEMG	Hausman	WG	PMG	MG	Hausman
Speed of adjustment	−0.422 [0.04]***	−0.921 [0.08]***	−1.000 [0.10]***	0.65	−0.418 [0.04]***	−0.479 [0.04]***	−0.582 [0.05]***	0.29
Long-run coefficient $FD_{i,t=1}$	0.008 [0.00]**	0.008 [0.00]***	0.028 [0.05]		0.008 [0.00]**	−0.005 [0.00]	0.068 [0.07]	
Short-run coefficient								
$\Delta FD_{i,t=1}$	0.000 [0.01]	−0.013 [0.01]	−0.016 [0.02]		0.000 [0.01]	0.003 [0.01]	−0.007 [0.01]	
$\Delta FD_{i,t=2}$	0.001 [0.01]	0.001 [0.01]	−0.021 [0.01]		0.001 [0.01]	0.004 [0.01]	−0.003 [0.01]	
Observations	968	968	968		968	968	968	
No. of countries	43	43	43		43	43	43	

Note: See Table 3.5 for notes.

92 Determinants of Financial Development

Tables 3.5 and 3.6, the PMG estimates indicate a significant long-run effect going from private investment to financial development, but not vice versa. This tends to underscore the importance of allowing for heterogeneity across countries in the sense that, compared to the PMG approach, the WG approach – ignoring the divergent performance across countries – is likely to produce misleading results. Moving from PMG to CCEPMG clearly highlights the importance of controlling for error dependence across countries.

After controlling for error dependence and heterogeneity across countries, the CCEPMG estimates clearly suggest positive long-run effects going in both directions between private investment and financial development. A note of caution may therefore be appropriate here: taking careful consideration of the integrated properties of the data, the error structure and the extent of heterogeneity are always worth keeping in mind in the econometric analysis of panel data.

In the following a set of experiments are conducted to test whether the above findings are robust to various model specifications. This research considers including GDP per capita in logs and trade openness separately as additional regressors.[57] Results clearly indicate that the inclusion of either GDP in log or trade openness does not alter the pattern of the findings.

In sum, after allowing for global interdependence and heterogeneity across countries, this analysis on annual data clearly shows positive long-run effects going in both directions between private investment and financial development. It is very likely that a single long-run relationship exists in this context. The findings in general suggest that surges of private investment stimulate the deepening of financial markets, and, on the other hand, financial development facilitates resource mobilization, and increases the quantity of funds available for investment.

3.5 Conclusion

This chapter aims to investigate the causality between aggregate private investment and financial development in a globalized world. Using a panel dataset with 43 developing countries over 1970–98, the analysis is conducted in two steps. One is system GMM estimation on data for five-year averages, indicating positive causal effects going in both directions and a high degree of persistence in the averaged data of private investment and financial development. The other is a common factor approach on annual data allowing for global interdependence and heterogeneity across countries. The analysis demonstrates that the series of both private investment and financial development are integrated, and two-way positive causal effects exist in the cointegrated system. In general, the chapter implies that, in a globalized world, private investment is both an engine and a follower of financial development, and vice versa.

This analysis has produced significant insights into the interactions between two important aspects of economic activities, aggregate private investment and financial development, in developing countries. The implications of the findings can be summarized in the following.

First, the finding in terms of a positive effect of private investment on financial development has rich implications for the development of financial markets. Since sound macroeconomic policies, and a favourable economic and legal environment, undoubtedly facilitate private investment, any efforts by government to reduce macroeconomic policy uncertainty, improve the regulatory framework and strengthen creditor and investor rights will be conducive to the development of financial markets. Moreover, the finding may shed light on a possible channel through which other variables drive financial development, for example, the effect of democracy and political stability on the speed of financial development (Girma and Shortland, 2008) and Chapter 4.

Second, the finding on better financial development leading to a private investment boom has clear implications for the conduct of macroeconomic policies in developing countries. This chapter suggests that as the financial system in a country becomes more sophisticated, more funds are channelled for productive investment so that firms find it easier to get access to them. This finding is in support of the financial development framework proposed by McKinnon (1973) and Shaw (1973), who emphasize that financial liberalization and financial development can foster economic growth by boosting investment and its productivity, substantially influencing macroeconomic policies in developing countries since the 1970s. This research contributes to the existing body of research on the links between financial development and economic growth, by suggesting that the former may enhance the latter through a private investment boom. This finding suggests that financial markets may well be the channel through which macroeconomic volatility or downturn leads to declines in private investment, which is consistent with what has happened during the 2007–2009 financial crisis.

Third, this research stresses the importance of taking careful account of error structure and heterogeneity in the econometric analysis of panel data. By considering the effects of common trends in a global economy and allowing for heterogeneity across countries, this analysis represents a significant improvement in comparison to existing research, which in general assumes error independence across countries. The results generated from existing research may deserve careful examination since the interactions and co-movements of economic factors, and the trends of globalization, have been central features of the world economy in recent decades.

Appendix tables

Table A3.1 The variables

Variable	Description	Source
FD	Index for financial development in this paper, mainly measuring the size of financial intermediary development. It is the first principal component of *LLY*, *PRIVO* and *BTOT*.	
LLY	Liquid Liabilities, the ratio of liquid liabilities of financial system (currency plus demand and interestbearing liabilities of banks and non-banks) to GDP.	Financial Development and Structure Database (FDS) in World Bank, 2008
PRIVO	Private Credit, the ratio of credits issued to private sector by banks and other financial intermediaries to GDP.	FDS, 2008
BTOT	Commercial-central Bank, the ratio of commercial bank assets to the sum of commercial bank and central bank assets.	FDS, 2008
PI	The ratio of nominal private investment to nominal GDP. It is replaced by PI/100.	Global Development Network (GDN), 2002
LGDP	Real GDP per capita (Chain) in log.	Penn World Table 6.2
OPENC	The sum of exports and imports over GDP (at current prices). It is replaced by $\log(1 + OPENC/100)$.	Penn World Table 6.2

Table A3.2 Descriptive statistics

Variable		Mean	Std. Dev.	Min	Max	Observations
FD	overall	−0.52	0.91	−2.65	4.14	N = 1198
	between		0.75	−2.13	1.66	n = 43
	within		0.52	−2.36	2.34	T-bar = 27.86
PI	overall	0.14	0.07	0.00	0.42	N = 1183
	between		0.05	0.02	0.25	n = 43
	within		0.04	0.00	0.42	T-bar = 27.51
LGDP	overall	3.47	0.35	2.76	4.19	N = 1183
	between		0.34	2.88	4.02	n = 43
	within		0.09	3.09	3.82	T-bar = 29
OPENC	overall	0.57	0.29	0.06	2.09	N = 1247
	between		0.26	0.16	1.23	n = 43
	within		0.14	0.04	1.43	T-bar = 29

Note: Appendix Table A3.1 describes all variables in detail.

Table A3.3 The list of countries in the full sample

East Asia & Pacific		Sub Sahara Africa		Latin America & Caribbean	
PHL	Philippines	GAB	Gabon	HND	Honduras
MYS	Malaysia	SEN	Senegal	TTO	Trinidad and Tobago
PNG	Papua New Guinea	NGA	Nigeria	GTM	Guatemala
THA	Thailand	NER	Niger	CRI	Costa Rica
KOR	Korea, Rep.	MUS	Mauritius	HTI	Haiti
		KEN	Kenya	SLV	El Salvador
South Asia		TGO	Togo	BRB	Barbados
IND	India	MDG	Madagascar	COL	Colombia
NPL	Nepal	GHA	Ghana	PER	Peru
PAK	Pakistan	GMB	Gambia, The	VEN	Venezuela
		RWA	Rwanda	ECU	Ecuador
Middle East & North Africa		CMR	Cameroon	MEX	Mexico
DZA	Algeria	CIV	Cote d'Ivoire	ARG	Argentina
MAR	Morocco	BDI	Burundi	URY	Uruguay
EGY	Egypt, Arab Rep.	ZAF	South Africa	CHL	Chile
				DOM	Dominican Rep.
				PRY	Paraguay

Table A3.4 Robustness test – GDP in log included (five-year-average data)

A. Does private investment cause financial development? 1970–98

Dependent variable: FD_{it}	OLS	WG	SYS-GMM	SYS-GMM-1	SYS-GMM-2
$FD_{i,t-1}$	0.879	0.427	0.753	0.638	0.693
	[15.21]***	[5.46]***	[6.38]***	[6.14]***	[3.78]***
$PI_{i,t-1}$	2.744	3.845	5.692	6.007	4.679
	[4.17]***	[4.25]***	[6.70]***	[4.65]***	[3.13]***
$LGDP_{it}$	0.014	2.215	0.634	0.972	1.240
	[0.12]	[4.41]***	[1.30]	[1.73]*	[2.11]**
M1 (p-value)			0.00	0.00	0.02
M2 (p-value)			0.99	0.80	0.46
Sargan (p-value)			0.51	0.35	0.30
Diff-Sargan (p-value)			0.98	1.00	0.71
Granger Causality (p-value)	0.00	0.00	0.00	0.00	0.00
LR effect point estimate	22.61	6.71	23.04	16.58	18.26
(Standard error)	[11.89]*	[1.81]***	[10.81]**	[5.41]***	[11.57]
Observations	212	212	212	212	212

B. Does financial development cause private investment? 1970–98

Dependent variable: PI_{it}	OLS	WG	SYS-GMM	SYS-GMM-1	SYS-GMM-2
$PI_{i,t-1}$	0.698	0.186	0.512	0.498	0.352
	[10.95]***	[2.39]**	[5.19]***	[5.01]***	[3.28]***
$FD_{i,t-1}$	0.007	0.004	0.004	−0.013	0.012
	[1.74]*	[0.55]	[0.54]	[1.36]	[1.43]
$LGDP_{it}$	0.016	0.081	0.092	0.095	0.103
	[1.60]	[1.88]*	[3.34]***	[1.19]	[3.08]***
M1 (p-value)			0.00	0.00	0.01
M2 (p-value)			0.40	0.47	0.26
Sargan (p-value)			0.45	0.27	0.46
Diff-Sargan (p-value)			0.88	0.67	0.97
Granger Causality (p-value)	0.08	0.58	0.59	0.18	0.16
LR effect point estimate	0.02	0.00	0.01	−0.03	0.02
(Standard error)	[0.01]*	[0.01]	[0.01]	[0.02]	[0.01]
Observations	198	198	198	198	198

Notes: Log GDP is included in the models to test the robustness of the findings of Tables 3.1 and 3.2. See Table 3.1 for more notes.

Table A3.5 Robustness test – OPENC included (five-year-average data)

A. Does private investment cause financial development? 1970–98

Dependent variable: FD_{it}	OLS	WG	SYS-GMM	SYS-GMM-1	SYS-GMM-2
$FD_{i,t-1}$	0.863	0.565	0.734	0.764	0.478
	[15.15]***	[7.86]***	[8.31]***	[6.78]***	[3.22]***
$PI_{i,t-1}$	2.699	4.206	4.759	7.494	2.713
	[4.85]***	[4.36]***	[3.09]***	[4.21]***	[1.93]*
$OPENC_{it}$	0.124	0.746	0.603	−0.143	1.305
	[0.80]	[2.41]**	[1.28]	[0.23]	[3.50]***
M1 (p-value)			0.01	0.00	0.06
M2 (p-value)			0.92	0.90	0.90
Sargan (p-value)			0.32	0.25	0.36
Diff-Sargan (p-value)			0.25	0.09	0.30
Granger Causality (p-value)	0.00	0.00	0.00	0.00	0.06
LR effect point estimate	19.67	9.68	17.88	31.74	5.20
(Standard error)	[7.87]**	[2.59]***	[8.47]**	[14.33]**	[3.73]
Observations	212	212	212	212	212

B. Does financial development cause private investment? 1970–98

Dependent variable: PI_{it}	OLS	WG	SYS-GMM	SYS-GMM-1	SYS-GMM-2
$PI_{i,t-1}$	0.742	0.228	0.455	0.340	0.305
	[13.87]***	[2.82]***	[3.61]***	[2.24]**	[2.38]**
$FD_{i,t-1}$	0.008	0.010	0.013	−0.010	0.019
	[1.80]*	[1.60]	[1.75]*	[0.80]	[2.13]**
$OPENC_{it}$	0.002	0.004	0.018	0.071	0.029
	[0.15]	[0.14]	[0.55]	[1.00]	[0.83]
M1 (p-value)			0.01	0.01	0.02
M2 (p-value)			0.33	0.39	0.21
Sargan (p-value)			0.24	0.36	0.15
Diff-Sargan (p-value)			0.10	0.13	0.03
Granger Causality (p-value)	0.07	0.11	0.09	0.43	0.04
LR effect point estimate	0.03	0.01	0.02	−0.01	0.03
(Standard error)	[0.02]*	[0.01]	[0.01]*	[0.02]	[0.01]**
Observations	198	198	198	198	198

Notes: Trade openness (*OPENC*) is included in the models to test the robustness of the findings of Tables 3.1 and 3.2. See Table 3.1 for more notes.

Table A3.6 Robustness test – two lags (five-year-average data)

A. Does private investment cause financial development? 1970–98

Dependent variable: FD_{it}	OLS	WG	SYS-GMM	SYS-GMM-1	SYS-GMM-2
$FD_{i,t=1}$	1.076	0.492	0.683	0.564	0.383
	[10.18]***	[5.07]***	[4.46]***	[2.95]***	[1.36]
$FD_{i,t=2}$	−0.194	−0.179	−0.216	−0.174	−0.079
	[1.67]*	[1.94]*	[1.54]	[1.17]	[0.67]
$PI_{i,t=1}$	3.647	4.767	5.735	7.524	5.605
	[3.75]***	[4.20]***	[2.85]***	[2.87]***	[2.88]***
$PI_{i,t=2}$	−1.118	3.385	3.305	3.983	2.812
	[1.00]	[2.88]***	[1.88]*	[2.55]**	[1.76]*
M1 (p-value)			0.02	0.09	0.37
M2 (p-value)			0.53	0.84	0.77
Sargan (p-value)			0.21	0.16	0.23
Diff-Sargan (p-value)			0.64	0.60	0.88
Granger Causality (p-value)	0.00	0.00	0.00	0.00	0.01
LR effect point estimate	21.5	11.87	16.96	18.89	12.09
(Standard error)	[11.94]*	[2.48]***	[6.36]**	[5.79]***	[5.52]**
Observations	169	169	169	169	169

B. Does financial development cause private investment? 1970–98

Dependent variable: PI_{it}	OLS	WG	SYS-GMM	SYS-GMM-1	SYS-GMM-2
$PI_{i,t=1}$	0.692	0.087	0.506	0.565	0.402
	[8.34]***	[0.99]	[4.24]***	[3.88]***	[2.82]***
$PI_{i,t=2}$	0.086	−0.081	−0.090	−0.038	−0.064
	[0.99]	[0.93]	[0.84]	[0.34]	[0.64]
$FD_{i,t=1}$	0.010	0.016	0.022	−0.003	0.027
	[1.30]	[2.09]**	[1.96]*	[0.25]	[2.08]**
$FD_{i,t=2}$	−0.004	0.002	−0.005	−0.002	−0.004
	[0.50]	[0.28]	[0.81]	[0.25]	[0.58]
M1 (p-value)			0.03	0.05	0.06
M2 (p-value)			0.14	0.16	0.08
Sargan (p-value)			0.61	0.47	0.45
Diff-Sargan (p-value)			0.54	0.27	0.25
Granger Causality (p-value)	0.20	0.03	0.09	0.73	0.10
LR effect point estimate	0.03	0.02	0.03	−0.01	0.03
(Standard error)	[0.02]	[0.01]**	[0.01]**	[0.03]	[0.01]**
Observations	155	155	155	155	155

Notes: AR(2) models are considered to test the robustness of the findings of Tables 3.1 and 3.2. See Table 3.1 for more notes.

Table A3.7 Determination of the numbers of common factors for FD and PI

	FD	PI
$r = 1$	2.654	3.339
$r = 2$	3.000	3.626
$r = 3$	3.202	3.823
$r = 4$	3.373	4.005
$r = 5$	3.539	4.183
$r = 6$	3.703	4.355
$r = 7$	3.866	4.522
$r = 8$	4.030	4.687

Note: This table reports the values of Information Criteria (IC1) (Bai and Ng, 2002) for different numbers of factors (r). The integer minimizing a criterion function, IC1 for example, is the estimated number of factors.

Appendix figures

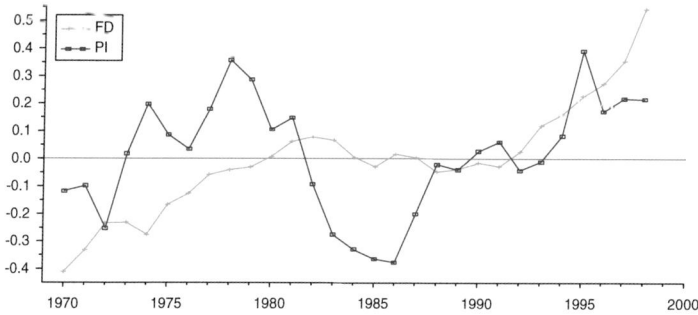

Figure AF3.1 Time series plots of FD and PI

Note: This graph depicts the time series plots of FD and PI over 1970–98.

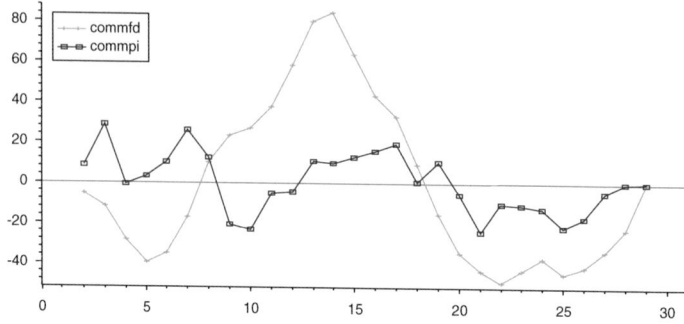

Figure AF3.2 Time series plots of common factors for *FD* and *PI*

Note: This graph depicts the time series plots of common factors for *FD* and *PI*, identified by using the PANIC approach of Bai and Ng (2004), over 28 years (1971–98). Here commfd denotes the common factor for the series of *FD*, while commpi denotes the common factor for the series of *PI*.

4
Political Institutions and Financial Development

4.1 Introduction

Over the last few decades, there has been a substantial increase in financial development in many developing countries. The average ratio of private credit to GDP increased from 23% in 1980 to 32% in 2000, while the average ratio of liquid liabilities to GDP rose from 32% in 1980 to 42% in 2000 in the developing world. On the political front, between 1980 and 2000 62 developing countries undertook significant institutional reforms towards democracy.[58] Do the above economic and political events in the developing world interact in important ways?

Much work has been done to explore the relationship between institutional improvement, especially political liberalization, and economic growth. The existing research in this field does not unanimously establish the consequences of political reform for economic development. Instead, it is made up of one line of research supporting positive consequences, another line stressing negative consequences and some maintaining ambiguous views. How does democratic process to improve institutional quality influence financial development, especially in countries with low GDP per capita, high ethnic and religious divisions or specific legal origins?

The importance of institutional improvement for financial development has been implicitly indicated by Clague *et al.* (1996) and Olson (1993), who argue that, in comparison to autocracies, democracies better facilitate property rights protection and contract enforcement, encouraging investment directly. In recent research on the political economy of financial development, Pagano and Volpin (2001), Rajan and Zingales (2003) and Beck *et al.* (2003) highlight the role of political intervention and institutions in financial development. In examining what forces lead

102 Determinants of Financial Development

governments to undertake reforms to enhance financial development, Chapter 5 finds that the extent of democracy is one of the significant forces. However, there has been little research which directly studies the impact of the democratic process for institutional improvement on financial development.

This analysis mainly carries out a dynamic panel data study, focusing on 90 developed and developing countries. It examines the impact on financial development of the democratic process in a broader sense, in terms of institutional improvement rather than political transformation.[59] The bias-corrected Least Square Dummy Variable (LSDV) estimator proposed by Kiviet (1995) and recently developed by Bruno (2005) is the central method of this study and is compared with the system GMM estimator proposed by Arellano and Bover (1995) and Blundell and Bond (1998).

Before proceeding to the econometric analysis, this research provides some preliminary evidence with a before-and-after event comparison to study probably the most important institutional change, namely political transformation from an autocratic regime to a democratic one. It focuses on 33 countries which underwent a democratic transformation during 1960–2000 subject to data availability for financial development. This exercise examines the responses of the level and volatility of financial development after a regime transition.

This chapter shows that improved institutional quality is associated with increases in financial development at least in the short run, especially for lower–income, ethnically divided and French legal origin countries. The before-and-after event study also indicates that, in general, democratic transitions are typically preceded by low financial development, but followed by a short-run boost in, and greater volatility of, financial development. The findings of this research underline the influence of institutional reform over the supply side of finance and shed light on the strong and robust relationship between institutional quality and economic performance.

The remainder of the chapter proceeds as follows. Section 4.2 presents a brief review of the literature on institutions, democratization and finance. Section 4.3 describes the sample and measures that are used in this study. The empirical results are presented in Section 4.5, following a description of dynamic panel data methods in Section 4.4. Section 4.6 concludes.

4.2 Institutions, democratization and finance

This section briefly outlines the theoretical background and motivation of this research. It discusses the role of institutions in financial development and the possible links between the democratic process and finance.

Research on the effect of institutional reform on general economic performance is associated with substantial controversies. Some argue that the democratic process enhances fundamental civil liberties, stable politics and an open society; promotes property rights protection and contract enforcement; discourages corruption and lawlessness and fosters economic growth (Olson, 1993; Clague et al., 1996; Minier, 1998 and Persson, 2005). On the contrary, under pressures from different interest groups, democratic structures may suffer from inefficiency in decision-making and difficulty in implementing viable policies for rapid growth. "Premature" democracy in developing countries possibly lowers the economic growth rate, and even results in economic disorder, political instability and ethnic conflict (Persson and Tabellini, 1992 and Blanchard and Shleifer, 2000). Tavares and Wacziarg (2001) show that "the overall effect of democracy on economic growth is moderately negative" – an increase in human capital accumulation is offset by a decrease in physical capital accumulation in the process of democratization.

Research on the role of institutions in financial development has been substantial, especially research on the effects of the legal and regulatory environment on the functioning of financial markets. A legal and regulatory system involving protection of property rights, contract enforcement and good accounting practices has been identified as essential for financial development. Most prominently, La Porta et al. (1997, 1998) have argued that the origins of the legal code substantially influence the treatment of creditors and shareholders, and the efficiency of contract enforcement.[60] Among others, Mayer and Sussman (2001) emphasize that regulations concerning information disclosure, accounting standards, permissible banking practices, and deposit insurance do appear to have material effects on financial development.

Another significant work in this context is Beck et al. (2003), which extends the settler mortality hypothesis of Acemoglu et al. (2001) to financial development. They argue that colonizers, often named as extractive colonizers, associated with an inhospitable environment aim to establish institutions that privilege the small elite group and potentially ignore private property rights, while colonizers, often called settler colonizers, in more favourable environments are more likely to create institutions that support private property and balance the power of the state. Accordingly, institutions in the extractive environment tend to block financial development, while those in settler colonies are more conducive to financial development.

The recently developed "new political economy" approach regards "regulation and its enforcement as a result of the balance of power between social and economic constituencies" (Pagano and Volpin, 2001). It centres on self-interested policy-makers who can intervene in financial markets either through overall regulation or individual cases for purposes such as career concerns and the promotion of group interests. Rajan and Zingales (2003) emphasize the role which the interest groups, especially the incumbent industrial firms and the domestic financial sector, can play in the process of financial development.[61]

Arguably, countries controlled by elite groups are more inclined to protect the interests of the elite from the bulk of society, restrict participation in the political system, and so on. The more power held by the elite groups and the more autocratic the system, the more obstacles there are for financial development. This tends to suggest that institutional reform intending to limit the influence of elite group over policy-making, widen suffrage in the political system, respect basic political rights and civil liberties, remove institutional obstacles and enhance institutional efficiency is beneficial to financial development. Girma and Shortland (2008) study the impact of democracy chrematistics and regime change on financial development, showing that both democracy and regime change promote financial development.[62] Apart from Girma and Shortland (2008), research directly exploring the impact of democratic process for institutional improvement on financial development has been lacking.

This research might contribute to our understanding of the structural determinants of financial development. Looking at this issue is also significant for examining whether institutional innovation contributes to an improved investment climate. This is because commonly used financial development indicators such as the ratio of liquid liabilities to GDP and the ratio of credit issued to the private sector to GDP are generally forward-looking. Better financial development is then an early indication of a better investment environment.

4.3 The measures and data

4.3.1 The sample

This research studies the impact of institutional improvement on financial development, controlling for GDP, trade openness, aggregate investment and the black market premium. The measures and data for financial development and institutional improvement are explained in more detail below. Information on the classifications of income levels, region dummies, ethnic fractionalization and legal origins is obtained from the

World Bank Global Development Network Database (GDN) (2002). The data for GDP, trade openness and aggregate investment are from the Penn World Table 6.2. Data for the black market premium are from the GDN (2002).

This study focuses on a panel of 90 non-transition economies over the period 1960–99 with five observations per country. Averaging data over non-overlapping, eight-year periods enables us to abstract from business cycle influences and to examine both short-run and long-run effects. The countries included for this analysis are those undertaking some political reforms to improve institutional quality, but not necessarily experiencing a democratic transition over 1960–99. The sample excludes the East European countries,[63] which became democracies and independent only following the end of the Cold War. The selection of countries is based on the Polity index, "polity2" of the PolityIV Database explained below. We naturally use data up to the end of the twentieth century, which is partly because of data availability for some important variables, like the black market premium,[64] and partly because annual data for 40 years are sufficient for a dynamic panel data study.

4.3.2 The measure and data for financial development

The aggregate measure of financial development in this context is denoted by *FD*. Since there is no single aggregate index in the literature, we use principal components analysis to produce a new aggregate index. Ideally, the principal component analysis should be based on indicators from the banking sector, stock market and bond market so as to capture different aspects of financial development. However, data on stock market and bond market development are rarely available for before 1975 or even later, so the analysis focuses on financial intermediary development.

The measure is based on three widely used indicators of financial intermediary development as follows:[65]

1. Liquid Liabilities (*LLY*), calculated as the liquid liabilities of banks and non-bank financial intermediaries (currency plus demand and interest-bearing liabilities) over GDP. It measures the size, relative to the economy, of financial intermediaries including three types of financial institutions: the central bank, deposit money banks and other financial institutions.

2. Private Credit (*PRIVO*), defined as the credit issued to the private sector by banks and other financial intermediaries divided by GDP, excluding the credit issued to government, government agencies and public enterprises, as well as the credit issued by the monetary authority

and development banks. This captures general financial intermediary activities provided to the private sector.

3. Commercial-Central Bank (*BTOT*), the ratio of commercial bank assets over the sum of commercial bank and central bank assets. It proxies the advantages of financial intermediaries in channelling savings to investment, monitoring firms, exerting corporate governance and undertaking risk management relative to the central bank.

Since these indicators are used to measure the size of the banking system,[66] *FD* mainly captures the size of bank-based intermediation. *FD* is the first principal component of these three indicators above, and accounts for 72% of their variation. The weights resulting from principal component analysis over the period 1990–99 are 0.59 for Liquid Liabilities, 0.63 for Private Credit and 0.50 for Commercial-Central Bank.

The data on these indicators are obtained from the World Bank's Financial Structure and Economic Development Database (2008).

4.3.3 The measure and data for institutional improvement

The research focuses on political institutions and studies their impact on financial development. The institutional improvement index is the Polity indicator "polity2" in the PolityIV Database (Marshall and Jaggers, 2009), denoted by *POLITY2*. It proxies the degree of democracy and seeks to measure institutional quality based on the freedom of suffrage, operational constraints and balances on executives and respect for other basic political rights and civil liberties. It is called the "combined polity score",[67] defined as the democracy score minus the autocracy score.[68]

To pick up any effect of institutional improvement on financial development, this exercise tries to incorporate all democratic reform episodes in the sense that any increase of the annual "polity2" score for a country will be considered even if it remains an autocratic regime or a democratic regime over the whole period.

To select democratic transition countries for the before-and-after event study, we also take into account the freedom index from Freedom House Country Survey (2008).

4.4 Methodology

To assess the relationship between institutional improvement and financial development, the following model is estimated:[69]

$$y_{it} = \alpha y_{i,t-1} + \beta x_{i,t-1} + z'_{i,t-1}\delta + \eta_i + \phi_t + v_{it} \quad (4.1)$$

$$i = 1, 2, \ldots 90 \text{ and } t = 2 \ldots 5$$

where y_{it} is the dependent variable *FD*, x_{it} is the explanatory variable *POLITY2*, z_{it} is a vector of controlling variables including the logarithm of the real GDP per capita (*LGDP*), trade openness (*OPENC*), aggregate investment (*CI*) and the black market premium (*BMP*). *OPENC* is the logarithm of one plus the trade share, the sum of exports and imports over GDP (at current prices), divided by 100. *CI* is the ratio of investment to real GDP per capita (using domestic prices), divided by 100. *BMP* is the logarithm of one plus the black market premium divided by 100. δ is a parameter vector, e.g. $(\delta_1, \ldots \delta_4)'$. η_i is an unobserved time-invariant country-specific effect and can be regarded as capturing the combined effect of all omitted variables. ϕ_t is the time effect. v_{it} is the transitory disturbance term.

We assume that the transient errors v_{it} are serially uncorrelated. In system GMM estimation all $x's$ and $z's$ are assumed to be potentially correlated with η_i and predetermined with respective to time-varying errors.[70] To avoid the potential endogeneity of explanatory variables, lagged values of $x_{i,t}$ and $z_{i,t}$ are included in the regression equation, which allows feedback from the past shocks onto $x_{i,t-1}$ and $z_{i,t-1}$ while the current and future realizations of y_{it} do not affect them. The assumption is inspired by Rodrik and Wacziarg (2005), who argue that "democratisations tend to follow periods of low growth rather than precede them". In contrast to the GMM approach, the following bias-corrected Least Squares Dummy Variable (LSDV) estimation assumes all $x's$ and $z's$ to be strictly exogenous, which rules out the possibility of feedbacks from the past, current and future shocks onto $x_{i,t-1}$ and $z_{i,t-1}$.

When the Ordinary Least Square (OLS) technique is used to estimate this model, the OLS estimate of α is inconsistent and likely to be biased upwards since the lagged values of y_{it} are positively correlated with the omitted fixed effects.

A number of methods have been developed to deal with the presence of fixed effects in the dynamic panel data model. By using a within group operator, the LSDV method eliminates any omitted variables bias created by the unobserved individual effect and estimates the new model below by OLS:

$$y_{it} - \bar{y}_i = \alpha(y_{i,t-1} - \bar{y}_{i,-1}) + (x_{i,t-1} - \bar{x}_{i,-1})\beta$$
$$+ (z_{i,t-1} - \bar{z}_{i,-1})\delta + (v_{it} - \bar{v}_i)$$
$$i = 1, 2, \ldots 90 \text{ and } t = 2 \ldots 5 \tag{4.2}$$

108 Determinants of Financial Development

where $\bar{y}_i$, $\bar{x}_i$ and $\bar{z}_i$ are the group means, that is, $\bar{y}_i = \sum_{t=2}^{5} y_{it}/5$, $\bar{x}_i = \sum_{t=2}^{5} x_{it}/5$ and $\bar{z}_i = \sum_{t=2}^{5} z_{it}/5$. Since the lagged value of y is correlated with the new error term, as shown by Nickell (1981), the LSDV estimate of α can be badly downwards biased for small T, even as N goes to infinity.

Another way commonly used to wipe out the individual effects is to apply first-differencing to Equation (3.1). By estimating the following first-difference equation, the first-difference 2SLS estimator of Anderson and Hsiao (1980, 1981), first-differenced GMM estimator of Arellano and Bond (1991) and the system GMM estimator of Arellano and Bover (1995) and Blundell and Bond (1998) are proposed among others:

$$\Delta y_{it} = \alpha \Delta y_{i,t-1} + \Delta x_{i,t-1}\beta + \Delta z'_{i,t-1}\delta + \phi_t - \phi_{t-1} + \Delta v_{it}$$

$$i = 1, 2, \ldots 90 \text{ and } t = 3 \ldots 5 \qquad (4.3)$$

Conventional wisdom suggests that the first-differenced GMM estimator is consistent and asymptotically more efficient than the first-differenced 2SLS estimator. However, it may suffer from finite sample bias by employing weak instruments, as argued by Blundell and Bond (1998), that is, that "when the autoregressive parameter α is close to unity or the variance of the individual effects (η_i) increases relative to the variance of the transient disturbances (v_{it}) in the standard AR(1) model, the instruments available for the first-differenced equation are likely to be weak".

To handle the weak instrument problem, Arellano and Bover (1995) and Blundell and Bond (1998) impose a mean stationarity assumption on initial conditions,[71] and combine the first-difference equations with suitably lagged levels as instruments and levels equations with suitably lagged first differences as instruments. More specifically, the system GMM estimator, one of the main focuses of this analysis, uses all lagged values of y, x and z as instruments for $\Delta y_{i,t-1}, \Delta x_{i,t-1}$ and $\Delta z_{i,t-1}$ in the first difference equation above,[72] and the lagged first differences of the series (y_{it}, x_{it}, z_{it}) dated $t{-}1$ as instruments for the untransformed equations in levels.[73] The system GMM estimator has been found to be more efficient than the first-differenced GMM estimator in the presence of persistent data and weak instruments for first differences.

The asymptotic properties of the system GMM estimator depend on having a large number of cross section units, however. One of the main problems in using this estimator is that it may have poor finite sample properties in terms of bias and imprecision. Starting from Kiviet (1995),

Political Institutions and Financial Development 109

a bias correction of LSDV has recently been developed for use in short dynamic panels. Kiviet (1995) derives an approach to approximating the small sample bias of the LSDV estimator and suggests that the bias approximation be evaluated at the estimates from some consistent estimates rather than the unobserved true parameter values, which makes bias correction operationally feasible. The Monte Carlo evidence from Kiviet (1995), Judson and Owen (1999) and Bun and Kiviet (2003) suggests that the bias-corrected LSDV estimator (LSDVC) is more efficient than LSDV, first-differenced 2SLS, first-differenced GMM and system GMM in terms of bias and root mean square error (RMSE) for small or moderately large samples. Bruno (2005) derives a bias approximation of various orders in dynamic unbalanced panels with a strictly exogenous selection rule.[74]

This analysis compares the OLS, LSDV, LSDVC and SYS-GMM, standing for the system GMM estimator, for the whole sample and three subsamples. The LSDVC estimator is regarded as the preferred estimator, especially for subsamples, even though the independent variables other than the lagged dependent variable are assumed to be strictly exogenous. The initial estimator for the LSDVC could be either first-differenced GMM or the SYS-GMM estimator. However, the SYS-GMM is selected since the Difference Sargan test of additional moments conditions could not reject the null, and the SYS-GMM may be a more reliable estimator than first-differenced GMM in this context.

4.5 Evidence

The econometric methods are applied to study the effect on financial development of a broader issue, that is institutional improvement, based on even a slight change of the Polity index, "polity2". Before proceeding to the econometric analysis, we look at some preliminary evidence on the effect of the establishment of representative government on financial development by applying a "before-and-after" approach to 33 countries which underwent transformation from autocratic regimes to complete or partial democracies at some point during 1960–2001.

4.5.1 Preliminary evidence

The sample selection for the "before-and-after" event study relies on both the "polity2" index and "freedom" index from the Freedom House Country Survey (2008). Countries with either their "polity2" index increasing from negative values to positive values or their "freedom" index jumping from "Not Free" to "Partly Free" or "Free" for at least ten years are considered for this analysis. In general, the "polity2" and "freedom" indices yield similar results on the timing of democratic transition for most cases. However, the "polity2" index excludes countries with small populations (less than half a million) and the "freedom" index is only available starting from 1972–73.[75] For completeness, the selection of democratic transition countries combines both indices when both are available and relies on either of them otherwise.

The "before-and-after" approach compares an individual country's financial development performance under autocratic and democratic regimes.[76] To ease interpretation, the *FD* measure has been rescaled[77] in Table 4.1. The five- or ten-year average of *FD* preceding democratic transition is compared with the mean of *FD* during the first five or ten years under democracy for 33 countries.

The ten-year average of standardized *FD* for the sample countries increases by 0.093 on average after the initiation of a democratic transition and more than half of the sample countries exhibit an improvement in financial development.[78] It is worth noting that the majority of countries which suffered from a dramatic drop in financial development after democratization are Latin American countries. In contrast, most African countries underwent a pick-up in financial development after their democratic transformations. The divergent performance in countries' financial development implies that, apart from democratization, the level of financial development in each country may be affected by numerous factors including macroeconomic risks and changes in the general investment climate.[79] On average, these results tend to suggest that the establishment of representative government is often associated with an increase in financial development, but the effect is only sizeable for a subset of countries.

The upper chart of Figure 4.1 displays the cross-country median *FD* ten years before and after transition for the whole sample. The lower chart of Figure 4.1 plots the coefficients on the fixed-effect estimate of 20 time dummies before and after democratisation to reflect the dynamic effect of a sustained democratization.[80] The two figures show that the sample countries in general experience a drop in *FD* prior to democratization, which is in accordance with the view that worsened economic conditions are associated with a subsequent democratization. After democratization, *FD* appears to move slightly upwards on average in one to five years, followed by a surge in five to ten years.

Figure 4.2 describes the standard deviation of the *FD* growth rate before and after a stable democratization for whole the sample and subsamples. Democratization has led to a substantial rise in the standard

Table 4.1 Change in FD standardized before and after democratization

Countries	Demo'tion year	1 [−10, 0)	2 (0, 10]	3 DIFF1	4 [−5, 0)	5 (0, 5]	6 DIFF2	7 [−10, −5)	8 (5, 10]	9 DIFF3
Argentina	1983	−0.375	−0.466	−0.092	−0.266	−0.723	−0.457	−0.483	−0.570	−0.087
Bolivia	1982	−1.055	−0.789	0.266	−1.000	−1.397	−0.396	−1.110	−0.844	0.266
Brazil	1985	−0.492	−0.341	0.151	−0.492	−0.610	−0.118		−0.408	
Chile	1989	−0.136	0.305	0.441	−0.138	0.040	0.178	−0.134	0.405	0.539
Dominican Rep.	1978	−0.527	−0.351	0.176	−0.337	−0.311	0.027	−0.717	−0.356	0.361
Ecuador	1979	−0.674	−0.486	0.188	−0.629	−0.451	0.178	−0.719	−0.697	0.022
Ethiopia	1994	−0.562	−0.615	−0.053	−0.547	−0.458	0.090	−0.577		
Ghana	1996	−1.295	−1.042	0.252	−1.256	−0.969	0.288	−1.333		
Grenada	1984	0.247	0.635	0.388	0.232	0.256	0.024	0.286	0.603	0.317
Guatemala	1986	−0.569	−0.411	0.157	−0.645	−0.532	0.114	−0.492	−0.185	0.307
Honduras	1980	−0.199	−0.278	−0.079	−0.142	−0.252	−0.110	−0.255	−0.192	0.064
Hungary	1989	−0.631	−0.335	0.296	−0.584	−0.323	0.261	−0.868	−0.446	0.421
Korea, Rep.	1987	0.307	1.031	0.724	0.482	0.874	0.393	0.133	1.428	1.295
Lesotho	1993	−0.300	−0.265	0.034	−0.572	−0.364	0.208	−0.028	−0.213	−0.185
Madagascar	1991	−0.942	−0.460	0.483	−0.983	−0.808	0.176	−0.902	−0.741	0.160
Mexico	1994	−0.592	−0.367	0.224	−0.404	−0.138	0.267	−0.779	−0.245	0.534
Mali	1992	−0.625	−0.532	0.093	−0.625	−0.559	0.066		−0.499	
Malawi	1994	−0.814	−0.737	0.078	−0.840	−0.783	0.056	−0.789	−0.750	0.039
Nicaragua	1990	−0.342	−0.548	−0.206	−0.667	−0.757	−0.090	−0.017	−0.506	−0.489
Nepal	1990	−0.735	−0.657	0.077	−0.745	−0.506	0.239	−0.725	−0.163	0.562
Pakistan	1988	−0.224	−0.266	−0.042	−0.186	−0.231	−0.045	−0.262	−0.127	0.135
Panama	1989	0.142	0.035	−0.106	0.093	0.039	−0.054	0.190	0.817	0.627
Peru	1979	−0.300	−0.351	−0.051	−0.230	−0.433	−0.203	−0.370	−0.554	−0.184

continued

Table 4.1 Continued

Countries	Demo'tion year	1 [−10, 0)	2 (0, 10]	3 DIFF1	4 [−5, 0)	5 (0, 5]	6 DIFF2	7 [−10, −5)	8 (5, 10]	9 DIFF3
Period covered										
Philippines	1986	−0.003	−0.113	−0.110	0.034	−0.363	−0.396	−0.040	0.076	0.116
Poland	1989	−0.398	−0.167	0.230	−0.610	−0.319	0.291	0.132	−0.125	−0.257
Paraguay	1989	−0.467	−0.588	−0.121	−0.588	−0.471	0.117	−0.346	−0.211	0.136
El Salvador	1982	−0.685	−0.740	−0.055	−0.724	−0.876	−0.151	−0.645	−0.925	−0.280
Suriname	1987	0.036	−0.110	−0.146	0.221	0.405	0.184	−0.149	−0.508	−0.359
Seychelles	1993	−0.299	0.029	0.328	−0.275	−0.128	0.148	−0.323	0.440	0.763
Thailand	1978	−0.193	0.903	1.096	−0.132	0.048	0.181	−0.254	0.452	0.706
Uruguay	1985	−0.145	−0.523	−0.378	0.246	−0.419	−0.666	−0.536	−0.398	0.139
South Africa	1994	0.453	0.514	0.061	0.434	0.562	0.128	0.465	0.731	0.266
Zambia	1991	−0.926	−1.341	−0.415	−0.926	−1.349	−0.423		−1.316	
Average				0.118			0.015			0.212
1st Quartile				−0.079			−0.110			−0.005
Median Value				0.078			0.090			0.149
3rd Quartile				0.252			0.181			0.450

Notes: This table compares the financial development performance for 33 countries before and after democratization. See text for the country selection. Columns 1 and 2 show the average of *FD* standardized ten years before or after transition, respectively. DIFF1 is the difference between them. Columns 4 and 5 show the average of *FD* standardized five years before or after transition. DIFF2 is the difference between the two columns. Columns 6 and 7 show the average of *FD* standardized ten to five years before transition and five to ten years after transition, respectively. DIFF3 is the difference between columns 6 and 7. In the lower section the average, 1st Quartile, median value and 3rd Quartile are caculated for DIFF1, DIFF2 and DIFF3. The *FD* measure has been divided by the cross-country standard deviation of *FD* in 1999.

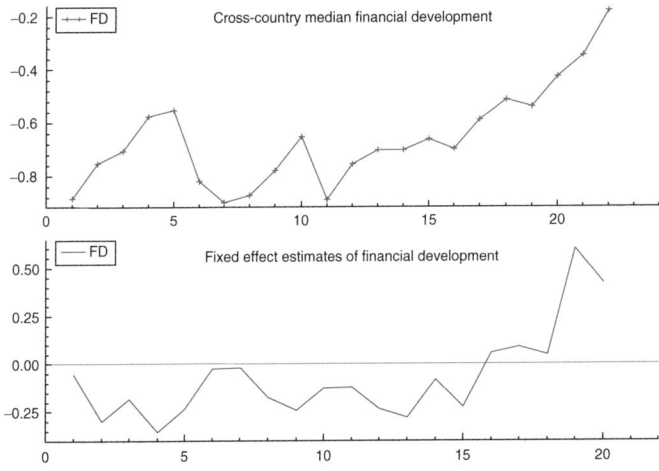

Figure 4.1 Financial development ten years before and after democratization

Note: 33 democratization countries, 1960–99. Upper figure shows the cross-country median financial development for these countries. Lower figure plots the coefficients of fixed-effect estimate of 20 time dummies before and after democratization. The regression is estimated by OLS, in which the country effects, time effects, controlling variables like *LGDP, OPENC, BMP* and *CI* are included.

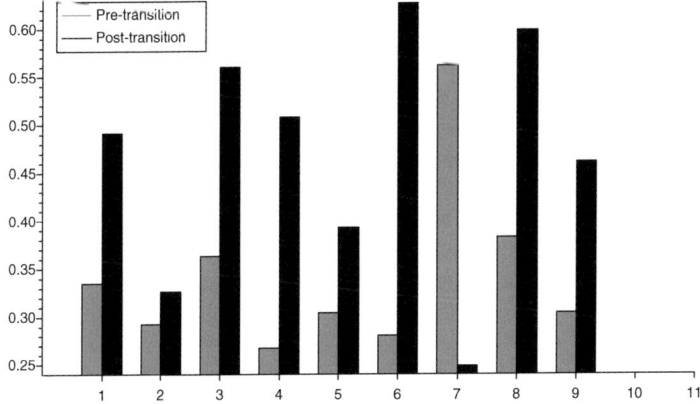

Figure 4.2 Volatility of financial development ten years pre/post-democratization

Note: 33 democratization countries, 1960–99. This figure shows the volatility of financial development, standard deviation of *FD* growth rate, for the whole sample and eight subsamples before and after democratization.

114 *Determinants of Financial Development*

deviation of the *FD* growth rate for the whole sample. Regional groups like Latin American (*LAC*) and Sub-Saharan African (*SSA*) countries experience a higher standard deviation of the *FD* growth rate, but Asian countries (*ASIA*) do not.[81] The standard deviations of the *FD* growth rate in income groups, like low-income countries (*INCLOW*) and middle-income countries (*INCMID*), and in legal origin groups, like British legal origin countries (*LEG_UK*) and French legal origin countries (*LEG_FR*), increases after their democratic transition. An increase in the standard deviation of the *FD* growth rate may reflect the fact that the removal of institutional obstacles after democratic transition could bring about short-run investment booms, reflected in a more volatile *FD* growth rate.

4.5.2 Regression results

Section 4.5.1 does provide some interesting results on the impact of democratic transition on financial development. However, this evidence is preliminary, and not convincing. In what follows we present the econometric evidence, for both the whole sample and three subsamples.[82]

4.5.2.1 Whole sample results

Table 4.2 reports the results for the whole sample, including estimation by OLS, LSDV, LSDVC and SYS-GMM. For each estimate, the first column is the baseline specification in which the income level and trade openness are present, while the second column controls for the black market premium and aggregate investment. The point estimate and the approximate standard error of the long-run effect for each model are reported. Given the estimated models, the OLS, LSDV, LSDVC and SYS-GMM estimates require that the long-run effect must have same sign as the short-run effect. For the SYS-GMM estimate, the table reports serial correlation tests, a Sargan test and a Difference Sargan test. The serial correlation tests are used to examine the null hypothesis of no first-order serial correlation and no second-order serial correlation respectively in residuals in first differences. Given the errors in levels are serially uncorrelated, we would expect to find significant first-order serial correlation, but no significant second-order correlation in the first-differenced residuals. The Sargan test of over-identifying restrictions is used to examine the overall validity of the instruments by comparing the sample moment conditions with their population analogue. The Difference Sargan test, proposed by Blundell and Bond (1998), is used to test the null hypothesis that the lagged differences of the explanatory variables are uncorrelated with the errors in the levels equations.

Table 4.2 Institutional improvement and financial development (whole sample), 1960–99

Dependent variable: $FD\_(it)$	OLS		LSDV		LSDVC		SYS-GMM	
$FD\_(i, t-1)$	0.951	0.863	0.379	0.320	0.825	0.796	0.689	0.848
	[0.00]***	[0.00]***	[3.00]***	[0.00]***	[0.00]***	[0.00]***	[0.01]***	[0.00]***
$POLITY2\_(i, t-1)$	0.015	0.015	0.025	0.026	0.018	0.020	0.080	0.028
	[0.04]**	[0.04]**	[0.04]**	[0.05]**	[0.19]	[0.15]	[0.03]**	[0.05]**
$LGDP\_(i, t-1)$	0.133	0.013	1.232	1.179	0.655	0.567	0.466	0.048
	[0.02]**	[0.85]	[0.00]***	[0.00]***	[0.02]**	[0.04]**	[0.20]	[0.74]
$OPENC\_(i, t-1)$	0.159	0.273	1.818	1.912	1.214	1.470	2.195	0.500
	[0.53]	[0.31]	[0.01]***	[0.02]**	[0.05]**	[0.06]*	[0.17]	[0.31]
$BMP\_(i, t-1)$		−0.240		−0.089		−0.050		−0.236
		[0.00]***		[0.45]		[0.73]		[0.02]**
$CI\_(i, t-1)$		2.372		0.798		0.755		2.785
		[0.00]***		[0.49]		[0.48]		[0.10]*
M1(p-value)[1]							0.03	0.04
M2(p-value)[1]							0.20	0.98
Sargan(p-value)[2]							0.28	0.34
Diff-Sargan (p-value)[2]							0.18	0.89
LR effect point estimate[3]	0.306	0.110	0.041	0.038	0.102	0.099	0.256	0.187
(Standard error)	[0.39]	[0.06]*	[0.02]*	[0.02]*	[0.08]	[0.07]	[0.23]	[0.17]
Observations	233	220	233	220	233	220	233	220

Notes: 82 countries. p-value is reported in brackets below point estimates. Year dummies included in all models. * significant at 5%; ** significant at 10%; *** significant at 1%. The LSDVC estimator is the corrected LSDV estimator developed by Kiviet (1995) for finite sample bias and contructed for dynamic unbalanced panels by Bruno (2005). The SYS-GMM results are two-step estimates with heteroscedasticity-consistent standard errors and test statistics; the standard errors are based on the finite sample adjustment of Windmeijer (2005).

[1] M1 and M2 are tests for null of no first-order and no second-order serial correlation in the first-differenced residuals, asymptotically $N(0,1)$.

[2] Sargan is a test of the over-identifying restrictions for GMM estimators, asymptotically χ^2. Diff-Sargan tests the null of mean stationarity for the system GMM estimator.

[3] LR measures the long-run effect of political liberalization on financial development. Its standard error is approximated using the delta method.

It is worth noting that, first, the autoregressive parameter estimated by LSDVC and SYS-GMM lies in the interval defined by the OLS levels and LSDV estimates. Recall that, in AR(1) models, the OLS levels estimate of the autoregessive parameter is biased upwards in the presence of fixed effects and the LSDV estimate is biased downwards in a short panel. A consistent estimate of the autoregressive parameter can be expected to lie in between the OLS levels and LSDV estimates. It is a simple indication of the presence of serious finite sample biases when particular estimates fail to fall into this interval or are very close to the bounds.

Both OLS and LSDV estimates indicate a significant positive effect of democratization on financial development although they are biased in opposite directions. The LSDVC estimator suggests evidence at the 20% significance level. The SYS-GMM estimate provides strong evidence that the improvement in institutional quality is associated with financial development, and the diagnostic tests, including the first- and second-order serial correlation tests, Sargan test and Difference Sargan test, support this. In general, the coefficients on the GDP level, trade openness and aggregate investment are positively signed, while the coefficient of the black market premium is negatively signed. The long-run effects in the cases of the OLS and LSDV estimates have been found to be positive and stable. However, the long-run effects for LSDVC and SYS-GMM are less precisely estimated.

In general, the table provides evidence, which is not due to unobserved heterogeneity or endogeneity biases, that democratization is followed by advances in financial development at least in the short run.

4.5.2.2 Subsamples

In principle, the system GMM and LSDVC estimates impose homogeneity on all slope coefficients. One concern over the above findings is that these parameters may be heterogeneous across countries. A natural way to confront this problem is to investigate subsamples, which are more homogeneous. We turn to three subsamples in this section: lower-income countries, ethnically diverse countries and French legal origin countries.[83] Since the cross section dimensions of these samples are relatively small, LSDVC is expected to be more appropriate than SYS-GMM for them.

Table 4.3 presents the results for the lower-income countries, made up of low-income and lower-middle-income countries, covering the majority of the developing countries. We find strong evidence of a positive effect of institutional improvement on financial development in the short run for every estimator. The LSDVC should be the most reliable

Table 4.3 Institutional improvement and financial development (lower-income countries), 1960–99

Dependent variable: $FD\_(it)$	OLS		LSDV		LSDVC		SYS-GMM	
$FD\_(i, t-1)$	0.932 [0.00]***	0.854 [0.00]***	0.387 [0.00]***	0.292 [0.04]**	0.840 [0.00]***	0.775 [0.00]***	0.991 [0.00]***	0.790 [0.00]***
$POLITY2\_(i, t-1)$	0.012 [0.11]	0.009 [0.25]	0.044 [0.00]***	0.048 [0.00]***	0.030 [0.04]**	0.032 [0.07]*	0.049 [0.07]*	0.027 [0.04]**
$LGDP\_(i, t-1)$	0.128 [0.05]*	0.049 [0.49]	0.662 [0.03]**	0.659 [0.04]**	0.249 [0.35]	0.245 [0.29]	0.238 [0.52]	0.255 [0.13]
$OPENC\_(i, t-1)$	−0.297 [0.33]	−0.348 [0.26]	1.676 [0.03]**	1.412 [0.10]*	1.177 [0.14]	1.123 [0.18]	0.603 [0.51]	0.363 [0.63]
$BMP\_(i, t-1)$		−0.244 [0.01]***		−0.123 [0.26]		−0.086 [0.47]		−0.223 [0.04]**
$CI\_(i, t-1)$		2.202 [0.01]***		0.847 [0.50]		0.554 [0.64]		2.213 [0.12]
M1 (p-value)[1]							0.00	0.00
M2 (p-value)[1]							0.26	0.22
Sargan (p-value)[2]							0.41	0.68
Diff-Sargan (p-value)[2]							0.84	0.97
LR effect point estimate[3]	0.180	0.054	0.072	0.068	0.186	0.142	5.454	0.13
(Standard error)	[0.18]	[0.05]	[0.02]***	[0.02]***	[0.11]*	[0.08]*	[141.51]	[0.09]
Observations	177	169	177	169	177	169	177	169

Notes: 57 countries. For other notes, please see Table 4.2.

estimator, given the above discussion. Moreover, it also indicates that the effect of improved institutional quality on financial development is sustained into the long run. Trade openness enters the models at the 20% significance level.

Table 4.4 shows the results for ethnically diverse countries which have a level of ethnic fractionalization greater than the sample median. We find strong evidence of the positive effect of institutional improvement on financial development in the short run. The autoregressive parameter estimates from LSDVC and SYS-GMM are very close. The LSDVC estimates suggest a positive effect of political liberalization on financial development at the 20% significance level with GDP and trade openness entering significantly. The SYS-GMM estimates provide much stronger evidence, in which GDP and trade openness are present at the 20% significance level. The long-run effects and approximate standard errors are in general less precisely estimated except for the case of the OLS and LSDV estimates.

The results for countries with French legal origin are reported in Table 4.5. This selection is essentially inspired by the work of La Porta *et al.* (1998), which regards legal origin as a main determinant of financial development. The experiments for British, German (LEG-GE) and Scandinavian (LEG-SC) legal origin groups produce no evidence in favour of a causal link from institutional improvement to financial development.

First it is worth noting that the autoregressive parameter estimated by SYS-GMM in the baseline model lies outside of the interval defined by the OLS and LSDV estimates, further implying the LSDVC may be a more reasonable estimator in this context. The LSDVC estimates typically show evidence in support of a positive effect of institutional improvement on financial development for French legal origin countries at the 15% significance level. The finding seems to be in line with La Porta *et al.* (1998), which claims that the main characteristic for countries with French legal origins is that private property rights are generally neglected, while British legal origin countries care more about private property owners. The finding supports a tentative hypothesis that democratization in French legal origin countries tends to change the status of private property owners in the national economy, and is thus conducive to financial development.

In sum, the above studies on subsamples have produced a coherent set of findings: improved institutional quality leads to greater financial development, at least in the short run. In the group of lower-income countries, a significant long-run effect is also observed. In general, we

Table 4.4 Institutional improvement and financial development (ethnically diverse countries), 1960–99

Dependent variable: $FD\_(it)$	OLS		LSDV		LSDVC		SYS-GMM	
$FD\_(i, t-1)$	0.913	[0.00]***	0.365	[0.00]***	0.820	[0.00]***	0.794	[0.00]***	0.857	[0.00]***	0.807	[0.00]***
$POLITY2\_(i, t-1)$	0.017	[0.02]**	0.026	[0.04]**	0.020	[0.16]	0.021	[0.17]	0.055	[0.11]	0.034	[0.06]*
$LGDP\_(i, t-1)$	0.144	[0.01]***	1.193	[0.00]***	0.585		0.501		0.378		0.206	
$OPENC\_(i, t-1)$	0.333	[0.51]	1.879	[0.00]***	1.318	[0.03]**	1.529	[0.08]*	1.447	[0.18]	0.816	[0.11]
$BMP\_(i, t-1)$		[0.17]		[0.01]***		[0.06]*		[0.07]*		[0.21]		[0.14]
	−0.237	[0.12]	−0.091	[0.44]			−0.055	[0.67]			0.218	[0.01]***
$CI\_(i, t-1)$	1.894	[0.00]***	0.458	[0.70]			0.530	[0.69]			1.304	[0.24]
		[0.02]**										
M1 (p-value)[1]									0.02		0.03	
M2 (p-value)[1]									0.19		0.54	
Sargan (p-value)[2]									0.12		0.24	
Diff-Sargan (p-value)[2]									0.73		0.61	
LR effect point estimate[3]	0.200		0.041		0.109		0.103		0.384		0.175	
(Standard error)	[0.15]		[0.02]**		[0.08]		[0.08]		[0.69]		[0.159]	
Observations	220		211		220		211		220		211	

Notes: 67 countries. For other notes, please see Table 4.2.

Table 4.5 Institutional improvement and financial development (French legal origin countries), 1960–99

Dependent variable: $FD\_(it)$	OLS		LSDV		LSDVC		SYS-GMM	
$FD\_(i, t-1)$	0.763	0.721	0.214	0.214	0.708	0.694	0.848	0.709
	[0.00]***	[0.00]***	[0.10]*	[0.12]	[0.00]***	[0.00]***	[0.00]***	[0.00]***
$POLITY2\_(i, t-1)$	0.018	0.020	0.027	0.030	0.027	0.032	0.038	0.042
	[0.12]	[0.07]*	[0.11]	[0.08]*	[0.12]	[0.14]	[0.11]	[0.04]**
$LGDP\_(i, t-1)$	0.144	0.042	0.643	0.572	0.294	0.155	0.319	0.129
	[0.04]**	[0.63]	[0.06]*	[0.12]	[0.47]	[0.65]	[0.10]*	[0.51]
$OPENC\_(i, t-1)$	0.468	0.755	2.691	2.110	2.421	1.997	0.522	1.250
	[0.23]	[0.04]**	[0.01]***	[0.06]*	[0.03]**	[0.07]*	[0.48]	[0.12]
$BMP\_(i, t-1)$		−0.185		−0.135		−0.088		−0.135
		[0.01]***		[0.35]		[0.61]		[0.06]*
$CI\_(i, t-1)$		1.836		1.110		1.558		1.445
		[0.04]**		[0.49]		[0.38]		[0.38]
M1 (p-value)[1]							0.08	0.06
M2 (p-value)[1]							0.12	0.19
Sargan (p-value)[2]							0.31	0.91
Diff-Sargan (p-value)[2]							0.51	0.95
LR effect point estimate[3]	0.075	0.070	0.034	0.038	0.094	0.104	0.251	0.144
(Standard error)	[0.05]	[0.04]*	[0.02]	[0.02]*	[0.06]	[0.08]	[0.27]	[0.12]
Observations	153	150	153	150	153	150	153	150

Notes: 49 countries. For other notes, please see Table 4.2.

find the black market premium has a negative effect, while GDP, trade openness and aggregate investment enter positively.

4.6 Conclusion

This research examines whether institutional improvement stimulates financial development using a panel of 90 economies over the period 1960–99. By comparing newly developed panel data techniques, including bias-corrected LSDV and system GMM estimators, this research shows that improved institutional quality is associated with increases in financial development at least in the short run, and this is particularly true for lower-income, ethnically divided and French legal origin countries. For the lower-income countries, this effect is expected to persist over longer horizons. The preliminary evidence from a "before-and-after" approach indicates that, in general, democratic transitions are typically preceded by low financial development, but followed by a short-run boost in, and greater volatility of, this.

The findings of this research highlight the influence of institutional innovation on the supply side of financial development. They shed light on the strong and robust relationship between institutional quality and economic performance, and present further grounds for institutional reform.

The findings in the panel data study on the coexistence of the effect of institutional innovation, GDP and trade openness on financial development are very significant. First, the study enriches the evidence for an openness-finance nexus. Huang and Temple (2005)'s cross section and panel data study suggests that trade openness is very likely to boost financial development, for which institutional improvement could serve as one channel. The IMF (2003) indicates the possible existence of such a channel by concluding that "greater openness to trade and stronger competition are conducive to institutional improvement, and thus to growth". However, the findings of this research tend to suggest that there are additional channels via which more open policies exert a positive effect on financial development. The findings are also consistent with Rajan and Zingales (2003)'s claim that trade openness is helpful for changing incumbents' willingness to promote financial development.

Second, the study has implications for economic and political reform. Giavazzi and Tabellini (2004) argue that "studying the effects of each reform (economic and political reform) individually can be misleading" and there are positive feedback effects and interaction effects between economic and political liberalization. The findings of this chapter seem to be consistent with their findings on the interaction effects, in the sense that institutional reform under an open economic environment exerts an additional boost to investment and economic growth, and thus to financial development.

Appendix tables

Table A4.1 The variables

Variable	Description	Source
FD	Index for financial development in this paper, mainly measuring the size of financial intermediary development. It is the first principal component of *LLY*, *PRIVO* and *BTOT*.	
LLY	Liquid Liabilities, the ratio of liquid liabilities of financial system (currency plus demand and interest-bearing liabilities of banks and nonbanks) to GDP.	Financial Development and Structure Database (FDS) in World Bank, 2008
PRIVO	Private Credit, the ratio of credits issued to private sector by banks and other financial intermediaries to GDP.	FDS, 2008
BTOT	Commercial-Central Bank, the ratio of commercial bank assets to the sum of commercial bank and central bank assets.	FDS, 2008
POLITY2	The index for the degree of democracy. It is the "polity2" in PolityIV Database.	PolityIV Database Marshall and Jaggers (2008)
LGDP	Real GDP per capita (Chain) in log.	Penn World Table 6.2
OPENC	The sum of exports and imports over GDP (at current prices). The regression uses log(1+OPENC/100).	Penn World Table 6.2
CI	The sum of investment over real GDP per capita (using domestic prices). The regression uses CI/100.	Penn World Table 6.2
BMP	Black market premium (%, means zero). The regression uses log(1+BMP/100).	Global Development Network (GDN), 2002
INCLOW	Dummy for low-income group	GDN, 2002
INCMID	Dummy for middle-income group, made up of lower-middle-income and low-income countries	GDN, 2002
ETHFRAC	Dummy for ethnic fractionalization	GDN, 2002
LEG_UK	Dummy for British legal origin	GDN, 2002
LEG_FR	Dummy for French legal origin	GDN, 2002
LEG_GE	Dummy for German legal origin	GDN, 2002
LEG_SC	Dummy for Scandinavian legal origin	GDN, 2002
ASIA	Dummy for Asian countries	GDN, 2002
LAC	Dummy for Latin American countries	GDN, 2002
SSA	Dummy for Sub-Sarahan African countries	GDN, 2002

Table A4.2 Descriptive statistics

Variable		Mean	Std. Dev.	Min	Max	Observations
FD	overall	−0.61	1.17	−2.91	1.85	N = 341
	between		1.09	−2.77	2.53	n = 90
	within		0.56	−2.45	4.48	T-bar = 3.79
POLITY2	overall	−1.83	6.39	−10.00	10.00	N=438
	between		5.37	−9.78	9.83	n=90
	within		3.56	−12.70	10.92	T-bar = 4.87
LGDP	overall	7.73	0.84	5.89	10.06	N = 399
	between		0.86	6.28	10.06	n = 86
	within		0.26	6.70	8.73	T-bar = 4.64
OPENC	overall	0.43	0.19	0.07	1.18	N = 399
	between		0.19	0.13	1.08	n = 86
	within		0.08	0.16	0.78	T-bar = 4.64
CI	overall	0.13	0.08	0.01	0.39	N = 399
	between		0.07	0.02	0.31	n = 86
	within		0.04	0.00	0.35	T-bar = 4.64
BMP	overall	0.33	0.66	−0.04	7.64	N = 402
	between		0.47	0.00	3.17	n = 88
	within		0.53	−1.65	5.88	T-bar = 4.57

Note: Appendix Table A4.1 describes all variables in detail.

5
Financial Reforms for Financial Development

5.1 Introduction

Financial liberalization has been one of the key trends characterizing the post-Bretton Woods era, with decreasing capital controls and an increasing participation of developing countries in international financial markets in recent decades. More broadly, domestic financial development, measured in terms of liquid liabilities or stock market capitalization, has risen dramatically over the same period. By using Bayesian Model Averaging (BMA) and General-to-specific (Gets) approaches, Chapter 2 examines the long-run determinants of financial development. However, what are the factors directly stimulating governments to liberalize the financial sector, aimed at enhancing financial development? Building on the framework of Abiad and Mody (2005) (AM hereafter), this chapter attempts to answer this question and to provide a more comprehensive view of the political economy of financial reform.

Although financial liberalization has been criticized as increasing the likelihood of financial crises and financial fragility, it is widely regarded as promoting the flow of financial resources, thereby reducing capital costs, stimulating investment and fostering financial development and economic growth (McKinnon, 1973; Shaw, 1973; Demirgüç-Kunt and Detragiache, 1998; Summers, 2000). In practice, governments in recent decades have been committed to reducing direct intervention in the financial system by easing or removing controls over interest rates, credit allocation and financial transactions domestically and internationally, opening up the banking system for foreign entry, and privatizing commercial banks or non-bank financial intermediaries. What are the main factors inducing governments to take these steps?

AM introduce an analytical framework to examine the factors that induce governments to undertake financial reforms. Using an ordered logit technique to estimate their specifications, AM argue that policy change in a country is positively related to its level of liberalization and any liberalization gap from the regional leader. The pace of reform is found to be affected by shocks or discrete changes such as a balance-of-payments crisis, a banking crisis, a new government's first year in office, participation in an IMF programme and a decline in US interest rates. However, they find that ideology and political and economic structures have "limited influence" on the likelihood of reform.

The AM analytical framework is attractive in many respects, but some aspects of their empirical analysis merit further attention. First, the ordered logit technique they apply may not be appropriate for this context, although the discrete and ordinal nature of the financial liberalization level, $FL_{i,t}$, and policy change, $\Delta FL_{i,t}$, may render the ordered logit method a natural choice at first glance. In the AM analysis, the dependent variable is *not the level of financial liberalization, but the change in the level of liberalization*. AM treat a movement from a score of 1 to 3 of the underlying index the same as they do a movement from 16 to 18, among many other possibilities for a specific change (say +2). However, the lack of cardinality in the scale of their original measure implies that movements along the scale for a specific change are not equivalent. Given this particular nature of the dependent variable, resorting to the ordered logit technique may not lead to the expected gains.[84] Second, as in most cross-country research, AM do not take into account the effects of common trends and the possibility of error dependence across countries and over time. The importance of error dependence seems especially relevant when the effects of domestic learning and regional diffusion are investigated, and is confirmed by the results of this analysis, including a formal test of dependence following Pesaran (2004).

In this analysis, four innovations are introduced. The first is that, rather than their ordered logit technique, this analysis centres on the Pesaran (2006) common correlated effect pooled (CCEP) approach that allows for the possibility of error dependence across countries. Second, to adjust for serial correlation in individual errors, the panel-robust standard errors after Arellano (1987) are computed for the CCEP estimates.[85] Third, it adds the extent of democracy into the AM framework, by introducing the Polity indicator, "polity2", in the PolityIV Database (Marshall and Jaggers, 2008), seeking to measure institutional quality. The level of democracy is a potentially important variable which reflects the political environment in which new policies are approved or rejected, and policy changes take place. Fourth, in addition to focusing on the original dataset used by AM, it takes up a further investigation based on a larger set of countries, in which the Abiad and Mody financial liberalization index is replaced by the Chinn-Ito index of capital account openness (2006).

This chapter produces the following findings. In general it confirms the negative effects of banking crises and high inflation on policy change, as observed by AM. It is also consistent with AM in suggesting that the effects of new governments in their first year and IMF programmes are strong when financial sectors are highly repressed, and become weaker as the level of financial liberalization goes up. However, this chapter points to the following three distinct conclusions. First, it shows that some of their findings on the effects of crises and shocks are fragile. Second, it is at odds with AM on the effects of domestic learning and regional diffusion. It suggests that policy change in a country is negatively rather than positively related to its liberalization level, and the liberalization gap from the regional leader appears less relevant than in AM. Third, this analysis observes a significant effect of the extent of democracy, the new variable added to the Abiad and Mody framework, on policy change. The findings on the negative effects of domestic learning and irrelevance of regional diffusion are supported by a larger sample of countries drawing on the Chinn-Ito index of capital account openness.

Section 5.2 provides a brief discussion of the model specifications and econometric methods. Section 5.3 presents the empirical results, based on the original dataset with the AM measure, and a larger set of countries with the Chinn-Ito measure, separately. Section 5.4 discusses the implications of the findings. Section 5.5 concludes.

5.2 Methodology

This section starts by briefly describing the models used in AM to study how financial reform is shaped, followed by a discussion of the econometric methods that will be applied in this chapter.

5.2.1 Model specifications

Below is the general model structure that captures the effects of domestic learning, regional diffusion, discrete changes and ideology and structure on policy changes.

$$\Delta FL_{it} = \alpha(FL_{it}^* - FL_{i,t-1})$$
$$+ \beta_1(REG\_FL_{i,t-1} - FL_{i,t-1})$$
$$+ \beta_2' SHOCKS_{it}$$
$$+ \beta_3' IDEOLOGY_{it}$$
$$+ \beta_4' STRUCTURE_{it}$$
$$+ \varepsilon_{it} \quad (5.1)$$

The dependent variable, ΔFL_{it}, is used to measure policy change, the difference between the level of financial liberalization in the current period, FL_{it}, and the past level of financial liberalization, $FL_{i,t-1}$. FL_{it}^{86} ranges between 0 and 1, with 0 and 1 corresponding to complete financial repression and complete financial liberalization, respectively. FL_{it}^* is the desired level of financial liberalization. The adjustment factor, α, measures the degree of status quo bias. A lower value of α is associated with more resistance to reform and a greater bias towards the status quo. The first term on the RHS is therefore used to examine domestic adjustment. The second term captures regional diffusion in which $REG\_FL_{i,t-1}$ is the maximum level of financial liberalization achieved in the region. $SHOCKS_{it}$ denotes discrete changes including four types of crises – balance-of-payments crises (BOP_{it}), banking crises ($BANK_{it}$), recessions ($RECESSION_{it}$) and high inflation periods ($HINFL_{it}$) – and three types of internal or external influences like the incumbent's first year in office ($FIRSTYEAR_{it}$), the influence of international financial institutions reflected by a dummy for an IMF programme of lending (IMF_{it}) and the influence of global factors proxied by the US Treasury Bill rate ($USINT_{it}$). $IDEOLOGY_{it}$ reflects political orientation including a dummy for left-wing government ($LEFT_{it}$) and a dummy for right-wing government ($RIGHT_{it}$). $STRUCTURE_{it}$ represents structural variables (either economic or political), for example the trade openness measure ($OPEN_{it}$) used in AM.

Overall, the Abiad and Mody framework is appealing, covering almost all possible aspects. However, a political structural variable, the extent of democracy ($POLITY2_{it}$), may be relevant to the analysis and is added to their framework. This is the Polity indicator "polity2" in the PolityIV Database (Marshall and Jaggers 2008) and seeks to measure institutional quality based on the freedom of suffrage, operational constraints on executives and respect for other basic political rights and civil liberties. It is called the "combined polity score", defined as the democracy score minus the autocracy score.[87]

5.2.1.1 Benchmark specification

The benchmark specification assumes that the desired level of financial liberalization, FL_{it}^*, is the perfect level of financial liberalization and the adjustment factor, α, is positively related to the level of financial liberalization to allow for the likelihood of domestic learning. Putting $FL^* = 1$ and $\alpha = \theta_1 FL_{i,t-1} (\theta_1 > 0)$ into Equation (5.1) above and reparameterizing, we have

$$\Delta FL_{it} = \theta_1 FL_{i,t-1}(1 - FL_{i,t-1})$$
$$+ \theta_2 (REG\_FL_{i,t-1} - FL_{i,t-1})$$
$$+ \theta_3' SHOCKS_{it}$$
$$+ \theta_4' IDEOLOGY_{it}$$
$$+ \theta_5' STRUCTURE_{it}$$
$$+ \varepsilon_{it} \qquad (5.2)$$

This equation is Equation (4) in AM.

5.2.1.2 Alternative specifications

Relaxing two assumptions used in the benchmark specification, three alternative specifications are considered:

First, rather than assuming the desired level of financial liberalization, FL_{it}^*, to be full liberalization, it is natural to adopt country-specific measures of the desired extent of liberalization. When plugging $FL^* = c$ ($0 < c < 1$) and $\alpha = \theta_1 FL_{i,t-1}$ into Equation (5.1) above, redefining the coefficients yields the following equation as in Equation (5) of AM[88]:

$$\Delta FL_{it} = \theta_1 FL_{i,t-1} + \theta_2 FL_{i,t-1}^2$$
$$+ \theta_3 (REG\_FL_{i,t-1} - FL_{i,t-1})$$
$$+ \theta_4' SHOCKS_{it}$$
$$+ \theta_5' IDEOLOGY_{it}$$
$$+ \theta_6' STRUCTURE_{it}$$
$$+ \varepsilon_{it} \qquad (5.3)$$

Second, the desired level of financial liberalization, FL^*_{it}, might be reasonably regarded to be increasing with the level of income. When $FL^* = a + bY_{it}$ and $\alpha = \theta_1 FL_{i,t-1}$ are considered, Equation (5.1) above can be rearranged and reparameterized as Equation (6) in AM:[89]

$$\Delta FL_{it} = \theta_1 FL_{i,t-1} + \theta_2 FL^2_{i,t-1}$$
$$+ \theta_3 (FL_{i,t-1}.Y_{it})$$
$$+ \theta_4 (REG\_FL_{i,t-1} - FL_{i,t-1})$$
$$+ \theta'_5 SHOCKS_{it}$$
$$+ \theta'_6 IDEOLOGY_{it}$$
$$+ \theta'_7 STRUCTURE_{it}$$
$$+ \varepsilon_{it} \tag{5.4}$$

Finally, when the possibility that shocks, ideology and structure variables may exert effects on the status quo bias is taken into account, the previous assumption $\alpha = \theta_1 FL_{i,t-1}$ is replaced by the following equation:

$$\alpha = \gamma_1 FL_{i,t-1}$$
$$+ \gamma_2 (REG\_FL_{i,t-1} - FL_{i,t-1})$$
$$+ \gamma'_3 SHOCKS_{it}$$
$$+ \gamma'_4 IDEOLOGY_{it}$$
$$+ \gamma'_5 STRUCTURE_{it}$$

Putting this expression as well as $FL^* = c$ into Equation (5.1) and redefining the coefficients yields the third specification, Equation (8) in AM, below:

$$\Delta FL_{it} = \theta_1 FL_{i,t-1} + \theta_2 FL^2_{i,t-1}$$
$$+ \theta_3 (REG\_FL_{i,t-1} - FL_{i,t-1})$$
$$+ \theta_4 (REG\_FL_{i,t-1} - FL_{i,t-1}).FL_{i,t-1}$$
$$+ \theta'_5 SHOCKS_{it} + \theta'_6 SHOCKS_{it}.FL_{i,t-1}$$
$$+ \theta'_7 IDEOLOGY_{it} + \theta'_8 IDEOLOGY_{it}.FL_{i,t-1}$$
$$+ \theta'_9 STRUCTURE_{it} + \theta'_{10} STRUCTURE_{it}.FL_{i,t-1}$$
$$+ \varepsilon_{it} \tag{5.5}$$

5.2.2 Econometric methods

AM use an ordered logit technique to estimate the benchmark specification and three alternative specifications with the results presented in Tables 7, 8 and 9 of their paper. A minor problem has been detected in their empirical results in which Singapore is misclassified as an African country while South Africa is misclassified as an East Asian country. The corrected results are presented in Appendix Table A5.4. In general, the pattern of Appendix Table A5.4 (part A) is similar to that of their Table 7. Appendix Table A5.4 (part B) presents stronger evidence for IMF_{it} and $REG\_FL_{i,t-1} - FL_{i,t-1}$.[90] It is worth noting that Appendix Table A5.4 (part C) shows that $FL_{i,t-1}$, $OPEN_{it}$ and $OPEN_{it} \times FL_{i,t-1}$ appear to be insignificant when country fixed effects are included, different from Table 9 of AM, which shows these variables to be significant when country fixed effects are included.

More importantly, the analyses conducted by AM may be questioned in the following two aspects.

The first is that the ordered logit technique they apply may not be natural for this context, although the discrete and ordinal nature of the financial liberalization level, $FL_{i,t}$, and policy change, $\Delta FL_{i,t}$, may render the ordered logit method an appropriate choice at first glance. Since the dependent variable is *not the level of financial liberalization, but policy change*, financial liberalization moving from a score of 1 to 3 in terms of their original measure[91] is treated the same as moving from 16 to 18, for example. However, given the ordinal feature of their original measure, in reality policy change reflected by moving from a score of 1 to 3, which could be at rather low levels, doesn't necessarily lead to the same extent of financial liberalization as moving from 16 to 18, which could be at much higher levels of financial liberalization. Given this particular nature of the dependent variable, resorting to the ordered logit technique may not lead to the expected gains.

Second, like in most cross-country research, AM do not take into account the effects of common trends and the possibility of error dependence across countries and over time. This seems especially relevant when the effects of domestic learning and regional diffusion are investigated. The assumption on the error term they use implies that the disturbances are uncorrelated between groups and over time. However, if the error term contains one or more unobserved factors which have different effects on every unit, as noted by Phillips and Sul (2003) among others, "the consequences of ignoring cross section dependence can be serious". On the other hand, the consequences of ignoring serial correlation and heteroscedasticity can also be serious, since this may lead to a downwards bias in standard errors, and therefore higher significance levels attached to the coefficients. In examining the origins of financial openness, Quinn and Inclán (1997) argue that it is critical to consider a common trend, such as changes in consumer tastes and technology, that may exert substantial effects on government liberalization policies as "fundamental but unobservable forces".

The particular nature of the dependent variable and the possibility of error dependence suggest that another estimation approach would be worthwhile. The wide range of scores on the original financial liberalization index from 1 to 18 and the policy change, $\Delta FL_{i,t}$, from -1 to 1 (after transformation) makes a simpler linear regression method a possible choice for this context. This chapter's approach centres on the Pesaran (2006) common correlated effect pooled (CCEP) estimator, a generalization of the fixed effects estimator which allows for the possibility of cross-section correlation.[92] To adjust for serial correlation in individual errors,[93] the panel-robust standard errors from Arellano (1987) are computed for the CCEP estimates, allowing the errors not only to be serially correlated for a given country, but also to have variances and covariances that vary across countries.

Pesaran (2006) proposes two common correlated effect (CCE) approaches for large heterogeneous panels whose error contains unobserved common factors. More specifically, this approach augments the one-way fixed effects model with the (weighted) cross-sectional means of the dependent variable and the individual specific regressors, analogous to a two-way fixed effects model. Including the (weighted) cross-sectional averages of the dependent variable and individual specific regressors is suggested by Pesaran (2006, 2007) as an effective way to filter out the impacts of common factors, which could be common technological or macroeconomic shocks, causing between group error dependence.

The Pesaran (2006, 2007) approach exhibits considerable advantages. It allows unobserved common factors to be possibly correlated with exogenous regressors and exert differential impacts on individual units. It permits unit root processes amongst the observed and unobserved common effects. The proposed estimator is still consistent, although it is no longer efficient, when the idiosyncratic components are not serially uncorrelated.

In this context, the cross sectional means of ΔFL_{it}, $FL_{i,t-1}$, $GDP_{i,t-1}$ and $OPEN_{it}$ are considered since these variables may be especially likely to reflect common effects. To allow the effects to be heterogeneous across regions, the models are augmented with the interactions between regional dummies and cross sectional means of the above variables, and time dummies. The CCEP estimator has been shown to be asymptotically unbiased and consistent as $N-> \infty$ for both T fixed or $T -> \infty$, and to have generally satisfactory finite sample properties.

Appendix Table A5.3 presents the time series properties for three continuous variables, the financial liberalization index ($FL_{i,t}$), GDP per capita in PPP terms ($GDP_{i,t}$) and trade openness ($OPEN_{i,t}$). It contrasts a panel unit root test proposed by Pesaran (2007) in the presence of cross section dependence with the Maddala and Wu (1999) Fisher test, which is associated with the assumption of cross section independence of the error term and does not require a balanced panel. The Pesaran (2007) approach augments the standard ADF regression with cross section averages of lagged levels and first differences of individual series, to control for cross section dependence. The Maddala and Wu (1999) Fisher test is then applied to this more general setting. With cross sectionally independent errors, the Maddala and Wu (1999) Fisher test cannot reject the null of non-stationarity for $FL_{i,t}$, $GDP_{i,t}$ and $OPEN_{i,t}$ when we do not allow for a trend. With a trend, the series of $GDP_{i,t}$ and $OPEN_{i,t}$ are close to being found as stationary. When we allow for a trend, Pesaran's test shows that we can almost reject the null of non-stationarity for $FL_{i,t}$, $GDP_{i,t}$ and $OPEN_{i,t}$ at the 10% significance level[94], suggesting that $FL_{i,t}$, $GDP_{i,t}$ and $OPEN_{i,t}$ may not be I(1) variables. However, this result should be interpreted with caution since there are reservations as to the power and reliability of these tests.

This analysis also employs a normal within groups (WG) approach to estimating the one-way fixed effects models (country fixed effects included), as estimated by AM, with non-robust standard errors. How important controlling for error dependence across countries and over time is for this context can be examined by comparing the WG estimates and CCEP estimates. The consistency of the one-way WG estimator for the dynamic homogeneous model is justified by the length of the time series,[95] but this estimator is biased in small samples because of the lagged dependent variable bias. The country fixed effects can be eliminated by an idempotent (covariance) transformation matrix as in within groups estimation.

5.3 Empirical evidence

By applying a within groups approach to the AM framework with the addition of the extent of democracy, this section presents empirical evidence in two steps on what shapes financial reform, an analysis on the original dataset with the AM measure in Section 5.3.1 and an analysis on a larger dataset with the Chinn-Ito (2006) measure in Section 5.3.2. In each step, the normal one-way fixed effects WG estimates with non-robust standard errors are contrasted with Pesaran (2006) CCEP estimates with panel-robust standard errors, with the former assuming that the errors are serially uncorrelated and independent across countries, while the latter approach allows for error dependence both across countries and over time.

5.3.1 Analysis on the original dataset

This section concerns the analyses on the benchmark specification (Equation 5.2) and three alternative specifications (Equations 5.3, 5.4 and 5.5) using AM's original dataset. The results are presented in Tables 5.1A/B, 5.2 and 5.3 corresponding to Tables 7, 8 and 9 in AM, respectively.

Table 5.1 (part A) and 5.1 (part B) reports the WG estimates and CCEP estimates of the benchmark specification (Equation 5.2). Table 5.1A strictly follows the model structure of AM^{96} while Table 5.1 (part B) reports $FL_{i,t-1}$ and $FL_{i,t-1}^2$ separately, presenting a direct link between policy change, ΔFL_{it}, and the level of liberalization, $FL_{i,t-1}$. In comparison to the ordered logit estimates in columns 4–6 (with country fixed effects) of Appendix Table A5.4A, the WG estimates in Table 5.1A (country effects are included by definition) not only confirm their findings, but also show that $FIRSTYEAR_{it}$ and $OPEN_{it}$ have positive effects on policy change.

To present a direct link between policy change, ΔFL_{it}, and the level of liberalization, $FL_{i,t-1}$, Table 5.1 (part B) reports $FL_{i,t-1}$ and $FL_{i,t-1}^2$ separately. The within R^2 associated with the CCEP estimates is much larger then those for the WG estimates, hinting at the importance of error dependence. With satisfactory finite sample properties, the CCEP estimates in Table 5.1 show that policy change is negatively rather than positively associated with the lagged level of financial liberalization, $FL_{i,t-1}$, and the regional liberalization gap, $REG\_FL_{i,t-1} - FL_{i,t-1}$. The CCEP estimates confirm the AM finding on a negative effect of $BANK_{it}$, and positive effects of BOP_{it} and $FIRSTYEAR_{it}$ on policy change. It also provides strong evidence for a negative effect of $POLITY2_{it}$, indicating that the extent of democracy tends to hinder the pace of reform.

Table 5.2 presents the within groups estimates, WG and CCEP, for the alternative specifications (Equations 5 and 6 in AM). The CCEP estimates confirm the previous observations of Table 5.1 in terms of the negative effects of the level of liberalization, regional liberalization gap, banking crises and the extent of democracy, and the positive effects of a balance-of-payments crisis and a new government's first year in office. A positive effect of $USINT_{it}$ is also observed.

Next we proceed to Table 5.3, which presents the within groups estimates of the most general specification (Equation 8 in AM). Note that the corrected Table 9 in AM shows that $FL_{i,t-1}$, $OPEN_{it}$ and $OPEN_{it} \times FL_{i,t-1}$ are insignificant in the presence of country fixed effects. Similarly, the

Table 5.1 Within estimates: Benchmark specification (Equation 4)

A. $FL_{i,t-1} \times (1 - FL_{i,t-1})$ reported

Estimators	WG	WG	WG	CCEP	CCEP	CCEP
$FL_{i,t-1} \times (1 - FL_{i,t-1})$	0.083 [0.038]**	0.098 [0.038]***	0.083 [0.039]**	0.046 [0.060]	0.070 [0.054]	0.075 [0.056]
$REG\_FL_{i,t-1} - FL_{i,t-1}$	0.076 [0.016]***	0.070 [0.016]***	0.083 [0.017]***	0.109 [0.025]***	0.111 [0.025]***	0.121 [0.027]***
BOP_{it}		0.017 [0.006]***	0.013 [0.006]**		0.019 [0.006]***	0.019 [0.006]***
$BANK_{it}$		−0.024 [0.007]***	−0.022 [0.007]***		−0.021 [0.010]**	−0.020 [0.009]**
$RECESSION_{it}$		−0.010 [0.008]	−0.009 [0.008]		−0.006 [0.008]	−0.007 [0.008]
$HINFL_{it}$		−0.003 [0.011]	−0.002 [0.011]		−0.009 [0.019]	−0.012 [0.021]
$FIRSTYEAR_{it}$			0.011 [0.006]*			0.011 [0.006]*
IMF_{it}			0.011 [0.007]*			0.008 [0.008]
$USINT_{it}$			−0.003 [0.001]***			0.001 [0.003]
$LEFT_{it}$			0.001 [0.010]			−0.001 [0.009]
$RIGHT_{it}$			0.000 [0.009]			0.005 [0.009]
$OPEN_{it}$			0.000 [0.000]*			0.000 [0.000]
$POLITY2_{it}$			−0.013 [0.014]			−0.034 [0.020]*
Observations	805	805	805	805	805	805
Number of countries	35	35	35	35	35	35
R-squared	0.03	0.05	0.07	0.13	0.15	0.17
CSD test (p-value)	0.00	0.00	0.00	0.03	0.01	0.01

continued

Table 5.1 Continued

B. $FL_{i,t-1}$ and $(FL_{i,t-1})^2$ reported separately

Estimators	WG	WG	WG	CCEP	CCEP	CCEP
$FL_{i,t-1}$	0.081	0.096	0.074	−0.208	−0.178	−0.202
	[0.038]**	[0.038]**	[0.040]*	[0.058]***	[0.061]***	[0.071]***
$(FL_{i,t-1})^2$	−0.104	−0.113	−0.113	−0.154	−0.175	−0.174
	[0.043]**	[0.043]***	[0.043]***	[0.066]**	[0.065]**	[0.064]***
$REG\_FL_{i,t-1}$ $-FL_{i,t-1}$	0.059	0.058	0.058	−0.144	−0.133	−0.148
	[0.022]***	[0.022]***	[0.023]**	[0.042]***	[0.047]***	[0.053]***
BOP_{it}		0.016	0.011		0.014	0.014
		[0.006]***	[0.006]*		[0.006]**	[0.005]**
$BANK_{it}$		−0.024	−0.020		−0.019	−0.018
		[0.007]***	[0.007]***		[0.010]*	[0.009]*
$RECESSION_{it}$		−0.010	−0.009		−0.002	−0.004
		[0.008]	[0.008]		[0.007]	[0.008]
$HINFL_{it}$		−0.003	−0.002		−0.014	−0.012
		[0.011]	[0.011]		[0.017]	[0.018]
$FIRSTYEAR_{it}$			0.011			0.011
			[0.006]*			[0.006]*
IMF_{it}			0.012			0.008
			[0.007]*			[0.008]
$USINT_{it}$			−0.003			0.003
			[0.001]***			[0.004]
$LEFT_{it}$			0.002			0.010
			[0.010]			[0.009]
$RIGHT_{it}$			0.003			0.008
			[0.009]			[0.008]
$OPEN_{it}$			0.000			0.000
			[0.000]*			[0.000]
$POLITY2_{it}$			−0.011			−0.038
			[0.014]			[0.022]*
Observations	805	805	805	805	805	805
Number of countries	35	35	35	35	35	35
R-squared	0.03	0.05	0.08	0.20	0.22	0.24
CSD test (p-value)	0.00	0.00	0.00	0.03	0.02	0.01

Notes: 35 countries (original dataset), 1973–96. Dependent variable is ΔFL_{it}. Using normal one-way within it groups estimator (WG) and Pesaran (2006)'s CCEP estimator, Table 5.1 A/B presents new results corresponding to models in Table 7 in Abiad and Mody (2005) with the addition of $POLITY2_{it}$. Table 5.1A reports results for $FL_{i,t-1} \times (1 - FL_{i,t-1})$, while Table 5.1B reports results for $FL_{i,t-1}$ and $FL_{i,t-1}^2$ separately. The within R-squared is reported. Non-robust standard errors are reported for WG estimates, while panel-robust standard errors are reported for CCEP estimates. CSD tests the null hypothesis of cross section independence in the panel data models using the test following Pesaran (2004).

* significant at 10%; ** significant at 5%; *** significant at 1%.

Table 5.2 Within estimates: Alternative specification (Equations 5 and 6)

Estimators	WG	WG	CCEP	CCEP
$FL_{i,t-1}$	0.074	0.092	−0.202	−0.175
	[0.040]*	[0.040]**	[0.071]***	[0.078]**
$(FL_{i,t-1})^2$	−0.113	−0.201	−0.174	−0.105
	[0.043]***	[0.053]***	[0.064]***	[0.066]
$FL_{i,t-1} \times Y_{i,t-1}$		0.007		−0.009
		[0.002]***		[0.004]**
$REG\_FL_{i,t-1} - FL_{i,t-1}$	0.058	0.063	−0.148	−0.094
	[0.023]**	[0.023]***	[0.053]***	[0.079]
BOP_{it}	0.011	0.011	0.014	0.016
	[0.006]*	[0.006]*	[0.005]**	[0.005]***
$BANK_{it}$	−0.020	−0.023	−0.018	−0.016
	[0.007]***	[0.007]***	[0.009]*	[0.009]*
$RECESSION_{it}$	−0.009	−0.010	−0.004	−0.004
	[0.008]	[0.008]	[0.008]	[0.008]
$HINFL_{it}$	−0.002	−0.004	−0.012	−0.015
	[0.011]	[0.011]	[0.018]	[0.018]
$FIRSTYEAR_{it}$	0.011	0.011	0.011	0.011
	[0.006]*	[0.006]*	[0.006]*	[0.006]*
IMF_{it}	0.012	0.012	0.008	0.009
	[0.007]*	[0.007]*	[0.008]	[0.008]
$USINT_{it}$	−0.003	−0.003	0.003	0.006
	[0.001]***	[0.001]***	[0.004]	[0.003]**
$LEFT_{it}$	0.002	0.001	0.010	0.011
	[0.010]	[0.010]	[0.009]	[0.010]
$RIGHT_{it}$	0.003	0.003	0.008	0.006
	[0.009]	[0.009]	[0.008]	[0.009]
$OPEN_{it}$	0.000	0.000	0.000	0.000
	[0.000]*	[0.000]**	[0.000]	[0.000]
$POLITY2_{it}$	−0.011	−0.010	−0.038	−0.039
	[0.014]	[0.014]	[0.022]*	[0.018]**
Observations	805	805	805	805
Number of countries	35	35	35	35
R-squared	0.08	0.09	0.24	0.25
CSD test (p-value)	0.00	0.00	0.01	0.01

Notes: This table, based on the original dataset, presents new results corresponding to models in Table 8 in AM except for the addition of $POLITY2_{it}$. See Table 5.1 for further notes.

CCEP estimates of Table 5.3 find less evidence for $FL_{i,t-1}$, $OPEN_{it}$ and $OPEN_{it} \times FL_{i,t-1}$. It confirms the negative effect of $REG\_FL_{i,t-1} - FL_{i,t-1}$ on policy reform.[97] A positive effect of $FIRSTYEAR_{it}$ and a negative effect of its interaction term with $FL_{i,t-1}$ are observed, highlighting that new

Table 5.3 Within estimates: Alternative specification (Equation 8)

Estimators	WG	CCEP
$FL_{i,t-1}$	−0.009	−0.175
	[0.072]	[0.121]
$(FL_{i,t-1})^2$	−0.011	−0.143
	[0.073]	[0.076]*
$REG\_FL_{i,t-1} - FL_{i,t-1}$	0.025	−0.147
	[0.023]	[0.055]**
$(REG - FL_{i,t-1} - FL_{i,t-1}) \times FL_{i,t-1}$	0.330	0.094
	[0.086]***	[0.098]
BOP_{it}	0.020	0.014
	[0.010]**	[0.010]
$BOP_{it} \times FL_{i,t-1}$	−0.029	−0.009
	[0.019]	[0.022]
$BANK_{it}$	−0.023	−0.023
	[0.013]*	[0.016]
$BANK_{it} \times FL_{i,t-1}$	0.004	0.011
	[0.027]	[0.026]
$RECESSION_{it}$	−0.015	−0.006
	[0.012]	[0.014]
$RECESSION_{it} \times FL_{i,t-1}$	0.020	0.008
	[0.023]	[0.024]
$HINFL_{it}$	0.030	0.014
	[0.015]*	[0.026]
$HINFL_{it} \times FL_{i,t-1}$	−0.156	−0.105
	[0.043]***	[0.073]
$FIRSTYEAR_{it}$	0.028	0.027
	[0.010]***	[0.012]**
$FIRSTYEAR_{it} \times FL_{i,t-1}$	−0.049	−0.046
	[0.020]**	[0.027]*
IMF_{it}	0.020	0.011
	[0.009]**	[0.008]
$IMF_{it} \times FL_{i,t-1}$	−0.050	−0.024
	[0.026]*	[0.018]
$USINT_{it}$	−0.003	−0.001
	[0.001]***	[0.005]
$LEFT_{it}$	−0.025	−0.019
	[0.014]*	[0.014]
$LEFT_{it} \times FL_{i,t-1}$	0.068	0.076
	[0.034]**	[0.039]*
$RIGHT_{it}$	0.006	0.008
	[0.012]	[0.012]
$RIGHT_{it} \times FL_{i,t-1}$	0.020	0.025
	[0.032]	[0.039]
$OPEN_{it}$	0.001	0.001
	[0.000]***	[0.001]

continued

Table 5.3 Continued

Estimators	WG	CCEP
$OPEN_{it} \times FL_{i,t-1}$	−0.001	−0.001
	[0.000]***	[0.001]
$POLITY2_{it}$	−0.030	−0.043
	[0.018]*	[0.031]
$POLITY2_{it} \times FL_{i,t-1}$	0.002	0.001
	[0.002]	[0.003]
Observations	805	805
Number of countries	35	35
R-squared	0.14	0.27
CSD test (p-value)	0.00	0.01

Notes: This table, based on the original dataset, presents new results corresponding to models in Table 9 in AM except for the addition of $POLITY2_{it}$. See Table 5.1 for further notes.

governments in their first year are likely to trigger reform, especially when the extent of financial liberalization is still at an early stage. The effect of the interaction between $LEFT_{it}$ and $FL_{i,t-1}$ is also shown to be positive.

The discrepancy between the WG estimates and CCEP estimates in the above study has pointed to the fundamental significance of relaxing assumptions on the error term. One may wonder which is more important, controlling for serial correlation in the errors or adjusting for cross section error dependence? To what extent does each relaxation make the results different from those associated with error independence? Answers may be found from Table 5.4, which reports the WG estimates with panel-robust standard errors, controlling for serial correlation of errors only, and the CCEP estimates with non-robust standard errors, controlling for cross section error dependence only. As it stands, both are important. Nevertheless, the quantitatively larger effects (coefficients) and much larger R^2 associated with the CCEP estimates than with the WG estimates may reflect that controlling for cross-country correlation is an especially crucial step for this context. One may notice from Table 5.4 that, suggested by either the WG estimates or CCEP estimates, the ideology and economic and political structure in general appear to have a substantial influence on policy change, especially for $LEFT_{it}$ and $OPEN_{it}$. This has raised a methodological concern that insufficient consideration of error dependence could lead to misleading findings.

Table 5.4 Error dependence across countries and over time considered separately

A. Within estimates corresponding to Table 5.1B

Estimators	WG	WG	WG	CCEP	CCEP	CCEP
$FL_{i,t-1}$	0.081	0.096	0.074	−0.208	−0.178	−0.202
	[0.049]	[0.045]**	[0.053]	[0.056]***	[0.057]***	[0.059]***
$(FL_{i,t-1})$	−0.104	−0.113	−0.113	−0.154	−0.175	−0.174
	[0.046]**	[0.045]**	[0.051]**	[0.049]***	[0.050]***	[0.050]***
$REG\_FL_{i,t-1} - FL_{i,t-1}$	0.059	0.058	0.058	−0.144	−0.133	−0.148
	[0.025]**	[0.027]**	[0.027]**	[0.037]***	[0.037]***	[0.040]***
BOP_{it}		0.016	0.011		0.014	0.014
		[0.006]**	[0.006]*		[0.006]**	[0.006]**
$BANK_{it}$		−0.024	−0.020		−0.019	−0.018
		[0.009]**	[0.009]**		[0.007]***	[0.007]**
$RECESSION_{it}$		−0.010	−0.009		−0.002	−0.004
		[0.010]	[0.009]		[0.008]	[0.008]
$HINFL_{it}$		−0.003	−0.002		−0.014	−0.012
		[0.019]	[0.020]		[0.010]	[0.011]
$FIRSTYEAR_{it}$			0.011			0.011
			[0.006]*			[0.006]*
IMF_{it}			0.012			0.008
			[0.009]			[0.007]
$USINT_{it}$			−0.003			0.003
			[0.001]**			[0.003]
$LEFT_{it}$			0.002			0.010
			[0.008]			[0.011]
$RIGHT_{it}$			0.003			0.008
			[0.008]			[0.010]
$OPEN_{it}$			0.000			0.000
			[0.000]*			[0.000]
$POLITY2_{it}$			−0.011			−0.038
			[0.013]			[0.015]***
Observations	805	805	805	805	805	805
Number of countries	35	35	35	35	35	35
R-squared	0.03	0.05	0.08	0.20	0.22	0.24
CSD test (p-value)	0.00	0.00	0.00	0.03	0.02	0.01

Notes: Panelrobust standard errors are reported for WG estimates, whilst non-robust standard errors are reported for CCEP estimates. See Table 5.1 for further notes.

Table 5.4 Continued

B. Within estimates corresponding to Table 5.2

Estimators	WG	WG	CCEP	CCEP
$FL_{i,t-1}$	0.074	0.092	−0.202	−0.175
	[0.053]	[0.053]*	[0.059]***	[0.062]***
$(FL_{i,t-1})^2$	−0.113	−0.201	−0.174	−0.105
	[0.051]**	[0.068]***	[0.050]***	[0.055]*
$FL_{i,t-1} \times Y_{i,t-1}$		0.007		−0.009
		[0.003]**		[0.003]***
$REG\_FL_{i,t-1} - FL_{i,t-1}$	0.058	0.063	−0.148	−0.094
	[0.027]**	[0.025]**	[0.040]***	[0.047]**
BOP_{it}	0.011	0.011	0.014	0.016
	[0.006]*	[0.006]*	[0.006]**	[0.006]**
$BANK_{it}$	−0.020	−0.023	−0.018	−0.016
	[0.009]**	[0.009]**	[0.007]**	[0.007]**
$RECESSION_{it}$	−0.009	−0.010	−0.004	−0.004
	[0.009]	[0.009]	[0.008]	[0.008]
$HINFL_{it}$	−0.002	−0.004	−0.012	−0.015
	[0.020]	[0.020]	[0.011]	[0.011]
$FIRSTYEAR_{it}$	0.011	0.011	0.011	0.011
	[0.006]*	[0.006]*	[0.006]*	[0.006]*
IMF_{it}	0.012	0.012	0.008	0.009
	[0.009]	[0.009]	[0.007]	[0.007]
$USINT_{it}$	−0.003	−0.003	0.003	0.006
	[0.001]**	[0.001]**	[0.003]	[0.003]*
$LEFT_{it}$	0.002	0.001	0.010	0.011
	[0.008]	[0.007]	[0.011]	[0.011]
$RIGHT_{it}$	0.003	0.003	0.008	0.006
	[0.008]	[0.009]	[0.010]	[0.010]
$OPEN_{it}$	0.000	0.000	0.000	0.000
	[0.000]*	[0.000]**	[0.000]	[0.000]
$POLITY2_{it}$	−0.011	−0.010	−0.038	−0.039
	[0.013]	[0.013]	[0.015]***	[0.015]***
Observations	805	805	805	805
Number of countries	35	35	35	35
R-squared	0.08	0.09	0.24	0.25
CSD test (p-value)	0.00	0.00	0.01	0.01

Note: Panelrobust standard errors are reported for WG estimates, whilst non-robust standard errors are reported for CCEP estimates. See Table 5.1 for further notes.

Table 5.4 Continued

C. Within estimates corresponding to Table 5.3

Estimators	WG	CCEP
$FL_{i,t-1}$	−0.009	−0.175
	[0.061]	[0.105]*
$(FL_{i,t-1})^2$	−0.011	−0.143
	[0.068]	[0.104]
$REG\_FL_{i,t-1} - FL_{i,t-1}$	0.025	−0.147
	[0.029]	[0.040]***
$(REG - FL_{i,t-1} - FL_{i,t-1}) \times FL_{i,t-1}$	0.330	0.094
	[0.082]***	[0.116]
BOP_{it}	0.020	0.014
	[0.010]*	[0.010]
$BOP_{it} \times FL_{i,t-1}$	−0.029	−0.009
	[0.021]	[0.019]
$BANK_{it}$	−0.023	−0.023
	[0.016]	[0.013]*
$BANK_{it} \times FL_{i,t-1}$	0.004	0.011
	[0.025]	[0.026]
$RECESSION_{it}$	−0.015	−0.006
	[0.015]	[0.012]
$RECESSION_{it} \times FL_{i,t-1}$	0.020	0.008
	[0.022]	[0.023]
$HINFL_{it}$	0.030	0.014
	[0.027]	[0.015]
$HINFL_{it} \times FL_{i,t-1}$	−0.156	−0.105
	[0.058]**	[0.043]**
$FIRSTYEAR_{it}$	0.028	0.027
	[0.010]***	[0.009]***
$FIRSTYEAR_{it} \times FL_{i,t-1}$	−0.049	−0.046
	[0.024]**	[0.019]**
IMF_{it}	0.020	0.011
	[0.011]*	[0.009]
$IMF_{it} \times FL_{i,t-1}$	−0.050	−0.024
	[0.022]**	[0.026]
$USINT_{it}$	−0.003	−0.001
	[0.001]**	[0.004]
$LEFT_{it}$	−0.025	−0.019
	[0.014]*	[0.014]
$LEFT_{it} \times FL_{i,t-1}$	0.068	0.076
	[0.037]*	[0.034]**
$RIGHT_{it}$	0.006	0.008
	[0.011]	[0.013]
$RIGHT_{it} \times FL_{i,t-1}$	0.020	0.025
	[0.034]	[0.032]

continued

Table 5.4 Continued

Estimators	WG	CCEP
$OPEN_{it}$	0.001	0.001
	[0.000]**	[0.000]**
$OPEN_{it} \times FL_{i,t-1}$	−0.001	−0.001
	[0.000]**	[0.000]**
$POLITY2_{it}$	−0.030	−0.043
	[0.025]	[0.018]**
$POLITY2_{it} \times FL_{i,t-1}$	0.002	0.001
	[0.002]	[0.002]
Observations	805	805
Number of countries	35	35
R-squared	0.14	0.27
CSD test (p-value)	0.00	0.01

Notes: Panelrobust standard errors are reported for WG estimates, whilst non-robust standard errors are reported for CCEP estimates. See Table 5.1 for further notes.

In sum, the above analyses based on the augmented specifications in which $POLITY2_{it}$ is included, allowing for the possibility of error dependence across countries and over time, produce interesting findings. On the one hand, this chapter confirms the significant effects of crises and shocks on policy reform identified by AM. More specifically, it confirms negative effects of banking crises and high inflation, and does agree with AM that a new government in its first year and an IMF programme have a strong effect when financial sectors are highly repressed and a weaker effect thereafter. On the other hand, it differs from AM in the following three aspects. First, it shows that the significant effects of balance-of-payments crises and US interest rates found by AM are fragile. The second aspect is that it yields opposite findings to AM on the effects of domestic learning. It shows that the extent of policy reform is negatively rather than positively affected by the existing liberalization level, while the regional liberalization gap does not appear relevant. Third, it addresses the importance of the extent of democracy for the process of financial reform and identifies a negative effect of the extent of democracy on policy change.

5.3.2 Analysis on a larger dataset

This section makes an effort to explore if the findings are robust to a larger set of countries. It makes use of the Chinn-Ito index of financial

144 *Determinants of Financial Development*

openness (2006) which is available for 108 countries over 1970–2000. But the Chinn-Ito index measures only a country's degree of capital account openness, one aspect of six policy dimensions on which the creation of the AM is based. Moreover, the country coverage in this analysis is confined to the data availability of crisis variables taken from Bordo *et al.* (2000) which contains only 55 countries. Since most of the added countries are OECD countries (listed in the Appendix Table A5.2), the effects of factors like balance-of-payment crises, banking crises, IMF programmes and the extent of democracy are expected to be weaker.[98] A variable description is presented in Appendix Table A5.1.

Tables 5.5A, 5.5B and 5.5C report the within groups estimates corresponding to Tables 5.1B, 5.2 and 5.3, respectively. As expected, these tables show weaker evidence for the effects of shocks, crises, ideology and economic and political structures on policy reform, except for US interest rates and high inflation. But, since the above analysis in general obtains findings consistent with AM on the effects of crises and shocks, more emphasis is placed on the robustness of the new findings regarding the negative effects of domestic learning and regional diffusion.

With a larger sample size, both the WG and CCEP estimates in these tables clearly indicate that policy reform is negatively linked to the level of liberalization, $FL_{i,t-1}$, at the 1% significance level. The tables further confirm that the effect of $REG\_FL_{i,t-1} - FL_{i,t-1}$ on policy change is ambiguous. Removing the variable $IMF_{i,t}$ doesn't alter the pattern of the results, as reported in Appendix Table A5.5 (A, B, C).

Hence, the findings summarized earlier on the negative effects of domestic learning and irrelevance of regional diffusion are largely supported by a larger sample of countries based on the Chinn-Ito index of capital account openness.

5.4 Discussions

The above findings have several implications. The negative link between policy change and the liberalization level suggests a convergence in the extent of financial liberalization in the sense that countries with highly repressed financial sectors have more potential to embark on reform, while countries with a highly liberalized financial sector have greater status quo bias – the reform likelihood is "saturated" (AM). Vivid examples can easily be picked up from the financial liberalization process in East Asia in recent decades. Since the 1970s, countries or areas with levels of liberalization much lower than those of the main developed countries (the US or UK for example) like the Republic of Korea, Singapore, Hong

Table 5.5 Augmented dataset with Chinn-Ito measure (2006)
A. Within estimates corresponding to Table 5.1B

Estimators	WG	WG	WG	CCEP	CCEP	CCEP
$FL_{i,t-1}$	−0.168	−0.170	−0.185	−0.204	−0.214	−0.301
	[0.044]***	[0.044]***	[0.048]***	[0.069]***	[0.068]***	[0.086]***
$(FL_{i,t-1})^2$	0.052	0.053	0.070	0.087	0.092	0.164
	[0.037]	[0.037]	[0.039]*	[0.049]*	[0.049]*	[0.058]***
$REG\_FL_{i,t-1}$	−0.016	−0.018	0.007	0.048	0.044	0.063
$-FL_{i,t-1}$	[0.027]	[0.027]	[0.030]	[0.036]	[0.037]	[0.046]
BOP_{it}		0.002	0.003		−0.005	−0.006
		[0.007]	[0.007]		[0.007]	[0.008]
$BANK_{it}$		−0.010	−0.012		−0.008	−0.010
		[0.009]	[0.009]		[0.010]	[0.011]
$RECESSION_{it}$		−0.001	0.004		0.001	0.002
		[0.007]	[0.007]		[0.008]	[0.009]
$HINFL_{it}$		−0.018	−0.015		−0.009	−0.007
		[0.012]	[0.013]		[0.017]	[0.018]
$FIRSTYEAR_{it}$			0.000			0.001
			[0.007]			[0.005]
IMF_{it}			0.000			0.007
			[0.009]			[0.007]
$USINT_{it}$			−0.005			−0.002
			[0.001]***			[0.002]
$LEFT_{it}$			−0.002			−0.010
			[0.010]			[0.010]
$RIGHT_{it}$			0.000			−0.003
			[0.010]			[0.012]
$OPEN_{it}$			0.000			0.000
			[0.000]			[0.000]
$POLITY2_{it}$			−0.003			0.004
			[0.018]			[0.027]
Observations	1263	1262	1150	1263	1262	1150
Number of countries	55	55	53	55	55	53
R-squared	0.04	0.04	0.07	0.22	0.22	0.26

Notes: 55 countries, 1973–97. Dependent variable is $\Delta FL_{i,t}$. Using normal one-way within groups estimator (WG) and Pesaran (2006)'s CCEP estimator, this table, based on a larger dataset associated with the Chinn-Ito measure (2006), presents new results corresponding to Table 5.1B. The within groups R-squared is reported. Variable descriptions are presented in the Appendix Table A5.1. Countries included are listed in the Appendix Table A5.2. Non-robust standard errors are reported for WG estimates, while panelrobust standard errors are reported for CCEP estimates.
* significant at 10%; ** significant at 5%; *** significant at 1%.

Table 5.5 Continued

B. Within estimates corresponding to Table 5.2

Estimators	WG	WG	CCEP	CCEP
$FL_{i,t-1}$	−0.185	−0.180	−0.301	−0.375
	[0.048]***	[0.048]***	[0.086]***	[0.122]***
$(FL_{i,t-1})^2$	0.070	0.028	0.164	0.138
	[0.039]*	[0.046]	[0.058]***	[0.071]*
$FL_{i,t-1} \times Y_{i,t-1}$		0.003		0.002
		[0.002]*		[0.004]
$REG\_FL_{i,t-1} - FL_{i,t-1}$	0.007	0.013	0.063	0.038
	[0.030]	[0.030]	[0.046]	[0.058]
BOP_{it}	0.003	0.002	−0.006	−0.012
	[0.007]	[0.007]	[0.008]	[0.010]
$BANK_{it}$	−0.012	−0.011	−0.010	−0.002
	[0.009]	[0.009]	[0.011]	[0.013]
$RECESSION_{it}$	0.004	0.005	0.002	0.002
	[0.007]	[0.007]	[0.009]	[0.010]
$HINFL_{it}$	−0.015	−0.018	−0.007	0.006
	[0.013]	[0.013]	[0.018]	[0.017]
$FIRSTYEAR_{it}$	0.000	0.000	0.001	0.000
	[0.007]	[0.007]	[0.005]	[0.006]
IMF_{it}	0.000	0.000	0.007	0.010
	[0.009]	[0.009]	[0.007]	[0.007]
$USINT_{it}$	−0.005	−0.005	−0.002	−0.002
	[0.001]***	[0.001]***	[0.002]	[0.002]
$LEFT_{it}$	−0.002	−0.004	−0.010	−0.013
	[0.010]	[0.010]	[0.010]	[0.011]
$RIGHT_{it}$	0.000	−0.002	−0.003	−0.008
	[0.010]	[0.010]	[0.012]	[0.017]
$OPEN_{it}$	0.000	0.000	0.000	0.000
	[0.000]	[0.000]	[0.000]	[0.001]
$POLITY2_{it}$	−0.003	−0.003	0.004	0.007
	[0.018]	[0.018]	[0.027]	[0.033]
Observations	1150	1150	1150	1150
Number of countries	53	53	53	53
R-squared	0.07	0.07	0.26	0.33

Note: See Table 5.5A for further notes.

Table 5.5 Continued

C. Within estimates corresponding to Table 5.3

Estimators	WG	CCEP
$FL_{i,t-1}$	−0.360	−0.681
	[0.096]***	[0.255]**
$(FL_{i,t-1})^2$	0.255	0.448
	[0.089]***	[0.232]*
$REG\_FL_{i,t-1} - FL_{i,t-1}$	−0.006	−0.009
	[0.031]	[0.057]
$(REG - FL_{i,t-1} - FL_{i,t-1}) \times FL_{i,t-1}$	0.274	0.436
	[0.107]**	[0.263]
BOP_{it}	−0.010	−0.013
	[0.012]	[0.017]
$BOP_{it} \times FL_{i,t-1}$	0.030	0.009
	[0.020]	[0.028]
$BANK_{it}$	−0.010	−0.002
	[0.014]	[0.024]
$BANK_{it} \times FL_{i,t-1}$	0.003	−0.002
	[0.025]	[0.036]
$RECESSION_{it}$	0.006	0.003
	[0.011]	[0.012]
$RECESSION_{it} \times FL_{i,t-1}$	−0.008	−0.006
	[0.021]	[0.019]
$HINFL_{it}$	0.041	0.046
	[0.018]**	[0.033]
$HINFL_{it} \times FL_{i,t-1}$	−0.254	−0.171
	[0.054]***	[0.147]
$FIRSTYEAR_{it}$	−0.008	−0.009
	[0.011]	[0.009]
$FIRSTYEAR_{it} \times FL_{i,t-1}$	0.019	0.019
	[0.021]	[0.017]
IMF_{it}	−0.002	0.018
	[0.011]	[0.012]
$IMF_{it} \times FL_{i,t-1}$	0.032	−0.006
	[0.039]	[0.050]
$USINT_{it}$	−0.005	−0.003
	[0.001]***	[0.002]
$LEFT_{it}$	−0.019	−0.045
	[0.016]	[0.028]
$LEFT_{it} \times FL_{i,t-1}$	0.028	0.068
	[0.031]	[0.051]
$RIGHT_{it}$	0.004	−0.015
	[0.015]	[0.031]
$RIGHT_{it} \times FL_{i,t-1}$	−0.011	0.022
	[0.031]	[0.048]

continued

Table 5.5 Continued

Estimators	WG	CCEP
$OPEN_{it}$	0.001	0.000
	[0.000]*	[0.001]
$OPEN_{it} \times FL_{i,t-1}$	0.000	0.000
	[0.000]	[0.000]
$POLITY2_{it}$	−0.010	0.008
	[0.020]	[0.041]
$POLITY2_{it} \times FL_{i,t-1}$	0.001	0.000
	[0.002]	[0.007]
Observations	1150	1150
Number of countries	53	53
R-squared	0.10	0.35

Note: See Table 5.5A for further notes.

Kong, Thailand and China have actively and progressively liberalized their financial systems.

This research finds that the significant effect of a regional liberalization gap on policy changes is hard to identify, although two opposite views have been proposed in the literature. AM suggest that countries with a level of liberalization far from that of the regional leader are found to be more likely to undertake reform, perhaps due to competitive pressure. The larger the gap in terms of liberalization levels within a region, the fiercer the competition amongst these countries for international capital and technologies. In contrast, Axelrod (1997) documents that the more similar a country is to its neighbouring nations in terms of economic, social and political developments, the more likely it is that it "adopts one of the neighbour's traits" while Simmons and Elkins (2004) predict that "governments' liberalization policies will be influenced by the policies of their most important foreign economic competitors". This line of research in general predicts that a greater gap from the regional leader tends to be associated with less incentive to compete and less chance to catch up with the regional leader in the short run, therefore a status quo bias is maintained.

In accordance with AM, the pattern suggested by their Table 3 that the coefficient on $REG\_FL_{i,t-1} - FL_{i,t-1}$ is positive and the coefficient on the interaction term is negative although insignificant, seems to be in line with the convergence story identified earlier in the sense that countries with lower levels of liberalization relative to that of the regional leader are more inclined to initiate reform, while the reform momentum fades as the liberalization gap from the regional leader shrinks. It implies that a greater gap from the regional leader tends to be associated with more incentives to engage in reform.

The finding concerning the negative effect of the extent of democracy on policy change is consistent with Fernandez and Rodrik (1991), who argue that there is uncertainty with respect to the distribution of benefits and costs from reform. They contrast democratic societies in which the majority would vote against the reform due to the presence of this uncertainty, just for safety, with authoritarian societies like Taiwan and the Republic of Korea (early 1960s), Chile (1970s) and Turkey (1980s), where "reform was imposed by the authoritarian regimes and against the wishes of business." The status quo appears to be more easily dislodged in autocratic societies than in democratic societies.

Chapter 4 shows that democratization is typically followed by financial development at least in the short run, which is in line with the argument of Rodrik and Wacziarg (2005) in terms of a short-run boost in economic growth and a decline in growth volatility after democratization. Together with the findings of Chapter 4, a clear picture seems to appear to us: a short-run increase in financial development emerges after democratization; however, once democracy has been established and enhanced, the extent of democracy may exert negative effects on the extent to which governments undertake financial reform.

This finding tends to suggest that ideology and political structure can have a *substantial influence* on policy change, contrary to some extent to the findings of AM, who claim that ideology and economic and political structure have *a limited influence* on policy change.

5.5 Conclusion

This chapter studies the forces that lead governments to undertake reforms to enhance financial development, based on AM. Given the particular nature of the dependent variable, it suggests replacing the ordered logit technique used by AM with a within groups approach, allowing for the possibility of error dependence across countries and over time, which seems of especial importance when the effects of domestic learning and regional diffusion in the process of financial liberalization are studied. Based on these innovations, the analysis shows that some of the AM findings are not robust to error dependence and the estimation method. It has produced the following significant findings, shedding new light on the political economy of financial reform.

This chapter finds that policy change in a country is negatively rather than positively associated with the initial extent of liberalization level, and the distance behind the regional leader. This indicates convergence in the extent of financial liberalization, in the sense that countries with highly repressed financial sectors have more potential to embark on reform, whilst countries with a highly liberalized financial sector have greater status quo bias.

This analysis suggests that some of AM findings on the effects of shocks and crises are robust whilst others are fragile. More specifically, it confirms the negative effects of banking crises and high inflation. It also agrees with AM that new governments in their first year and IMF programmes have a strong effect when financial sectors are highly repressed, and a weaker effect thereafter. But it finds no evidence in support of the effects of balance-of-payments crises and US interest rates on policy change.

Furthermore, it shows that economic and political structure and ideology can have a substantial influence on policy change, and the extent of democracy, the added variable, has a significantly negative effect on policy reform.

Appendix tables

Table A5.1 The variables (mainly used with the larger dataset)

Variable	Description	Source
FL	It is the financial liberalization index, produced by rescaling the Chinn-Ito index to interval [0, 1]. The Chinn-Ito index, the KAOPEN index, measures a country's degree of capital account openness, taking on higher values the more open the country is to cross-border capital transactions.	Chinn and Ito (2006)
Y	GDP per capita in PPP terms.	Penn World Table 6.2
BOP	As in Abiad and Mody (2005) (originally taken from Bordo et al. (2000)), it is the balance-of-payments crisis variable identified by "a forced change in parity, abandonment of a pegged exchange rate, or an international rescue," or if an index of exchange market pressure (a weighted average of exchange rate, reserve and interest rate changes) exceeds a critical threshold of one and a half standard deviations above its mean. It is set equal to 1 if a balance of payments crisis has occurred within the past two years, and 0 otherwise.	Bordo et al. (2000)
BANK	As in Abiad and Mody (2005) (originally taken from Bordo et al. (2000)), it is the bankig crisis identified by periods of "financial distress resulting in the erosion of most or all of aggregate banking system capital". It is set equal to 1 if a banking crisis has occurred within the past two years, and 0 otherwise.	Bordo et al. (2000)
RECESSION	As in Abiad and Mody (2005), it is the recession dummy variable, set equal to 1 where the annual real GDP growth rate is negative, and 0 otherwise.	Penn World Table 6.2 (PWT62) (Heston et al., 2006)

continued

Table A5.1 Continued

Variable	Description	Source
HINFL	As in Abiad and Mody (2005), it is the high inflation dummy variable, set equal to 1 where the annual inflation exceeds 50%, and 0 otherwise.	World Bank World Development Indicators (WDI), 2008
FIRSTYEAR	Based on the *YRSOFFC* variable (how many years the chief executive has been in office), it is the first year in office dummy as in Abiad and Mody (2005).	World Bank's Database of Political Institutions (2005)
IMF	As in Abiad and Mody (2005), it is the IMF programme dummy variable constructed using the programme dates from the IMF "History of Lending Arrangements".	Abiad and Mody (2005), and IMF's "History of Lending".
USINT	As in Abiad and Mody (2005), it is the US Treasury Bill rate used as the world interest rate.	IMF's International Financial Statistics (2005)
LEFT	As in Abiad and Mody (2005), it denotes a left-wing government where its associated party is named or described as "communist", "socialist", "Social Democratic" or "left-wing".	World Bank's Database of Political Institutions (2005)
RIGHT	As in Abiad and Mody (2005), it denotes the right-wing government where its associated party is named or described as "conservative", or "right-wing".	World Bank's Database of Political Institutions (2005)
OPEN	The sum of exports and imports over GDP (at current prices), averaged over 1973–97.	Penn World Table 6.2
DEMO	Index of democracy. It is called combined the polity score, and is the democracy score minus the autocracy score, averaged over 1973–97. It is also used with the original dataset. The index has been converted to range from 0 to 1.	PolityIV Database (Marshall and Jaggers 2008)

Table A5.2 The list of countries in the augmented dataset

East Asia		South Asia		OECD countries	
CHN	China	BGD	Bangladesh*	AUS	Australia*
HKG	Hong Kong	IND	India*	AUT	Austria
IDN	Indonesia*	LKA	Sri Lanka*	BEL	Belgium
KOR	Korea, Rep.*	NPL	Nepal*	CAN	Canada*
MYS	Malaysia*	PAK	Pakistan*	CHE	Switzerland
PHL	Philippines*			DEU	Germany*
SGP	Singapore*			DNK	Denmark
THA	Thailand*			ESP	Spain
TWN	Taiwan*			FIN	Finland
				FRA	France*
Latin America		**Middle East**		GBR	United Kingdom*
& Caribbean		**& Africa**		GRC	Greece
ARG	Argentina*	EGY	Egypt*	IRL	Ireland
BRA	Brazil*	GHA	Ghana*	ISL	Iceland
CHL	Chile*	ISR	Israel*	ITA	Italy*
COL	Colombia*	MAR	Morocco*	JPN	Japan*
CRI	Costa Rica	NGA	Nigeria	NLD	Netherlands
ECU	Ecuador	ZAF	South Africa*	NOR	Norway
JAM	Jamaica	ZWE	Zimbabwe*	NZL	New Zealand*
MEX	Mexico*			PRT	Portugal
PER	Peru*			SWE	Sweden
PRY	Paraguay			TUR	Turkey*
URY	Uruguay			USA	USA*
VEN	Venezuela*				

Note: Countries with * are in the original dataset of Abiad and Mody (2005).

Table A5.3 Unit root test in heterogeneous panels

Variables	FL		GDP		OPEN	
Trend	Yes	No	Yes	No	Yes	No
Maddala and Wu (1999)'s Fisher test	43.82 [0.99]	25.39 [1.00]	77.84 [0.24]	52.81 [0.94]	75.23 [0.31]	64.11 [0.68]
Pesaran (2007)'s cross sectionally augmented Fisher test	74.85	50.23	67.65	54.98	63.01	62.31

Notes: Maddala and Wu (1999)'s Fisher test is for the case of cross sectionally independent error. Under the null of a unit root, the test statistic is asymptotically distributed as a standard normal. Pesaran (2007)'s test is the Maddala and Wu (1999)'s Fisher test applied to the cross sectionally augmented Dickey-Fuller regression. The 10% critical values provided by H.M. Pesaran for the pair of $N = 30$ and $T = 30$ is 82.89 with a trend and 82.18 without a trend.

154 *Determinants of Financial Development*

Table A5.4 Corrected version of Tables 7, 8 and 9 in Abiad and Mody (2005)

A. Corrected version of Table 7 in Abiad and Mody (2005)

Country dummy included	No	No	No	Yes	Yes	Yes
$FL_{i,t-1}$ $\times (1 - FL_{i,t-1})$	3.933 [4.39]***	4.562 [4.94]***	4.106 [4.48]***	6.794 [4.44]***	7.284 [4.83]***	6.574 [4.07]***
$REG\_FL_{i,t-1} - FL_{i,t-1}$	1.032 [4.18]***	1.050 [3.76]***	1.195 [3.93]***	2.285 [3.23]***	2.089 [2.71]***	2.529 [3.21]***
BOP_{it}		0.521 [2.60]***	0.430 [2.21]**		0.550 [2.19]**	0.475 [1.94]*
$BANK_{it}$		−1.020 [2.74]***	−0.983 [2.67]***		−0.995 [2.68]***	−0.935 [2.57]**
$RECESSION_{it}$		−0.018 [0.05]	0.002 [0.00]		−0.055 [0.15]	−0.026 [0.07]
$HINFL_{it}$		−0.136 [0.35]	−0.238 [0.62]		−0.317 [0.50]	−0.302 [0.48]
$FIRSTYEAR_{it}$			0.178 [0.78]			0.234 [0.87]
IMF_{it}			0.327 [1.81]*			0.253 [0.98]
$USINT_{it}$			−0.071 [1.82]*			−0.090 [2.13]**
$LEFT_{it}$			0.282 [1.14]			−0.035 [0.10]
$RIGHT_{it}$			0.153 [0.85]			−0.132 [0.39]
$OPEN_{it}$			−0.001 [1.01]			0.009 [1.14]
Observations	805	805	805	805	805	805
Number of countries	35	35	35	35	35	35

Notes: This is a corrected version of Table 7 in Abiad and Mody (2005), which treated Singapore as an African country and South Africa as an East Asian country. Except for the difference in magnitude, this table shows a similar pattern to Table 7 in Abiad and Mody (2005). Robust t-statistics in brackets.

* significant at 10%; ** significant at 5%; *** significant at 1%.

Financial Reforms for Financial Development 155

Table A5.4 Continued

B. Corrected version of Table 8 in Abiad and Mody (2005)

Country dummy included	No	No	Yes	Yes
$FL_{i,t-1}$	4.110	4.307	6.546	7.189
	[4.49]***	[4.69]***	[4.02]***	[4.34]***
$(FL_{i,t-1})^2$	−4.052	−5.720	−6.638	−9.893
	[3.94]***	[4.19]***	[3.35]***	[3.90]***
$FL_{i,t-1} \times Y_{i,t-1}$		0.095		0.247
		[2.34]**		[2.55]**
$REG\_FL_{i,t-1} - FL_{i,t-1}$	1.231	0.965	2.465	2.714
	[2.72]***	[1.88]*	[2.09]**	[2.45]**
BOP_{it}	0.429	0.476	0.473	0.457
	[2.19]**	[2.40]**	[2.02]**	[1.95]*
$BANK_{it}$	−0.985	−0.976	−0.932	−1.007
	[2.70]***	[2.70]***	[2.70]***	[2.92]***
$RECESSION_{it}$	−0.002	−0.005	−0.027	0.001
	[0.00]	[0.01]	[0.07]	[0.00]
$HINFL_{it}$	−0.235	−0.206	−0.303	−0.398
	[0.63]	[0.53]	[0.48]	[0.64]
$FIRSTYEAR_{it}$	0.178	0.141	0.233	0.245
	[0.78]	[0.62]	[0.86]	[0.91]
IMF_{it}	0.332	0.414	0.255	0.288
	[1.74]*	[2.12]**	[0.96]	[1.06]
$USINT_{it}$	−0.070	−0.074	−0.090	−0.086
	[1.80]*	[1.87]*	[2.07]**	[1.99]**
$LEFT_{it}$	0.280	0.190	−0.029	−0.098
	[1.15]	[0.82]	[0.08]	[0.28]
$RIGHT_{it}$	0.146	0.153	−0.125	−0.072
	[0.77]	[0.84]	[0.38]	[0.21]
$OPEN_{it}$	−0.001	0.000	0.009	0.013
	[1.00]	[0.04]	[1.14]	[1.40]
Observations	805	805	805	805
Number of countries	35	35	35	35

Notes: This table corresponds to the Table 8 in Abiad and Mody (2005), which treated Singapore as an African country and South Africa as an East Asian country, and consequently indicates that IMF in column 1 and REG_FL-FL in columns 2 and 3 are insignificant. Robust t-statistics in brackets.

* significant at 10%; ** significant at 5%; *** significant at 1%.

Table A5.4 Continued

C. Corrected version of Table 9 in Abiad and Mody (2005)

Country dummy included	No	Yes
$FL_{i,t-1}$	3.719	3.475
	[2.16]**	[1.61]
$(FL_{i,t-1})^2$	−3.827	−1.82
	[2.19]**	[0.70]
$REG\_FL_{i,t-1} - FL_{i,t-1}$	0.508	1.459
	[0.81]	[1.21]
$(REG - FL_{i,t-1} - FL_{i,t-1}) \times FL_{i,t-1}$	2.87	10.256
	[1.51]	[3.95]***
BOP_{it}	0.811	0.809
	[2.69]***	[1.89]*
$BOP_{it} \times FL_{i,t-1}$	−0.892	−0.989
	[1.47]	[1.11]
$BANK_{it}$	−0.883	−1.043
	[1.65]*	[1.85]*
$BANK_{it} \times FL_{i,t-1}$	−0.093	0.016
	[0.09]	[0.01]
$RECESSION_{it}$	−0.487	−0.503
	[1.12]	[0.91]
$RECESSION_{it} \times FL_{i,t-1}$	1.235	1.164
	[1.43]	[1.21]
$HINFL_{it}$	0.292	0.37
	[0.64]	[0.50]
$HINFL_{it} \times FL_{i,t-1}$	−2.203	−3.471
	[1.65]*	[2.35]**
$FIRSTYEAR_{it}$	0.566	0.592
	[1.98]**	[1.86]*
$FIRSTYEAR_{it} \times FL_{i,t-1}$	−1.163	−1.055
	[1.84]*	[1.45]
IMF_{it}	0.775	0.65
	[2.94]***	[1.83]*
$IMF_{it} \times FL_{i,t-1}$	−1.523	−1.741
	[2.26]**	[1.94]*
$USINT_{it}$	−0.078	−0.091
	[1.93]*	[2.10]**
$LEFT_{it}$	−0.116	−0.616
	[0.29]	[1.16]
$LEFT_{it} \times FL_{i,t-1}$	1.049	1.282
	[1.01]	[1.09]
$RIGHT_{it}$	0.257	0.192
	[0.87]	[0.50]
$RIGHT \times FL_{i,t-1}$	0.087	−0.221
	[0.09]	[0.19]

continued

Financial Reforms for Financial Development   157

Table A5.4 Continued

Country dummy included	No	Yes
$OPEN_{it}$	3.719	3.475
	[2.16]**	[1.61]
$OPEN_{it} \times FL_{i,t-1}$	−3.827	−1.82
	[2.19]**	[0.70]
Observations	805	805
Number of countries	35	35

Notes: This table corresponds to the Table 9 in Abiad and Mody (2005), which treated Singapore as an African country and South Africa as an East Asian country, and consequently indicates that $(REG\_FL-FL) \times FL$ is significant but $OPEN$ and $OPEN \times FL$ are insignificant in column 1, and FL, $OPEN$ and $OPEN \times FL$ are significant in column 2. Robust t-statistics in brackets.

* significant at 10%; ** significant at 5%; *** significant at 1%.

Table A5.5 Augmented dataset with Chinn-Ito measure (2006): IMF dropped

A. Within estimates corresponding to Table 5.1B

Estimators	WG	WG	WG	CCEP	CCEP	CCEP
$FL_{i,t-1}$	−0.168	−0.170	−0.174	−0.204	−0.214	−0.261
	[0.044]***	[0.044]***	[0.045]***	[0.069]***	[0.068]***	[0.084]***
$(FL_{i,t-1})^2$	0.052	0.053	0.056	0.087	0.092	0.119
	[0.037]	[0.037]	[0.038]	[0.049]*	[0.049]*	[0.059]**
$REG\_FL_{i,t-1}$	−0.016	−0.018	0.002	0.048	0.044	0.044
$-FL_{i,t-1}$	[0.027]	[0.027]	[0.028]	[0.036]	[0.037]	[0.036]
BOP_{it}	0.002	0.001	−0.005	−0.006		
	[0.007]	[0.007]	[0.007]	[0.008]		
$BANK_{it}$	−0.010	−0.010	−0.008	−0.009		
	[0.009]	[0.009]	[0.010]	[0.011]		
$RECESSION_{it}$	−0.001	0.000	0.001	0.001		
	[0.007]	[0.007]	[0.008]	[0.009]		
$HINFL_{it}$	−0.018	−0.017	−0.009	−0.009		
	[0.012]	[0.013]	[0.017]	[0.017]		
$FIRSTYEAR_{it}$	0.000	0.001	[0.007]	[0.006]		
$USINT_{it}$	−0.005	−0.002				
	[0.001]***	[0.002]				
$LEFT_{it}$	−0.004	−0.008				
	[0.010]	[0.009]				
$RIGHT_{it}$	0.000	0.000				
	[0.010]	[0.011]				

continued

Table A5.5 Continued

Estimators	WG	WG	WG	CCEP	CCEP	CCEP
$OPEN_{it}$	0.000	0.000				
	[0.000]*	[0.000]				
$POLITY2_{it}$	−0.002	0.012				
	[0.016]	[0.022]				
Observations	1263	1262	1213	1263	1262	1213
Number of countries	55	55	53	55	55	53
R-squared	0.04	0.04	0.07	0.22	0.22	0.25

Note: See Table 5.5A for notes.

B. Within estimates corresponding to Table 5.2

Estimators	WG	WG	CCEP	CCEP
$FL_{i,t-1}$	−0.174	−0.169	−0.261	−0.343
	[0.045]***	[0.045]***	[0.084]***	[0.118]***
$(FL_{i,t-1})^2$	0.056	0.006	0.119	0.079
	[0.038]	[0.044]	[0.059]**	[0.081]
$FL_{i,t-1} \times Y_{i,t-1}$		0.004	0.004	
		[0.002]**	[0.004]	
$REG\_FL_{i,t-1} - FL_{i,t-1}$	0.002	0.007	0.044	0.012
	[0.028]	[0.028]	[0.036]	[0.048]
BOP_{it}	0.001	0.001	−0.006	−0.011
	[0.007]	[0.007]	[0.008]	[0.009]
$BANK_{it}$	−0.010	−0.010	−0.009	0.000
	[0.009]	[0.009]	[0.011]	[0.013]
$RECESSION_{it}$	0.000	0.001	0.001	0.002
	[0.007]	[0.007]	[0.009]	[0.009]
$HINFL_{it}$	−0.017	−0.020	−0.009	0.000
	[0.013]	[0.013]	[0.017]	[0.016]
$FIRSTYEAR_{it}$	0.000	0.000	0.001	0.000
	[0.007]	[0.007]	[0.006]	[0.006]
$USINT_{it}$	−0.005	−0.004	−0.002	−0.001
	[0.001]***	[0.001]***	[0.002]	[0.002]
$LEFT_{it}$	−0.004	−0.006	−0.008	−0.012
	[0.010]	[0.010]	[0.009]	[0.010]
$RIGHT_{it}$	0.000	−0.001	0.000	−0.004
	[0.010]	[0.010]	[0.011]	[0.015]
$OPEN_{it}$	0.000	0.000	0.000	0.000
	[0.000]*	[0.000]*	[0.000]	[0.000]

continued

Table A5.5 Continued

Estimators	WG	WG	CCEP	CCEP
$POLITY2_{it}$	−0.002 [0.016]	−0.002 [0.016]	0.012 [0.022]	0.019 [0.028]
Observations	1213	1213	1213	1213
Number of countries	53	53	53	53
R-squared	0.07	0.07	0.25	0.31

Note: See Table 5.5A for notes.

Table A5.5 Continued

C. Within estimates corresponding to Table 5.3

Estimators	WG	CCEP
$FL_{i,t-1}$	−0.303 [0.089]***	−0.599 [0.232]**
$(FL_{i,t-1})^2$	0.190 [0.081]**	0.355 [0.208]*
$REG\_FL_{i,t-1} - FL_{i,t-1}$	−0.024 [0.029]	−0.040 [0.053]
$(REG - FL_{i,t-1} - FL_{i,t-1}) \times FL_{i,t-1}$	0.216 [0.096]**	0.360 [0.224]
BOP_{it}	−0.010 [0.011]	−0.010 [0.015]
$BOP_{it} \times FL_{i,t-1}$	0.027 [0.020]	0.000 [0.025]
$BANK_{it}$	−0.008 [0.014]	0.002 [0.023]
$BANK_{it} \times FL_{i,t-1}$	−0.003 [0.025]	−0.009 [0.035]
$RECESSION_{it}$	0.006 [0.010]	0.009 [0.011]
$RECESSION_{it} \times FL_{i,t-1}$	−0.017 [0.020]	−0.023 [0.022]
$HINFL_{it}$	0.027 [0.017]	0.022 [0.031]
$HINFL_{it} \times FL_{i,t-1}$	−0.201 [0.049]***	−0.103 [0.143]
$FIRSTYEAR_{it}$	−0.005 [0.011]	−0.005 [0.009]
$FIRSTYEAR_{it} \times FL_{i,t-1}$	0.010 [0.020]	0.010 [0.018]

continued

Table A5.5 Continued

Estimators	WG	CCEP
$USINT_{it}$	−0.005	−0.002
	[0.001]***	[0.002]
$LEFT_{it} \times FL_{i,t-1}$	−0.017	−0.034
	[0.015]	[0.025]
$LEFT_{it} \times FL_{i,t-1}$	0.022	0.048
	[0.030]	[0.049]
$RIGHT_{it}$	0.009	−0.004
	[0.014]	[0.025]
$RIGHT_{it} \times FL_{i,t-1}$	−0.019	0.006
	[0.030]	[0.043]
$OPEN_{it}$	0.001	0.000
	[0.000]**	[0.000]
$OPEN_{it} \times FL_{i,t-1}$	0.000	0.000
	[0.000]	[0.000]
$POLITY2_{it}$	−0.002	0.020
	[0.019]	[0.033]
$POLITY2_{it} \times FL_{i,t-1}$	0.002	0.002
	[0.002]	[0.005]
Observations	1213	1213
Number of countries	53	53
R-squared	0.09	0.33

Note: See Table 5.5A for notes.

6
Geographic Determinants of Carbon Markets (CDM)

6.1 Introduction

Global warming has emerged as one of the most critical issues of our age, and a key issue in the global economic and environmental debates. In recent years, the global carbon market has become a newly developed area for research and practice. It essentially consists of allowance-based markets and project-based markets which use market-based mechanisms to allocate and trade carbon credits that represent CO_2 emission reductions in order for the participants to meet their compliance requirements at the lowest possible cost. In allowance-based markets, the buyers purchase emission allowances created and allocated (or auctioned) by regulators under cap-and-trade regimes like Assigned Amount Units (AAUs) under the Kyoto Protocol, or EU Allowances (EUAs) under the EU Emissions Trading Scheme (EU ETS). Within project-based markets, the buyers purchase emission credits from investing into a project that can demonstrate a reduction of CO_2 emissions in comparison to the level of emissions in the absence of the project investment. The most notable examples of such activities are the Clean Development Mechanism (CDM) and the Joint Implementation (JI) schemes under the Kyoto Protocol.

As part of the emerging global carbon market, CDM is the only Kyoto mechanism which involves developing countries in the climate change negotiations. Under the Kyoto Protocol, the CDM is designed to realize the benefits in terms of capital flow, technological transfer, sustainable development and cost-effective emission abatement. However, the geographic distribution of CDM projects by host country and region has been found to be highly uneven. This chapter addresses the issue of whether the geographic endowments in the host countries matter for

CDM development using recently developed spatial econometric techniques, with an aim of encouraging further research into economic, institutional and policy determinants of CDM development.

In response to climate change, the global community adopted the Kyoto Protocol in 1997. It came into force in February 2005 and calls for legally binding limits on the greenhouse gas (GHG) emissions by developed countries (or Annex I countries) by at least 5% in comparison to the 1990 levels over the first commitment period (i.e. 2008–12). Although each Annex I country is assigned an amount of CO_2 equivalents (expressed in Assigned Amount Units, AAUs) to be used over the period 2008–12, some Annex I countries still face a projected shortfall in GHG emission reductions. To meet their commitments, these countries usually seek emission reduction credits through the three "flexibility mechanisms" defined under the Kyoto Protocol: International Emission Trading (IET), Joint Implementation (JI) and the CDM.

The CDM is defined in Article 12 of the Kyoto Protocol, and is the only such mechanism that involves developing countries. By joining in the CDM, on the one hand, developing countries can get access to significant foreign capital flows and technology transfer to achieve more sustainable, less GHG-intensive pathways of development. On the other hand, the Annex I countries can purchase and utilize the emission reduction credits, called Certified Emission Reductions (CERs), generated from CDM projects towards meeting their quantified emission targets under the Protocol.

The geographic distribution of CDM projects by host country and region has been observed as being lopsided, in terms of both the number of projects and the volume of credits. More specifically, two regions, Asia and the Pacific, and Latin America, together dominate the distribution of CDM projects and CER flows, such that by the end of September 2008 China, India, Brazil and Mexico accounted for 45%, 23%, 5% and 1% of CDM projects, respectively.[99] Developing countries with large populations and economies are expected to account for a large number of CDM projects and CER flows. However, do countries with particular geographic characteristics like higher absolute latitudes, higher elevations and richer resource endowments have more CDM projects and CER flows?

Economists have long noted the crucial role of geography in economic development: transport costs, human health, agricultural productivity and ownership of natural resources. The climate theory of underdevelopment has been widely recognized in the sense that certain geographic endowments have an adverse impact on economic development. For example, some geographic endowments (like mineral resource endowments) may influence the inputs into the production function, while others (like tropical location) may make the production technologies much harder to employ and affect technological development in the very long term (Sachs, 2003; Sachs and Warner, 1995; Diamond, 1997; Gallup *et al.* 1999).

While there is considerable research examining the sustainable development impacts of CDM development, much less work has aimed to explore the fundamental determinants of CDM development across countries. This chapter evaluates whether cross-sectional differences in CDM development can be explained by cross-sectional differences in geographic characteristics and resource endowments, once controlling for other potential factors.

The cross-country experience of CDM project selection and foreign direct investment indicates the existence of neighbourhood effects or spillovers among countries.[100] The neighbourhood effects of CDM projects, together with "a new and deeper version of globalization" since 1970 (Crafts, 2000) which causes a closer interdependence across countries, suggest that spatial correlation is an important phenomenon to be considered in this application. By employing the spatial econometric method recently developed by Kelejian and Prucha (2010), this chapter conducts a cross-country study on 48 developing countries over the period from December 2003 up to September 2008.

This research has led to two significant findings. First, it provides evidence that positive spatial dependence among observations exists in this context. More specifically, the CDM credit flows in a country increase by about 0.34 to 0.48 units if those in its neighbouring countries increase by one unit; and countries with larger CDM credit flows tend to be geographically clustered with other large CDM host countries. Second, by allowing for spatial dependence and accounting for the size of the economy (initial population and initial GDP per capita), this research finds that absolute latitude and elevation have positive impacts on CDM credit flows, suggesting that countries further from the equator and having higher elevations tend to initiate more CDM projects and issue more CDM credit flows. Larger service exporting countries seem to have more advantages in getting access to CDM projects, while on the contrary, larger natural resource exporting countries have smaller CDM credit flows, indicating that natural resource abundance may not necessarily be attractive to CDM projects.

This finding sheds light on the geographic determinants of uneven CDM project development across countries. It has rich implications for developing countries in terms of international cooperation and national capacity building in order to access effectively the CDM for their national sustainable development objectives. This research also suggests that the geographic considerations should be introduced into the econometric and theoretical cross-country studies of climate change and mitigation.

The remainder of the chapter proceeds as follows. Section 6.2 describes the data and shows some stylized facts. The empirical results are presented in Section 6.4, following a description of econometric methods in section 6.3. Section 6.5 concludes.

6.2 Data and stylized facts

This section outlines the measures and data for CDM, key geographic variables and the control variables.

The dependent variable is the Clean Development Mechanism credit flows, simply denoted by *CDM*. The indicator for *CDM* is the average of the Certified Emission Reductions (2012 kCERs) generated by the CDM projects in the pipeline over the period from December 2003 to September 2008.[101] One country has one observation. To diminish the impacts of outliers and measurement errors, it is taken in logs. The CDM projects in the pipeline include not only those called "confirmed projects" which have been at the registration stage, having either registered or requested registration, but also those called "probable projects" which are at the validation stage, waiting to be registered and implemented over the next three years. One CER equals to one metric tonne of CO_2e.[102] Data on CER flows are from the UNEP Risoe Centre (2008).

To examine the impacts of particular geographic characteristics on CDM project development, three geographic variables – absolute latitude, elevation and land area – are considered. Absolute latitude (*LATITUDE*) equals the absolute distance from the equator of a country. The closer the countries are to the equator, the more tropical climate they have. Elevation (*ELEV*) is the mean elevation (metres above sea level) calculated in geographic projection, and used in logs. The land area (*AREA*) in square kilometres for each country is in logs. Data on latitude, elevation and land area are taken from the physical factors dataset of Center for International Development (CID) at Harvard University.[103]

To assess the role of natural resource endowments, this research uses two groups of variables. One group of variables consists of dummies for the manufactured goods exporting countries (*EXPMANU*), service exporting countries (*EXPSERV*) and non-fuel primary goods exporting countries (*EXPPRIM*) from the Global Development Network of the World Bank (GDN). The other group of variables, taken from Isham *et al.* (2005), includes dummies for the exporters of point source natural resources (e.g. oil, diamonds, plantation crops) (*RESPOINT*), "diffuse" natural resources (e.g. wheat, rice, animals) (*RESDIFF*) and coffee/cocoa natural resources (*RESCOFF*).

Control variables included in this analysis are the initial GDP per capita (*GDP03*), the initial population (*POP03*), an ethnic fractionalization index (*ETHNIC*), a religious fractionalization index (*RELIGION*) and legal origin dummies, *COMLEG* and *CIVLEG*.

The inclusion of the initial GDP per capita and population is to control for the size of the economy where *GDP03* is the real GDP per capita in 2003 in constant 2000 US$ (chain series), and *POP03* is the population in 2003. Both *GDP03* and *POP03* are used in logs and taken from the Penn World Table 6.2 in Heston *et al.* (2006). The variables *ETHNIC* and *RELIGION* characterize social divisions and cultural differences. The data on *ETHNIC* and *RELIGION* are taken from Alesina *et al.* (2003).[104] *COMLEG* is the Common Law legal origin dummy for countries with British legal origin, while *CIVLEG* is the Civil Law legal origin dummy for countries with French, German or Scandinavian legal origins. Data on *CIVLEG* and *COMLEG* are from the GDN.[105]

The sample includes 48 CDM host countries from Asia and the Pacific, Latin America and the Caribbean, the Middle East and North Africa, Sub-Saharan Africa and Europe and Central Asia as listed in the Appendix Table A6.1. Countries with fewer than three monthly non-zero observations (up to September 2008) in terms of credit flows (2012 kCERs) have been removed.

Figure 6.1 presents the scatter plots between CDM credit flows and absolute latitude and elevation, respectively. Despite the existence of outliers such as China and Paraguay, the positive associations between absolute latitude and CDM credit flows, and between elevation and CDM credit flows, can be observed. Countries with higher absolute latitudes and higher elevations are more likely to have more CDM projects as well as CER credit flows.

Figure 6.2 demonstrates, in the upper chart, that CDM credit flows in coffee exporters, diffuse exporters and point source exporters are in general smaller than those in the non-exporters of the relevant resources. The lower chart shows that manufactured goods exporters, service exporters and non-fuel primary goods exporters tend to have fewer CDM credit flows in comparison to their counterparts.

166 *Determinants of Financial Development*

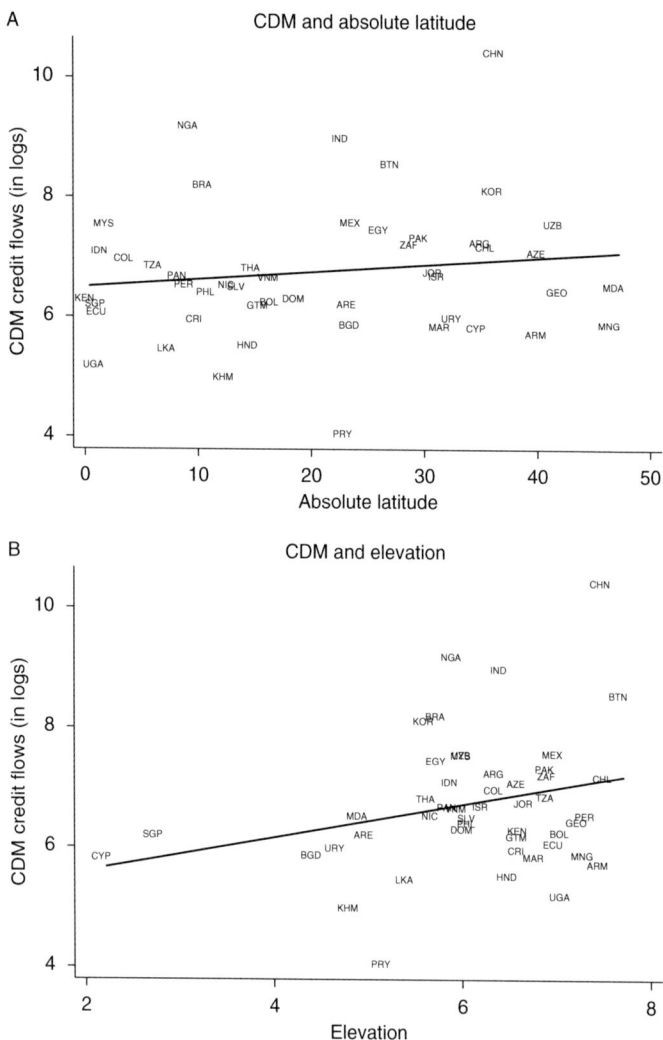

Figure 6.1 Scatter plots of CDM and geography
Note: Variables and data sources are described in the text. These figures show scatter plots of absolute latitude and elevation against CDM credit flows (CERs).

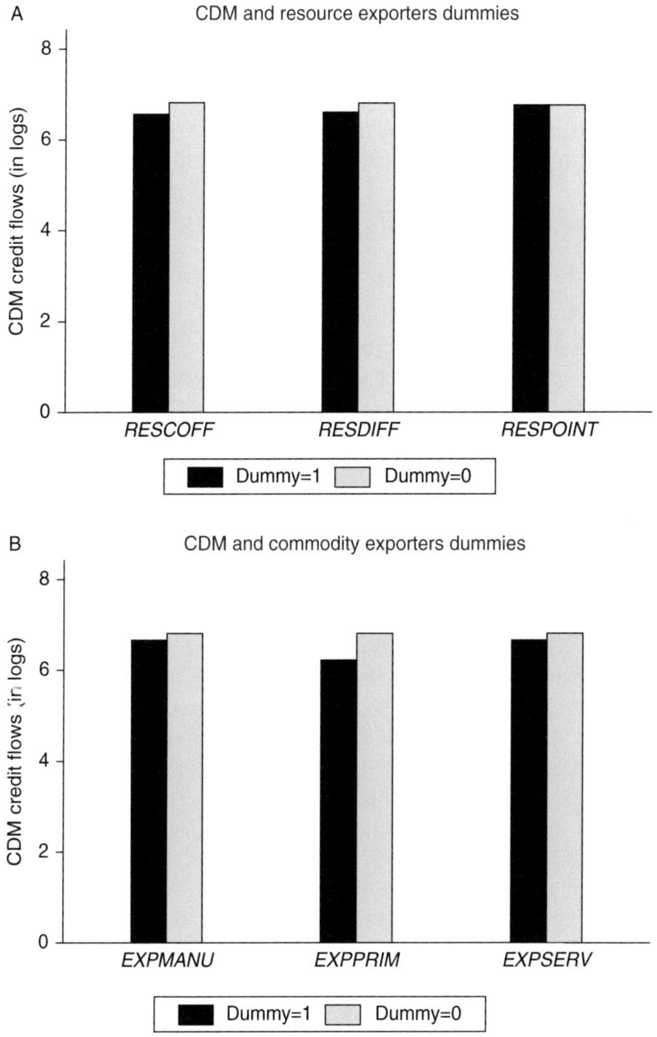

Figure 6.2 CDM and resource endowments

Note: Variables and data sources are described in the text. These figures show the comparisons of CDM credit flows (CERs) for different dummies of exporters.

6.3 Econometric method: Spatial econometric approach

To study the impacts of geography on CDM project development, this research conducts a cross-sectional study allowing for spatial correlation on 48 countries over the period from December 2003 to September 2008. It starts from an Ordinary Least Square (OLS) estimation on a basic model:

$$Y_n = X'_n \beta + \epsilon_n$$
$$n = 1, 2, \ldots 48 \qquad (6.1)$$

where Y_n is an $n \times 1$ (n is the number of cross section units) vector of observations on dependent variable *CDM*.

X_n is an $n \times k$ matrix of observations on k exogenous explanatory variables which consist of geographic variables (*LATITUDE, ELEV, AREA, EXPSERV, EXPPRIM, RESPOINT, RESDIFF* and *RESCOFF*) and the control variables including *GDP03, POP03, ETHNIC, RELIGION* and legal origin dummies (*CIVLEG, COMLEG*).

β is a $k \times 1$ parameter vector. The error term ϵ_n is an $n \times 1$ vector with $E(\epsilon) = 0$ and $E(\epsilon \epsilon') = \delta^2 I$.

The OLS specification typically follows the assumption of no spatial interdependence or spatial correlation. However, spatial dependence associated with social interactions or unobserved common shocks has been widely recognized. On the one hand, considerable research has been done to explore the implications of social or spatial interactions in terms of neighbourhood effects, spatial spillovers or networks effects (Manski, 2000; Brock and Durlauf, 2001). The fact that one agent's decision variable is affected by those of other agents is typically formulated as a spatial lagged dependent variable, or a spatial lag term to be included in the right-hand side of the regression model. In the context of financial liberalization and reform, Abiad and Mody (2005, henceforth AM) find that regional diffusion in terms of the liberalization gap from the regional leader is significantly associated with the policy change.

On the other hand, in a globalized world, common shocks – either observed global shocks like macroeconomic shocks or unobserved global shocks like technological shocks – are believed to cause closer interdependence across countries. Andrews (2005) analyses the impact of common shocks in the cross section regression in which the observations are i.i.d. across population units conditional on common shocks, providing a general framework for spatially correlated errors.[106] In examining the origins of financial openness, Quinn and Inclán (1997) argue that the common trend, such as changes in consumer tastes and technology, may substantially affect government liberalization policies as "fundamental but unobservable forces".

Obviously, the OLS estimation provides the foundation for spatial analysis. This research incorporates the spatial correlation structure into the basic linear model to account for both spatial lag dependence and spatial error dependence.

A spatial lag model is a formal specification of spatial lag dependence due to the presence of social and spatial interactions. Its basic form is the mixed regressive, spatial autoregressive model:[107]

$$Y_n = X'_n\beta + \lambda W_n Y_n + \epsilon_n, |\lambda|<1 \qquad (6.2)$$

where λ is the spatial autoregressive coefficient or spatial interdependence coefficient, measuring the dependence of Y_i on neighbouring Y_n. W_n is an $n \times n$ spatial weighting matrix of known constants, reflecting the neighbouring relationships with zero across diagonals and a row-standardized form. The added variable, $\lambda W_n Y_n$, an average of the neighbouring values, is referred to as a spatially lagged dependent variable, or a spatial lag of Y_n. The error term, ϵ_n, is an $n \times 1$ idiosyncratic error vector, assumed to be distributed independently across the cross-sectional dimension with zero mean and constant variances σ_ϵ^2.

When the spatial dependence exists in the error term due to unobserved effects of common shocks (for example, macroeconomic shocks, political shocks or environmental shocks), a spatial error model can be used as follows:[108]

$$Y_n = X'_n\beta + u_n$$
$$u_n = \rho M_n u_n + \epsilon_n, |\rho|<1 \qquad (6.3)$$

where ρ is the spatial autoregressive coefficient, measuring the amount of spatial correlation in the errors. M_n is the spatial weighting matrix, may or may not be the same as W_n. u_n is spatially correlated residuals and ϵ_n is the independent and identically distributed disturbances with zero mean and constant variances σ_ϵ^2. $M_n u_n$ is known as a spatial lag of u_n.

By plugging the error term of the spatial error model (6.3) into the spatial lag model (6.2), one can generate the spatial autoregressive model with autoregressive disturbances of order (1,1), that is the SARAR(1,1) model, as follows,

$$Y_n = X_n\beta + \lambda W_n Y_n + u_n, \quad |\lambda|<1$$
$$u_n = \rho M_n u_n + \epsilon_n, \quad |\rho|<1 \qquad (6.4)$$

The above model is believed to be very general in the sense that it allows for spatial spillovers stemming from endogenous variables, exogenous variables and disturbances. It can be rewritten as:

$$Y_n = Z_n' \delta + u_n$$
$$u_n = \rho M_n u_n + \epsilon_n \tag{6.5}$$

where $Z_n' = [X_n, W_n Y_n]$, $\delta = [\beta', \lambda]'$

The corresponding transformed model can be obtained by pre-multiplying (6.5) by $I_n - \rho M_n$,

$$Y_{n*}(\rho) = Z_{n*}'(\rho) \delta + \epsilon_n \tag{6.6}$$

where $Y_{n*}(\rho) = Y_n - \rho M_n Y_n$ and $Z_{n*}(\rho) = Z_n - \rho M_n Z_n$.

To estimate a general spatial model like (6.4), a number of approaches have been proposed in the literature, for example, Kelejian and Prucha (1998, 1999), Kelejian et al. (2004), Lee (2003, 2007) and Lee and Liu (2006). However, these approaches in general assume that the innovations in the disturbance process are homoscedastic, which may not hold in many applications. To fill this gap, Kelejian and Prucha (2010) develop a Generalized Spatial Two-Step Least Square (GS2SLS) estimator with a three-stage procedure of inference for the SARAR(1,1) model that allows for unknown heteroscedasticity in the innovations. Arraiz et al. (2010) provide simulation evidence showing that, when the disturbances are heteroscedastic, the GS2SLS estimator produces consistent estimates while the ML estimator produces inconsistent estimates.

This chapter examines the impacts of geography on CDM development within a general SARAR(1,1) framework. To estimate the SARAR(1,1) model, it employs the three-stage procedure of Kelejian and Prucha (2010), which can be summarized in the following.

In the FIRST step, the model (6.5) is estimated by the Two-Stage Least Square (2SLS) estimator using the instrument H_n. The instrument H_n is the matrix of instruments which is formed as a subset of linearly independent columns of $(X_n, W_n X_n, W_n^2 X_n \ldots)$. The first step 2SLS estimator is as follows:

$$\tilde{\delta}_n = (\tilde{Z}_n' Z_n)^{-1} \tilde{Z}_n' Y_n \tag{6.7}$$

$$\tilde{u}_n = Y_n - Z_n \tilde{\delta}_n \tag{6.8}$$

where $\tilde{Z}_n = P_H Z_n = [X_n, \widehat{W_n Y_n}]$, $\widehat{W_n Y_n} = P_H W_n Y_n$ and $P_{H_n} = H_n (H_n' H_n)^{-1} H_n'$.

In the SECOND step, ρ_n and σ_ϵ^2 are estimated, where ρ_n is the spatial autoregressive parameter and σ_ϵ^2 is the variance of the innovation term ϵ_n. They are estimated by applying GMM to the model (6.5), based on the 2SLS residuals $\tilde{u}_n$ obtained from the First step. More specifically, this estimator is $\tilde{\rho}_n$, defined as

$$\tilde{\rho}_n = \underset{\rho \in [-a^\rho, a^\rho]}{\arg\min} \; [m(\rho, \tilde{\delta}_n)' \, \tilde{\Psi}_n^{-1} \, m(\rho, \tilde{\delta}_n)] \tag{6.9}$$

where $\tilde{\Psi}_n$ is an estimator of the variance-covariance matrix of the limiting distribution of the normalized sample moments $n^{\frac{1}{2}} m(\rho, \tilde{\delta}_n)$.

$$m(\rho, \tilde{\delta}_n) = g_n(\tilde{\delta}_n) - G_n(\tilde{\delta}_n) \rho \rho^2$$

$$g_n(\tilde{\delta}_n) = \frac{1}{n} \begin{bmatrix} \tilde{u}_n' \tilde{u}_n \\ \tilde{\bar{u}}_n' \tilde{\bar{u}}_n \\ \tilde{u}_n' \tilde{\bar{u}}_n \end{bmatrix}$$

$$G_n(\tilde{\delta}_n) = \frac{1}{n} \begin{bmatrix} 2\tilde{u}_n' \tilde{\bar{u}}_n & -\tilde{\bar{u}}_n' \tilde{\bar{u}}_n & n \\ 2\tilde{\bar{u}}_n' \tilde{\bar{\bar{u}}}_n & -\tilde{\bar{\bar{u}}}_n' \tilde{\bar{\bar{u}}}_n & Tr(M_n' M_n) \\ \tilde{u}_n' \tilde{\bar{\bar{u}}}_n + \tilde{\bar{u}}_n' \tilde{\bar{u}}_n & -\tilde{\bar{u}}_n' \tilde{\bar{\bar{u}}}_n & 0 \end{bmatrix}$$

$$\tilde{\bar{u}}_n = M_n \tilde{u}_n$$

$$\tilde{\bar{\bar{u}}}_n = M_n^2 \tilde{u}_n$$

In the THIRD step, δ in the transformed model (6.6) can be estimated by a generalized spatial 2SLS procedure (GS2SLS) after replacing ρ by $\tilde{\rho}_n$. The GS2SLS estimator of δ is defined as:

$$\hat{\delta}_n(\tilde{\rho}_n) = [\hat{Z}_{n*}(\tilde{\rho}_n)' Z_{n*}(\tilde{\rho}_n)]^{-1} [\hat{Z}_{n*}(\tilde{\rho}_n) Y_{n*}(\tilde{\rho}_n)] \tag{6.10}$$

where $Y_{n*}(\tilde{\rho}_n) = Y_n - \tilde{\rho}_n M_n Y_n$, $Z_{n*}(\tilde{\rho}_n) = Z_n - \tilde{\rho}_n M_n Z_n$, and $\hat{Z}_{n*}(\tilde{\rho}_n) = P_H Z_{n*}(\tilde{\rho}_n)$.

6.4 Empirical evidence

This section presents the empirical evidence for the impacts of various geographic variables on CDM credit flows. Before proceeding to detailed

172 Determinants of Financial Development

econometric analysis, we briefly test for spatial dependence of CDM credit flows across countries with evidence presented in Figure 6.3 and Table 6.1.

Figure 6.3 plots the averaged CDM credit flows of all sample countries against the distance to the country with the largest CDM credit flows in

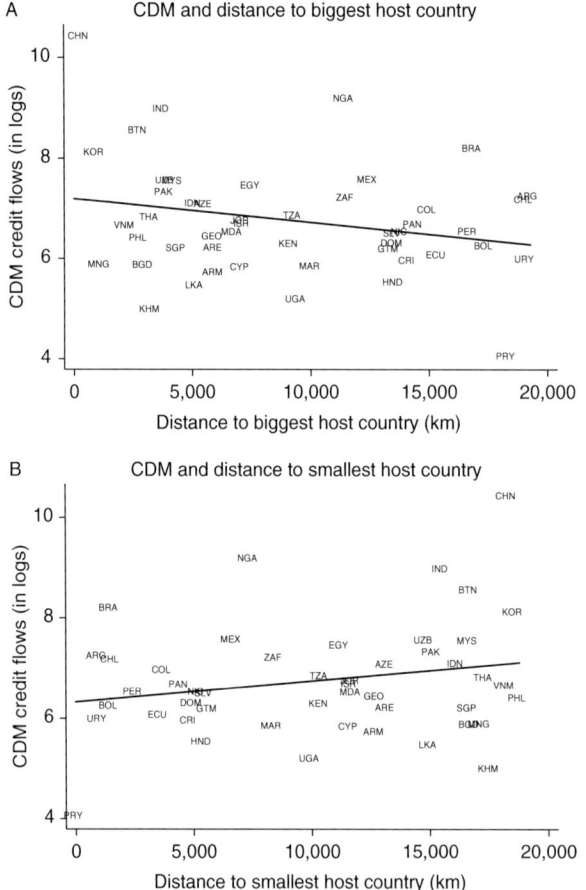

Figure 6.3 CDM and distance to biggest and smallest host countries

Note: Variables and data sources are described in the text. These figures show scatter plots of the distances to the biggest CDM host country (China) and to the smallest host country (Paraguay) against CDM credit flows (CERs).

Geographic Determinants of Carbon Markets (CDM) 173

the upper chart, and the distance to the country with the smallest CDM credit flows in the lower chart. Data on the great circle distances are from Gleditsch *et al.* (2001). This figure clearly shows that countries closer to the biggest CDM host country, which is China, tend to have more CDM credit flows, whereas countries closer to the smallest CDM host country, which is Paraguay, tend to have fewer CDM credit flows.[109] Countries with more (fewer) CDM credit flows appear to be geographically clustered with other larger (smaller) CDM host countries.

By using two different spatial weighting matrices, an inverse-distance spatial weighting matrix and a binary spatial weighting matrix, two standard test statistics of spatial autocorrelation have been calculated (Table 6.1). The inverse-distance spatial weighting matrix gives the inverse of the distance to each sample point within a 4000 km neighbourhood, and zero otherwise, while the binary spatial weighting matrix gives a weight of 1 to all sample points within a 4000 km neighbourhood, and zero otherwise.[110] Both matrices are row-standardized of one. Following Kelejian and Prucha (1999), the spatial weighting matrices have been "idealized" so that each unit has the same number of neighbours with "one neighbour ahead and one neighbour behind" in a wraparound world.

Table 6.1 contrasts Moran's I and Gearcy's C statistics for CDM credit flows. Both Moran's I and Gearcy's C statistics examine the null hypothesis of no spatial dependence. No matter which matrix is chosen, the two Moran's I statistics are greater than the expected value (-0.021) and the two Gearcy's C statistics are smaller than the expected value (1.000), suggesting positive spatial dependence of CDM credit flows

Table 6.1 Moran's I and Geary's C for CDM

	Moran's I	E(I)	SD(I)	z-statistic	p-value
Inverse-distance Weights	0.086	−0.021	0.084	1.250	[0.102]
Binary Weights	0.094	−0.021	0.067	1.714	[0.043]**
	Gearcy's C	E(C)	SD(C)	z-statistic	p-value
Inverse-distance Weights	0.902	1.000	0.092	−1.064	[0.144]
Binary Weights	0.870	1.000	0.074	−1.748	[0.040]**

Notes: This table reports Moran's I and Gearcy's C tests for spatial autocorrelation for the averaged CDM credit flows in logs for 48 CDM host countries listed in the Appendix Table A6.1. The test statistics are calculated using an inverse-distance weighting matrix and a binary weighting matrix, respectively, as described in the text.
* significant at 10%; ** significant at 5%; *** significant at 1%.

across countries.[111] Moreover, both Moran's I and Gearcy's C statistics reject the null at about 10% significance level with an inverse-distance spatial weighting matrix, and at 5% significance level with a binary spatial weighting matrix. This shows that the positive spatial dependence of the CDM credit flows is significant across countries.

Tables 6.2 and 6.3 investigate whether countries with particular geographic endowments are more likely to attract CDM projects, for which eight geographic endowment variables, as explained earlier, are selected from various sources.[112]

Column 1 of Table 6.2 reports the OLS estimates for the non-spatial model (6.1). Firstly, an OLS heteroscedasticity test following White (1980) and Koenker (1981) is conducted to examine whether there is heteroscedasticity in the estimation regression which is related to any of the geographic variables we examine.[113] The White/Koenker test rejects the null at 10% significance level, indicating that heteroscedasticity exists in the estimations and should be taken into account for this context.

To test for which type(s) of spatial dependence, spatial lag dependence or spatial error dependence or both, exist(s) in this context, we carry out two simple Lagrange Multiplier tests (LM) separately. The hypothesis of no spatially lagged dependent variable is rejected at about 10% significance level while the hypothesis of no spatially autocorrelated error term can not be rejected. Furthermore, the p-values for the robust LM tests following Anselin et al. (1996) and the log-likelihood statistics are reported to test for whether a spatial lag model is more appropriate than a spatial error model for this context. The evidence that the robust LM test doesn't reject the null hypothesis of no spatially autocorrelated error term, but does reject the null of no spatially lagged dependent variable (at about 10% significance level), together with the evidence that the log-likelihood statistic for the spatial lag model (-41.03) is bigger than that for the spatial error model (-41.61), suggest that a spatial lag model is preferred to a spatial error model.

Columns 2 to 4 report the ML estimates for the spatial lag model (6.2) and spatial error model (6.3), and the GS2SLS estimates following Kelejian and Prucha (2010) for the SARAR(1,1) model (6.4). An inverse-distance spatial weighting matrix has been used to calculate the ML estimates and GS2SLS estimates.[114]

The spatial autocorrelation parameter, "ρ" appears to be insignificant in both the spatial error model and the SARAR(1,1) model. For the spatial autoregressive parameter, "λ", ρ has been found weakly significant in the spatial lag model and significant in the SARAR(1,1) model, with larger coefficient in the SARAR(1,1) model. The GS2SLS estimate of "λ" in the

Geographic Determinants of Carbon Markets (CDM) 175

Table 6.2 Geography and CDM (by inverse-distance weights)

	Non-spatial model	Spatial Lag model	Spatial Error model	SARAR(1,1)
λ		0.185		0.339
		[0.135]		[0.033]**
ρ			0.315	−0.300
			[0.226]	[0.239]
LATITUDE	0.016	0.017	0.016	0.018
	[0.090]*	[0.088]*	[0.111]	[0.140]
ELEVATION	0.276	0.270	0.255	0.274
	[0.048]**	[0.008]***	[0.012]**	[0.031]**
AREA	0.155	0.135	0.125	0.118
	[0.150]	[0.173]	[0.219]	[0.331]
EXPSERV	0.965	0.888	0.851	0.860
	[0.004]***	[0.002]***	[0.004]***	[0.020]**
EXPPRIM	−0.287	−0.320	−0.337	−0.307
	[0.368]	[0.211]	[0.184]	[0.333]
RESPOINT	−1.587	−1.642	−1.565	−1.678
	[0.013]**	[0.000]***	[0.000]***	[0.002]***
RESDIFF	−1.059	−1.098	−0.998	−1.147
	[0.013]**	[0.002]***	[0.005]***	[0.010]***
RESCOFF	−1.368	−1.484	−1.435	−1.525
	[0.022]**	[0.001]***	[0.001]***	[0.011]**
GDP03	0.258	0.236	0.279	0.185
	[0.259]	[0.090]*	[0.056]*	[0.264]
POP03	0.360	0.366	0.367	0.360
	[0.004]***	[0.001]***	[0.001]***	[0.007]***
ETHNIC	1.336	1.467	1.367	1.606
	[0.050]*	[0.015]**	[0.031]**	[0.027]**
REGLIGION	2.077	2.067	2.061	2.001
	[0.013]**	[0.000]***	[0.000]***	[0.001]***
COMLEG	0.557	0.541	0.520	0.552
	[0.261]	[0.117]	[0.135]	[0.190]
CIVLEG	1.278	1.354	1.393	1.331
	[0.046]**	[0.004]***	[0.003]***	[0.022]**
Constant	−4.312	−5.175	−4.064	−5.571
	[0.074]*	[0.003]***	[0.018]**	[0.006]***
Observations	48	48	48	48
R-squared	0.73	0.74	0.72	
Log Likelihood		−41.03	−41.61	
White/Koenker test	[0.105]			
Spatial lag:				
LM	[0.107]			
Robust LM	[0.107]			
Spatial error:				
LM	[0.572]			
Robust LM	[0.570]			

Notes: Dependent variable is the averaged CDM credit flows (2012 kCERs) in logs. Robust p-values are reported in brackets. Variables and data sources are described in text. λ is the spatial autoregressive parameter in dependent variable in the spatial lag model and SARAR (1,1) model, whilst ρ is the spatial autoregressive parameter in the disturbance in spatial error model and SARAR(1,1) model. The White/Koenker test is to examine the null of no heteroscedasticity. The spatial weighting matrix used here is a row-standardized inverse-distance weighting matrix described in the text. Robust p-values are reported in brackets.

* significant at 10%; ** significant at 5%; *** significant at 1%.

SARAR(1,1) model shows that the CDM credit flows in a country increase by 0.34 units if those in its neighbouring countries increase by one unit.

The explanatory variables described in Section 6.2, except for *EXPMANU*, have been found to be closely related to CDM credit flows with the expected signs. In particular, the GS2SLS estimates show that the the geographic variables *LATITUDE* and *ELEV* are positively associated with CDM development. For the resource and commodity exporter dummies, *EXPSERV* is positively related, while *RESPOINT*, *RESDIFF* and *RESCOFF* are negatively related, to CDM development. All of the control variables including *GDP03*, *POP03*, *ETHNIC*, *RELIGION* and legal origin dummies (*CIVLEG*, *COMLEG*) are in general found significantly associated with CDM development and should be included in the model.[115]

With a row-standardized binary weighting matrix, Table 6.3 in general confirms the findings of Table 6.2 in terms of positive impacts of *LATITUDE*, *ELEV* and *EXPSERV*, and negative impacts of *RESPOINT*, *RESDIFF* and *RESCOFF* on CDM credit flows. Table 6.3 seems to provide stronger evidence than Table 6.2, especially for the spatial autoregressive coefficients, "λ" and "ρ". According to the SARAR(1,1) model, the degree of neighbourhood effects for the CDM credit flows increases to 0.48.

The finding on the positive association between absolute latitude and CDM credit flows is consistent with the literature. On the one hand, research by Diamond (1997), Gallup *et al.* (1999) and Sachs (2003a) suggests that countries in a tropical location in terms of a smaller absolute latitude are often associated with poor crop yields and production due to adverse ecological conditions such as fragile tropical soils, unstable water supply and prevalence of crop pests. On the other hand, tropical location can be characterized as an inhospitable disease environment, believed to be a primary cause for "extractive" institutions, in conjunction with weaker institutions according to the settler mortality hypothesis of Acemoglu *et al.* (2001). Countries further from the Equator are more likely to have better climate conditions and stronger institutions, which are conducive to CDM project development.

The finding on the positive association between elevation and CDM credit flows is in line with recent research. It is widely known that the Earth's average surface temperature rose by approximately 0.6°C in the twentieth century and will rise a few degrees C in this century. Global warming is likely to raise the sea level and change the land area and elevation above sea level for many countries. Countries with higher elevations are therefore supposed to have more potential to attract CDM projects.

Table 6.3 Geography and CDM (by binary weights)

	Non-spatial model	Spatial Lag model	Spatial Error model	SARAR(1,1)
λ		0.288		0.476
		[0.068]*		[0.023]**
ρ			0.495	−0.299
			[0.041]**	[0.205]
LATITUDE	0.016	0.018	0.016	0.020
	[0.090]*	[0.065]*	[0.094]*	[0.108]
ELEVATION	0.276	0.255	0.232	0.256
	[0.048]**	[0.011]**	[0.018]**	[0.047]**
AREA	0.155	0.115	0.118	0.087
	[0.150]	[0.244]	[0.232]	[0.479]
EXPSERV	0.965	0.831	0.779	0.796
	[0.004]***	[0.004]***	[0.006]***	[0.034]**
EXPPRIM	−0.287	−0.334	−0.401	−0.319
	[0.368]	[0.187]	[0.118]	[0.306]
RESPOINT	−1.587	−1.671	−1.574	−1.717
	[0.013]**	[0.000]***	[0.000]***	[0.002]***
RESDIFF	−1.059	−1.127	−1.023	−1.182
	[0.013]**	[0.001]***	[0.003]***	[0.008]***
RESCOFF	−1.368	−1.515	−1.529	−1.546
	[0.022]**	[0.001]***	[0.001]***	[0.009]***
GDP03	0.258	0.220	0.267	0.162
	[0.259]	[0.111]	[0.063]*	[0.325]
POP03	0.360	0.382	0.358	0.392
	[0.004]***	[0.000]***	[0.001]***	[0.004]***
ETHNIC	1.336	1.581	1.395	1.765
	[0.050]*	[0.009]***	[0.027]**	[0.018]**
REGLIGION	2.077	1.940	2.011	1.834
	[0.013]**	[0.000]***	[0.000]***	[0.006]***
COMLEG	0.557	0.559	0.482	0.602
	[0.261]	[0.101]	[0.150]	[0.155]
CIVLEG	1.278	1.407	1.408	1.457
	[0.046]**	[0.002]***	[0.002]***	[0.014]**
Constant	−4.312	−5.591	−3.544	−6.221
	[0.074]*	[0.001]***	[0.042]**	[0.003]***
Observations	48	48	48	48
R-squared	0.73	0.75	0.71	
Log Likelihood		−40.56	−40.99	
White/Koenker test	[0.105]			
Spatial lag:				
LM	[0.055]*			
Robust LM	[0.070]*			
Spatial error:				
LM	[0.385]			
Robust LM	[0.563]			

Notes: The spatial weighting matrix used for the spatial lag model, spatial error model and SARAR(1,1) model in this table is a row-standardized binary weighting matrix described in the text. See Table 6.2 for more notes.

Some growth literature indicates that natural resource abundance is connected with social and economic instability and weak institutional quality, which hamper CDM project development. Isham *et al.* (2005) find that, in comparison to manufacturing exporters, the exporting countries of "point source" natural resources (e.g. oil, diamonds, plantation crops) and coffee/cocoa natural resources are more likely to have severe social and economic divisions, and less likely to develop socially cohesive mechanisms and effective institutional capacities for managing shocks.

In sum, this research produces the following significant findings. First, it provides evidence for the presence of positive spatial dependence amongst observations for this context, especially the spatial lag dependence associated with neighbourhood effects and social interactions. CDM credit flows in a country are significantly affected by those of its neighbouring countries, more specifically, the CDM credit flows in a country increase by about 0.34 to 0.48 units if those in its neighbouring countries increase by one unit. Second, by allowing for spatial dependence and accounting for the size of the economy (initial population and initial GDP per capita), this research finds that the absolute latitude and elevation have positive impacts on CDM credit flows, suggesting that countries further from the Equator and having a higher elevation tend to initiate more CDM projects and issue more CDM credit flows. Countries with more exports of services seem to have more advantages in attracting CDM projects, whilst in contrast countries with more exports of natural resources have smaller CDM credit flows, indicating that natural resource abundance may not necessarily be conducive to CDM development.

6.5 Concluding remarks

Under the Kyoto Protocol, the Clean Development Mechanism (CDM) is designed to provide the non-Annex I countries (developing countries and transition economies) with access to the flows of technology and capital which could contribute to their sustainable development objectives, whilst allowing Annex I countries to earn credits to meet their Kyoto commitments by investing in GHG emission reduction projects in non-Annex I countries.

This chapter investigates whether the cross-sectional differences in geographic endowments can explain the cross-sectional differences in CDM credit flows. It conducts a cross-country study allowing for both spatial error dependence and spatial lag dependence for 48 CDM host countries over December 2003–September 2008.

This research leads to two significant findings. First, it provides evidence for a positive relationship between CDM credit flows in a country and those in its neighbours, more specifically, the CDM credit flows in a country increase by about 0.34 to 0.48 units if those in its neighbours increase by one unit. Countries with larger (smaller) CDM credit flows have been found to be geographically clustered with other larger (smaller) CDM host countries. Second, by allowing for spatial dependence and accounting for the size of the economy (initial population and initial GDP per capita), this research finds that absolute latitude and elevation have positive impacts on CDM credit flows, suggesting that countries further from the equator and having higher elevations are in better positions to attract CDM projects. Countries with more exports of service are more associated with larger CDM credit flows, whilst in contrast countries with more exports of natural resources have fewer CDM credit flows, indicating that natural resource abundance doesn't necessarily play a large role in promoting CDM development. These findings are robust to the choices of different spatial weighting matrices – an inverse-distance spatial weighting matrix and a binary spatial weighting matrix. The research also controls for an ethnic fractionalization index, a religious fractionalization index and legal origin dummies.

This finding sheds light on the geographic determinants of uneven CDM project development across countries, and has rich implications for developing countries in terms of international cooperation and national capacity building to access effectively CDM for their national sustainable development objective. This research may contribute to our understanding of the cross-country differences in CDM development and contain some merits for the UNFCCC in terms of improving the geographic distribution of CDM project activities and capacity building. This research also suggests that geographic considerations should be introduced into the econometric and theoretical cross-country studies of climate change and mitigation.

Appendix table

Table A6.1 The list of countries in the full sample

Code	Country name	Code	Country name
ARE	United Arab Emirates	KHM	Cambodia
ARG	Argentina	KOR	Korea, Rep.
ARM	Armenia	LKA	Sri Lanka
AZE	Azerbaijan	MAR	Morocco
BGD	Bangladesh	MDA	Moldova, Rep.
BOL	Bolivia	MEX	Mexico
BRA	Brazil	MNG	Mongolia
BTN	Bhutan	MYS	Malaysia
CHL	Chile	NGA	Nigeria
CHN	China	NIC	Nicaragua
COL	Colombia	PAK	Pakistan
CRI	Costa Rica	PAN	Panama
CYP	Cyprus	PER	Peru
DOM	Dominican Rep.	PHL	Philippines
ECU	Ecuador	PRY	Paraguay
EGY	Egypt, Arab Rep.	SGP	Singapore
GEO	Georgia	SLV	El Salvador
GTM	Guatemala	THA	Thailand
HND	Honduras	TZA	Tanzania
IDN	Indonesia	UGA	Uganda
IND	India	URY	Uruguay
ISR	Israel	UZB	Uzbekistan
JOR	Jordan	VNM	Vietnam
KEN	Kenya	ZAF	South Africa

Note: This table lists the country codes and country names for 48 CDM host countries considered in this analysis. Data are from the UNEP Risoe Centre CDM/JI Pipeline Analysis and Database (2008).

Conclusion

This research studied the fundamental issues related to financial market development and carbon market development in the context of globalization, using recently developed econometric and statistical methods. Chapter 1 contained an overall review of the literature on the development of financial markets. Chapters 2 to 5 examined specific issues related to financial development whilst Chapter 6 was about the geographic determinants of CDM development, which is an important part of carbon markets, especially for developing countries.

Chapter 2 sought to investigate the political, economic and geographic determinants of the development of financial markets. By jointly applying two prominent tools for addressing model uncertainty, BMA and Gets approaches, it suggested that initial GDP, initial population, legal origin and institutional quality are fundamental determinants of the cross-country differences in financial development.

Chapters 3 and 4, respectively specifically focused on the economic and political determinants of financial development in the context of globalization. By using GMM estimation on averaged data and a common factor approach on annual data, Chapter 3 indicated a positive causal effect going from aggregate private investment to financial development, and vice versa. From a political viewpoint, Chapter 4 revealed a positive effect of institutional improvement on financial development at least in the short run, and an increase in financial development after democratic transformation.

Chapter 5 analysed what induces governments to undertake financial reforms, and what causes financial development. Starting from AM and allowing for error dependence across countries and over time, Chapter 5 found that some of the AM findings are robust, but others are fragile. It also identified a negative effect of the extent of democracy on policy reform. Together with Chapter 4, it seems to indicate that a short-run increase in financial development emerges after democratization, but that once democracy has been established and enhanced, its extent may exert negative effects on the likelihood of financial reform.

The last chapter found that countries with larger (smaller) CDM credit flows tend to be geographically clustered with other larger (smaller) CDM host countries and countries with higher absolute latitude, higher elevations and more exports of services tend to have more CDM credit flows than others.

This research to some extent contributes to our understanding of the causes of financial development, and adds to the growing research in this area. However, what I have done so far merely represents a start being made in this direction, much remains to be done. A number of areas for further research are summarized below:

1. While it is suggested that the level of financial development in a country is determined by its institutional quality, macroeconomic policies and geographic characteristics, as well as the level of income and cultural characteristics, further research into the more fundamental factors behind these characteristics is obviously worthwhile. To this end, other approaches may be considered, for example, recursive methods or dynamic programming applied to the theoretical models.

2. This research suggests that economic reforms with more open trade policies and attractive investment policies, and political reforms aimed at a more democratic society, should be conducive to financial development. Other research suggests that legal and regulatory reforms boost financial development. However, how to undertake these reforms, and in what sequence, has not yet been fully understood.

3. Although this research takes into account in Chapters 3 and 4, the effects of globalization on financial development, much work is still needed to explore the link between domestic and international financial markets, the impact of financial market integration on the development of domestic financial markets and the role of foreign financial institutions in domestic financial development.

4. As time goes, with more data available on the number of CDM projects and/or the volume of CDM credit flows, time series studies or panel data studies can be carried out to find whether or not a more open trade policy is conducive to CDM development, whether or not institutional quality is important for CDM, whether or not financial development promotes CDM development, and so on.

Notes

1. See Levine (1997, 2005) for a review.
2. The 39 potential determinants considered for this analysis are grouped under four headings: institutions, policy, geography and others. See Section 2.2.3 for details.
3. The description of these measures relies heavily on Demirgüç-Kunt and Levine (1996, 1999).
4. Since data for the efficiency of the bond market are not available whilst data for the size of the bond market are mainly available for developed countries in the World Bank's Financial Structure and Economic Development Database (2008), to avoid resulting in smaller sample sizes in the principal component analysis, bond market development is not included here. A simple analysis of the determinants of bond market development (for a smaller sample) is presented in Appendix Table A2.8.
5. Measures of financial liberalization and financial openness are not used here due to the concern that the effects of other variables on financial development may work through them.
6. ccounting standards data in La Porta *et al.* (1998) forms another interesting variable, but this variable has to be excluded due to its limited country coverage.
7. To some extent, absolute latitude serves as an alternative indicator for the zero-one tropical dummy in the GDN.
8. The EBA proposed by Leamer (1983, 1985) regards a variable to be robust if its extreme bounds lie strictly to one side or the other side of zero, where the extreme bounds for the coefficients of a particular variable are defined as "the lowest estimate of its value minus two times its standard error and the highest estimate of its value plus two times its standard error, respectively". The interval formed by two extreme bounds constitutes the maximum scope by which a variable may vary in the presence or absence of others, and indicates the confidence one may have in the coefficient estimates.
9. A computer program for the Bayesian approach to model uncertainty has been developed by Raftery *et al.* (1997).
10. A computer algorithm designed for implementing the general-to-specific approach, called PcGets, has been developed by Krolzig and Hendry (2001), following earlier work by Hoover and Perez (1999).
11. As argued by Granger and Hendry (2005) and echoed by Hansen (2005), none of the model selection methods currently available is immune from four possible conceptual errors of model selection methods: parametric vision, the assumption of a true data generating process, evaluation based on fit and ignoring of the impact of model uncertainty on inference.
12. Sala-i-Martin (1997a, 1997b) criticizes the standard of robustness employed by Levine and Renelt (1992) as too restrictive, and suggests a different version of extreme bounds analysis by saying that a variable is robust as long as 95% or more of the distribution of estimates lies to one side of zero. By this

methodology, relatively more variables are found to be robustly related to growth. However, the methodology of Sala-i-Martin (1997a, 1997b) is not Bayesian, although it uses weights proportional to the likelihoods of each model.

13. Fernandez et al. (2001) re-examine the Sala-i-Martin (1997a, 1997b) dataset using a full BMA explained below and Markov Chain Monte Carlo techniques to deal with the huge range of possible models. The full BMA of Fernandez et al. (2001) requires full specification of the prior distribution for every parameter conditional on each possible model and calculates the average of the parameter estimates across all possible models by using corresponding posterior model probabilities as weights. Their research has produced findings in support of the conclusions of Sala-i-Martin (1997a, 1997b). However, fully specifying the prior distribution for all potential parameters is very difficult and "essentially arbitrary" (Sala-i-Martin et al. 2004) when the number of possible regressors is large.
14. The computational procedure for the Occam's Window technique is implemented using the bicreg software for *S*-Plus or *R* written by Adrian Raftery and revised by Chris Volinsky.
15. The Occam's Window approach can be divided into two types, corresponding to two approaches. One is the symmetric Occam's Window in which models "much less likely than the most likely model" are excluded, the other is the strict Occam's Window in which the models having "more likely submodels nested within them" are excluded from the subset left in the symmetric Occam's Window (Raftery, 1995).
16. The modification used to calculate the sign certainty index is developed by Malik and Temple (2009) based on the original bicreg code.
17. The summary below is heavily drawn from Hoover and Perez (1999), Krolzig and Hendry (2001), Hendry and Krolzig (2005) and Granger and Hendry (2005).
18. Since any variable removed at the pre-search stage is permanently eliminated, the F pre-search testing (top-down) at step 1 in the "liberal strategy" default setting has been increased from 0.75 to 1, so as not to risk omitting any potential factor which is not significant in the GUM.
19. The effect of institutions, policy and geography on financial development are also examined in isolation. The results are not reported here, but are available from the author.
20. MC^3 is essentially a shorthand for the Markov Chain Monte Carlo technique, which is applied in this table only as a robustness test.
21. The Chow tests are F tests and used to test parameter constancy. The Normality test, a Chi-squared statistic, is used to check the normality of the distribution of the residuals. The Heteroscedasticity test is for unconditional heteroscedasticity.
22. The variable *EURFRAC* is closely associated with legal origins as noted earlier.
23. Many experiments suggest that the results are sensitive to the inclusion of the variable *EXPMANU*.
24. It is the share of population who can speak one of the main European languages.
25. It is the proportion of the population near a coast a river navigable to the ocean.

26. The sketch in this section heavily relies on Raftery (1995), Sala-i-Martin et al. (2004) and Malik and Temple (2009).
27. A saturated model (M_S) in which each data point is fitted exactly can be also used as a baseline model.
28. Financial intermediaries emerge endogenously under certain conditions, as widely addressed by Diamond (1984) and Williamson (1986), to avoid the duplication of monitoring costs (to minimize the monitoring costs by pooling projects), to channel savings from households to firms for use in the production process and to pool risk.
29. Among others, Chapter 2 examines the long-run determinants of financial development by using BMA and Gets approaches. That chapter suggests that "the level of financial development in a country is determined by its institutional quality, macroeconomic policies, and geographic characteristics, as well as the level of income and cultural characteristics". Chapter 4 reveals that institutional improvement is typically followed by a higher level of financial development at least in the short run, while Chapter 5 suggests that, once democracy has been established and enhanced, the extent of democracy may exert negative effects on the extent to which governments undertake reform aimed at financial development.
30. Among others, Doms and Dunne (1993) show that microeconomic lumpiness is very important for aggregate investment. Bertola and Caballero (1994) argue that microeconomic irreversibilities play an important role in smoothing investment dynamics in the presence of idiosyncratic uncertainty. In the industrial organization literature, Dixit (1989), Leahy (1993) and Caballero and Pindyck (1996) discuss the consequences of the entry (creation) decision of new (incumbent) entrepreneurs and exit decisions of some incumbents for variation in the aggregate stock of capital.
31. Benhabib and Spiegel (2000) show that financial development positively influences the investment rate. Schich and Pelgrin (2002) indicate a positive effect going from financial development to private investment in 19 OECD countries over 1970–97. Ndikumana (2000, 2005) finds that the development of banks and stock markets tends to stimulate domestic investment.
32. Details on these indicators can be found in Section 3.2.
33. Kose, Prasad and Terrones (2003) show that the overall volume of international trade and gross private capital flows has increased dramatically over the past three decades: in particular, "the growth of world trade has been larger than that of world income in almost all years since 1970".
34. This source could be the most reliable one for private investment ratio, while we can calculate it by deducting the net inflows of FDI and public investment from the gross fixed capital formation. Although data for private investment are only for up to 1998, they are sufficient (or long enough) to conduct this analysis.
35. Essentially, the principal component analysis takes N specific indicators and produces new indices (the principal components) $X_1, X_2,...X_N$ which are mutually uncorrelated. Each principal component, a linear combination of the N indicators, captures a different dimension of the data. Typically the variances of several of the principal components are low enough to be negligible, and hence the majority of the variation in the data will then be captured by a small number of indices.

186 Notes

36. The summary below is heavily drawn from Demirgüç-Kunt and Levine (1996, 1999).
37. The precision of the principal component analysis used to derive this new index depends on having a relatively large number of variables. Given that there are only three indices on which the principal component analysis is based, the new index of financial development is almost the mean of the three individual indices.
38. Two measures for the efficiency of financial intermediation widely used are Overhead Costs, the ratio of overhead costs to total bank assets, and Net Interest Margin, the difference between bank interest income and interest expenses, divided by total assets. Due to the incompleteness of the available data, they are not included in this analysis.
39. In the growth and convergence context, both the panel data analysis of Caselli *et al.* (1996) and the cross section analysis of Mankiw *et al.* (1992) find a negative effect of initial income on growth, but the former identifies a much larger effect than the latter, implying a 10% convergence rate relative to 2–3% suggested by Mankiw *et al.* (1992).
40. Starting from a general model with three lags of the dependent and independent variables and testing the null hypothesis of the coefficients being zero for the longest lag, we end up with one lagged independent variable and one lagged dependent variable appearing in the model for this context, given that the relevant specification tests are satisfied.
41. Caselli *et al.* (1996) treat some variables like the investment rate and population growth rate as predetermined and argue that these variables are potentially both causes and effects of economic growth.
42. Alonso-Borrego and Arellano (1999) propose the symmetrically normalized GMM estimator and the Limited Information Maximum Likelihood estimator. Recently Kruiniger (2008) has developed the Maximum Likelihood estimator and Newey and Windmeijer (2009) have proposed the new variance estimator for the generalized empirical likelihood estimator.
43. Bond *et al.* (2001) and Bond (2002) illustrate that in principle the first-differenced GMM estimates for the AR(1) coefficient should lie between the within group estimates (being downwards biased) and the OLS estimates (being upwards biased) from a straightforward pooled regression.
44. For the case of r=2, when $f_t = (1\ \eta_t)'$ and $\lambda_i' = (\alpha_i\ 1)$, we have $\lambda_i' f_t = \alpha_i + \eta_t$, where α_i and η_t are the individual effect and time effect, respectively.
45. Bai (2004) suggests that differenced data can also be used to calculate the number of factors.
46. The normalization that $\frac{\Lambda^{k'}\Lambda^k}{N} = I_k$ is used when $T > N$.
47. Bai and Ng (2004) recommend standardizing the data first, although the PANIC approach does not require it.
48. The standardized *FD* and *PI* are used here and the rest of the study. The PANIC approach essentially requires a balanced panel. To overcome the problem of missing data, imputation within each region is conducted, since countries in a region tend to have similar income levels, closer economic relations and to be more dependent on each other. There are 49 observations imputed for *FD* and 64 observations for *PI*, corresponding to 4% and 5% of complete observations in the resulting balanced panels, respectively. Appendix Table A3.3 presents the list of countries in each region.

49. When time trends are included, the presence of a deterministic trend in the data-generating process is assumed while the absence of such a trend is assumed when time trends are not allowed. Including time trends is less general than excluding them. In particular, including trends improves fit to some extent but may cause a large loss of power and possibly severe multicollinearity in the ADF regressions.
50. Four "panel" statistics are a "variance ratio" statistic ($Z_{\hat{v}NT}$), a "panel-t" statistic ($Z_{\hat{t}NT}$), a "panel-rho" statistic ($Z_{\hat{\rho}NT-1}$) and a "panel-ADF" statistic ($Z_{\widehat{adf}NT}$).
51. Three "group mean" statistics are a "group-t" statistic ($\tilde{Z}_{\hat{t}NT}$), a "group-rho" statistic ($\tilde{Z}_{\hat{\rho}NT-1}$) and a "group-ADF" statistic ($\tilde{Z}_{\widehat{adf}NT}$).
52. The Pedroni test based on defactored data should be interpreted with caution, since the defactored data are estimated and may be subject to particular forms of measurement errors.
53. More specifically, the MG estimator and its standard errors are calculated as

$$\widehat{\theta}_{MG} = \bar{\theta} = \frac{\sum_{i=1}^{N} \widehat{\theta}_i}{N} \text{ and } se(\widehat{\theta}_{MG}) = \frac{\sigma(\widehat{\theta}_i)}{\sqrt{N}} = \frac{\sqrt{\sum_{i=1}^{N} \frac{(\widehat{\theta}_i - \bar{\theta})^2}{N-1}}}{\sqrt{N}}, \text{ respectively.}$$

54. To overcome the problem of missing data, imputation within each region is conducted, since countries in a region tend to have similar income levels, closer economic relations and be more dependent on each other. There are 49 observations imputed for FD and 64 observations for PI, corresponding to 4% and 5% of complete observations in the resulting balanced panels, respectively.
55. The short-run coefficients reported in Tables 3.5 and 3.6 are in general less informative. The CCEP and WG assume the short-run coefficients to be identical across countries, ignoring the heterogeneity widely recognized. The CCEPMG and CCEMG (as well as PMG and MG) allow the short-run coefficients to vary across countries, which is a more realistic assumption to make. However, the short-run coefficients reported are the cross-country averages, and therefore they are highly influenced by the outliers.
56. The number of lags is constrained by the number of observations. As shown by Pesaran et al. (1999), the PMG estimator seems quite robust to outliers and the choice of ARDL order.
57. Data on GDP per capita and trade openness are taken from Heston et al. (2006).
58. Countries are considered as experiencing a political transition when either their "polity2" scores in the PolityIV Database by Marshall and Jaggers (2009) change from negative values to positive values or when their "freedom" indices, defined in this paper from the Freedom House Country Survey (2008), change from "Not Free" to "Free" or "Partly Free".
59. One of the channels through which democratization affects financial development is property rights protection and contract enforcement. Olson (1993) and Clague et al. (1996) argue that democracies tend to result in better protection of property rights and more efficient contract enforcement, which are conducive to financial development (La Porta et al., 1997, 1998).

188 Notes

60. La Porta *et al.* (1997, 1998) document that countries with a legal code like Common Law tend to protect private property owners, while countries with a legal code like Civil Law tend to care more about the rights of state and less about the rights of the masses. Countries with French legal origins are said to have comparatively inefficient contract enforcement and more corruption, and less well-developed financial systems, while countries with British legal origins enjoy higher levels of financial development.
61. They argue that incumbents have strong incentives to block the development of a more transparent and competitive financial sector, although these incentives may be weakened by openness to external trade and international flows of capital.
62. Based on annual data on developed and developing countries over 1975–2000, Girma and Shortland (2008) use approaches such as the system GMM approach from Arellano and Bover (1995) and Blundell and Bond (1998). In contrast to their study, this research uses the system GMM and LSDVC approaches, based on averaged data on 90 developed and developing countries over 1960–99 to see if democratization brings about financial development.
63. The main reason for this is that, data prior to 1990 for these countries generated by the centrally planned economy are largely incomplete, while data after 1990 are highly problematic or doubtful since most of these countries underwent severe economic disorder for several years in the early stage of the transformation process to a market-oriented economy. A research area in the future will be to see if the transition countries fit the pattern observed for the sample countries of this study.
64. Data for the black market premium from the GDN are available up to 1998.
65. The description here is mainly from Demirgüç-Kunt and Levine (1996, 1999).
66. Two measures for the efficiency of financial intermediation which are sometimes used are Overhead Costs, the ratio of overhead costs to total bank assets, and Net Interest Margin, the difference between bank interest income and interest expenses, divided by total assets. Due to the incompleteness of the relevant data, they are not included in this analysis.
67. In this polity coding system, zero is the threshold by which a country with a positive "polity2" score is regarded as a democracy whilst a country with a negative "polity2" score is regarded as an autocracy.
68. The democracy and autocracy scores are derived from six authority characteristics (regulation, competitiveness and openness of executive recruitment; operational independence of chief executive or executive constraints and regulation and competition of participation). Based on these criteria, each country is assigned a democracy score and an autocracy score ranging from 0 to 10. The larger the democracy score, the fairer the election of executive power, the more open the political process and the higher the extent of the constraints on executive power. In contrast, a larger autocracy score reflects a less open political process in a country in terms of less competitiveness and fairness in election, narrower participation and fewer constraints on executive power.
69. By experimenting with five-year and eight-year averages, respectively, I start from a general model with three lags of the dependent and independent

variables and test the null hypothesis of the coefficients being zero for the longest lag. I end up with one lagged dependent variable, one lagged independent variable, one lag of log GDP and one lag of the trade openness measure appearing in the model with eight-year averages for this context, given that the relevant specification tests are satisfied.

70. The series $x_{i\,t-1}$ is defined as being predetermined with respective to $v_{i,\,t}$ when $x_{i\,t-1}$ is correlated with $v_{i,\,t-1}$ and earlier shocks, but is uncorrelated with $v_{i\,t}$ and subsequent shocks. The series $x_{i\,t}$ is strictly exogenous when $x_{i\,t}$ is uncorrelated with earlier, current and future errors. See Bond (2002) and Arellano (2003) for details.

71. For the multivariate autoregressive model, Blundell and Bond (2000) show that a sufficient condition for the additional moment conditions to be valid is the joint mean stationarity of all the series.

72. In this analysis the instrument set used is restricted (to avoid the possible over-fitting bias) in the sense that all lagged values of y, x and z at dates $t-2$ and $t-3$ are used as instruments for $\Delta y_{i,t-1}$, $\Delta x_{i,t-1}$ and $\Delta z_{i,t-1}$ in the first difference equation.

73. Note that when the instrument set is not restricted, the lagged first differences of the series (y_{it}, x_{it}, z_{it}) dated $t-1$ are used as instruments for the untransformed equations in levels. Differences lagged two periods or more are redundant as instruments for the levels equations because the corresponding moment conditions are linear combinations of those already in use. In this analysis, the lagged first-differences of the series (y_{it}, x_{it}, z_{it}) dated $t-1$ and $t-2$ are employed due to the use of restricted instrument set.

74. Essentially, in the bias approximation of Bruno (2005), the within operator is adjusted to include an exogenous selection rule which selects only the observations with observable current and one-time lagged values, by which missing observations for some individuals are allowed.

75. Since the freedom index has data starting from the period 1972–73, it is not used for the panel data study, but is used for selecting the democratic transition countries.

76. The event identification methodology of Papaioannou and Siourounis (2008) has been found useful for selecting the democratic transition countries, but the selection method in this analysis differs from their method in the following ways. First, for simplicity this analysis selects the sample exclusively depending on the changes from autocratic rule to democratic regimes without any further divisions, while Papaioannou and Siourounis (2008) divide democratizations into "full", "partial" and "borderline" with different thresholds in terms of either the "polity2" or the "freedom" index. Second, this analysis is interested in the effect of a *stable* regime change on financial development. Hence, the sample includes only the countries whose regime changes last for at least ten years.

77. The *FD* measure has been standardized. More specifically, it is divided by the cross-country standard deviation of *FD* in 1999.

78. When we compare the five-year averages before and after democratization, we find that the five-year average of standardized *FD* post-democratization for 33 countries is larger by 0.015 cross-country standard deviations of *FD* than before their democratization, and about two-thirds of the sample countries benefit from this process. Columns 7 to 9 show that the average of

Notes

standardized *FD* five to ten years post-democratisation for 33 countries is larger by 0.212 cross-country standard deviations of *FD* than ten to five years before their democratization, and much more sample countries benefit from this process. The median values of the increase in standardized *FD* for three cases of comparison are positive.

79. Looking at the financial development performance of each individual country, we find enormous heterogeneity across countries, ranging from an increase of 1.096 of a cross-country standard deviation of *FD* in the ten-year average of standardized *FD* for Thailand to a decline of 0.415 of a cross-country standard deviation of *FD* for Zambia. The Republic of Korea and Madagascar also witnessed a drastic increase in the ten-year average of standardized *FD*, whilst Nicaragua and Uruguay experienced a tremendous drop in *FD* following their democratization. Case studies on how democratization helped the financial development process are interesting areas for future research.
80. The regression is estimated by OLS in which the unobserved country specific effects, time effects and control variables such as trade openness, GDP, aggregate investment and the black market premium are included.
81. The financial development performance in Asian countries and other economic performances in East Asian and Pacific countries are largely different from those in South Asian countries.
82. Results regarding the impacts on specific financial development measures such as private credit, liquidity liabilities and commercial-central bank are available from the author upon request.
83. The selection of these subsamples is mainly stimulated by Rodrik and Wacziarg (2005) in which low-income countries, ethnically diverse countries and Sub-Saharan African countries are studied. However, I find no evidence in support of a positive/negative link between institutional improvement and financial development for the Sub-Saharan African countries. Experiments were also conducted for the Asian countries and Latin American countries, again finding no evidence.
84. In addition, the ordered logit approach imposes strong distributional assumptions relative to a linear model, and the estimates of individual effects and other parameters may be inconsistent because of an incidental parameter problem.
85. Other ways to address either cross section correlation or serial correlation in this context have also been done (results are available from author upon request).
86. FL_{it} is generated by dividing the original AM financial liberalization index by 18. The original financial liberalization index, ranging from 0 to 18, is based on six policy dimensions (credit controls, interest rate controls, entry barriers in the banking sector, operational restrictions, privatization in the financial sector and restrictions on international financial transactions) with each dimension taking on values between 0 and 3.
87. The democracy and autocracy scores are derived from six authority characteristics (regulation, competitiveness and openness of executive recruitment; operational independence of chief executive or executive constraints and regulation and competition of participation). Based on these criteria, each country is assigned a democracy score and an autocracy score ranging from

0 to 10. The larger the democracy score, the fairer the election of executive power, the more open the political process and the higher the extent of the constraints on executive power. In contrast, a larger autocracy score reflects a less open political process in a country in terms of less competitiveness and fairness in elections, narrower participation and fewer constraints on the executive.

88. Here $\theta_1 c$ and $-\theta_1$ are renamed as θ_1 and θ_2, respectively. β_1, β_2', β_3' and β_4' are reparameterized as θ_3, θ_4', θ_5' and θ_6', respectively.
89. Here $\theta_1 c$, $-\theta_1$ and $b\theta_1$ are renamed as θ_1, θ_2 and θ_3, respectively. β_1, β_2', β_3' and β_4' are reparameterized as θ_4, θ_5', θ_6' and θ_7', accordingly.
90. More specifically, IMF_{it} has been found to be significant when country fixed effects are excluded, while $REG\_FL_{i,t-1} - FL_{i,t-1}$ appears to be significant no matter whether the country fixed effects are included or not.
91. Divided by 18, the original measure has been rescaled to get an index, $FL_{i,t}$, ranging between 0 and 1.
92. This analysis first experiments with including time dummies in the original AM models in the within group estimation to control for cross section correlation. However, this approach is not as general as Pesaran's (2006) approach which, besides other advantages, allows common factors to have differential impacts across countries. Including time dummies controls only for a common component, whose effect is common across countries.
93. Although serial correlation in the errors can be alleviated once country fixed effects are included, it may not be fully removed. The standard robust standard errors do not allow for serial correlation in errors, only for heteroscedasticity.
94. The test statistic takes the form of $-2\sum_{i=1}^{N}\ln(p_{iT})$ in which p_{iT} is the p-value corresponding to the unit root test of the ith individual cross section unit for the cross-sectionally augmented DF regression. The critical values for the Fisher P-test on a cross-sectionally augmented regression (Pesaran, 2007) are provided by M. Hashem Pesaran.
95. Since the lagged dependent variable bias arising from the within group transformation can be alleviated when T is large in a dynamic panel (Nickell, 1981).
96. $FL_{i,t-1}(1 - FL_{i,t-1})$ is reported here.
97. Although the coefficients on $REG\_FL_{i,t-1} - FL_{i,t-1}$ and its interaction term are negative and positive, respectively, the range of $FL_{i,t-1}$ from 0 to 1 determines the derivative of ΔFL_{it} with respect to $REG\_FL_{i,t-1} - FL_{i,t-1}$, $-0.147 + 0.094 \times FL_{i,t-1}$, is always negative.
98. The panel is unbalanced mainly because data on IMF programs are missing for the following six countries over period 1973–83: China, Costa Rica, Ecuador, Jamaica, Nigeria, Portugal and Uruguay.
99. Data are from the UNEP Risoe Centre (2008).
100. For example, as the only two CDM host countries in Asia in 2003, India and the Republic of Korea were immediately followed by four Asian host countries in 2004 and nine other Asian host countries in 2005 (UNEP Risoe Centre, 2008).
101. A country with k monthly non-zero observations (up to September 2008) has its averaged CDM being its total CERs divided by k.

102. CO_2e is the Carbon Dioxide Equivalent, the unit of measurement used to indicate the global warming potentials defined in decision 2/CP.3 of the Marrakech Accords or as subsequently revised in accordance with Article 5 of the Kyoto Protocol.
103. Data on latitude, elevation and land area for Singapore are added to the physical factors dataset of CID.
104. This inclusion is stimulated by the works of Alesina *et al.* (2003) and Stulz and Williamson (2003), for example. Alesina *et al.* (2003) argue that the ethnic and religious fractionalizations in a country are associated with its economic success and institutional quality. Stulz and Williamson (2003) show that culture, proxied by ethnic, religious and language differences, explain why investor protection differs across countries and how investor rights are enforced among countries.
105. The inclusion is due to La Porta *et al.* (1998) who suggest that the legal origin of a country is helpful in explaining the extent to which investor rights are protected in it. More specifically, countries with a Common Law tradition tend to place more emphasis on private rights protection and less on the rights of the state, while countries which have adopted a Civil Law tradition do the opposite.
106. The Andrews (2005) approach is very general in the sense that the effects of common shocks, which are ς-measurable, may differ across population units, in a discrete or continuous fashion, and may be local or global in nature.
107. The addition of the spatially lagged dependent variable results in a form of endogenity, rendering the OLS an inapplicable method for spatial lag model. To estimate the spatial lag model consistently, the Generalized 2SLS and Maximum Likelihood approach (ML) have been proposed (Kelejian and Prucha, 1998, 1999; Lee, 2003, 2007; Kelejian *et al.*, 2004; Anselin, 2006).
108. Since the spatial error model is a special case of a regression specification with a non-spherical error variance-covariance matrix, more specifically, the off-diagonal elements are non-zero. OLS estimates remain unbiased whilst the standard errors are biased. The OLS method can therefore be applied to this model with the standard errors adjusted to allow for error correlation. The spatial error model can be consistently estimated by GMM or ML (Kelejian and Prucha, 1998, 1999; Anselin, 2006).
109. This evidence is preliminary. One might find that countries like Brazil, closer to Paraguay, have large CDM credit flows. This suggests that, apart from geographic distance, other geographic variables are also important in the process of CDM development, and so are the institutional variables and financial variables.
110. Data on the great circle distances are also from Gleditsch et al. (2001).
111. If Moran's I is greater (smaller) than its expected value, E(I), and/or Gearcy's C is smaller (larger) than its expected value, E(C), the overall distribution of the variable in question can be reflected by positive (negative) spatial autocorrelation.
112. In this analysis, we also explore the impacts on CDM credit flows of other geographic factors such as being landlocked, the minimum distance from one of the three capital-goods-supplying centres (New York, Rotterdam and Tokyo), mean distance to the nearest coastline or a river navigable to the

ocean, the proportion of a country's total land area with 100 km of the ocean or such a river, and the proportion of a country's total land area in Koeppen-Geiger temperate zones. In general we find no evidence to support any significant associations between these factors and CDM credit flows. This may suggest that, as more and more modern technologies have been employed in the areas of transportation and telecommunications, and more and more railways, automobiles, air transport and all forms of telecommunications become available, the geographic advantages in terms of easy access to the sea and/or international trade centres tend to be diminish in the process of economic development.
113. Under the null of no heteroscedasticity, the test statistic is distributed as Chi-square with degree of freedom being the total number of the regressors.
114. The spatial weighting matrices, W_n and M_n, are treated as the same.
115. The GS2SLS estimates suggest that the impacts of *AREA* and *EXPPRIM* have been less precisely estimated.

Bibliography

Abiad, A. and A. Mody. 2005. Financial reform: What shakes it? What shapes it? *American Economic Review*, 95, 66–88.

Acemoglu, D., S. Johnson and J. Robinson. 2001. Colonial origins of comparative development: An empirical investigation. *American Economic Review*, 91(5), 1369-1401.

Ahn, S.C. and P. Schmidt. 1995. Efficient estimation of models for dynamic panel data. *Journal of Econometrics*, 68, 5–28.

Alesina, A., A. Devleeschauwer, W. Easterly and S. Kurlat. 2003. Fractionalization. *Journal of Economic Growth*, 8(2), 155–94.

Alonso-Borrego, C. and M. Arellano. 1999. Symmetrically normalised instrumental-variable estimation using panel data. *Journal of Business Economic Statistics*, 17, 36–49.

Anderson, T.W. and C. Hsiao. 1981. Estimation of dynamic models with error components. *Journal of the American Statistical Association*, 76, 598–606.

Anderson, T.W. and C. Hsiao. 1982. Formulation and estimation of dynamic models using panel data. *Journal of Econometrics*, 18, 47–82.

Andrews, D. W. K. 2005. Cross-section regression with common shocks. *Econometrica*, 73(5), 1551–85.

Anselin, L. 2006. Spatial Econometrics. In Mills, T. and K. Patterson (eds) *Palgrave Handbook of Econometrics*, vol. 1, Econometric Theory, Basingstoke: Palgrave Macmillan, 901–69.

Anselin, L., A. Bera, R. Florax and M. Yoon. 1996. Simple diagnostic tests for spatial dependence. *Regional Science and Urban Economics*, 26 (1), 77–104.

Arellano, M. 1987. Computing robust standard errors for within-group estimators. *Oxford Bulletin of Economic and Statistics*, 49, 431–34.

Arellano, M. 2003. *Panel Data Econometrics*, New York Oxford. University Press: Advanced Texts in Econometrics.

Arellano, M. and S. Bond. 1991. Some tests of specification for panel data: Monte carlo evidence and an application to employment equations. *Review of Economic Studies*, 58, 277–97.

Arellano, M. and O. Bover. 1995. Another look at the instrumental-variable estimation of error-components models. *Journal of Econometrics*, 68, 29–51.

Arraiz, Irani, D. M. Drukker, H. H. Kelejian, I. R. Prucha. 2010. A spatial Cliff-Ord-type model with heteroskedastic innovations: Small and large sample results. *Journal of Regional Science*, 50(2), 592–614.

Axelrod, R. 1997. The Dissemination of Culture: A Model with Local Convergence and Global Polarization. *Journal of Conflict Resolution*, 41(2), 203–26.

Bagehot, W. 1873. *Lombard Street: A Description of the Money Market*. London: Henry S. King.

Bai, J. 2009. Panel data models with interactive fixed effects. *Econometrica*, 77(4), 1229–79.

Bai, J. and S. Ng. 2002. Determine the number of factors in approximate factor models. *Econometrica*, 70, 191–221.

Bibliography 195

Bai, J. and S. Ng. 2004. A PANIC attack on unit roots and cointegration. *Econometrica*, 72, 1127–77.

Bailliu, J. N. 2000. Private capital flows, financial development, and economic growth in developing countries. Bank of Canada Working Paper 2000-15.

Baltagi, B. H., P. O. Demetriades and S. H. Law. 2009. Financial development and openness: Evidence from panel data. *Journal of Development Economics*, 89(2), 285–96.

Banerjee, A., M. Marcellino and C. Osbat. 2004. Some cautions on the use of panel methods for integrated series of macro-economic data. *Econometrics Journal*, 7(2), 322–40.

Beck, T., A. Demirguc-Kunt and R. Levine. 2003. Law, endowment and finance. *Journal of Financial Economics*, 70, 37–81.

Bekaert, G., R. H. Campbell and R. Lumsdaine. 2002. Dating the integration of world equity markets. *Journal of Financial Economics*, 65(2), 203–47.

Bencivenga, V. R., B. D. Smith. 1991. Financial intermediation and endogenous growth. *Review of Economic Studies*, 58, 195–209.

Benhabib, J. and M. M. Spiegel. 2000. The financial development in growth and investment. *Journal of Economic Growth*, 5, 341–60.

Bernanke, B. S. and M. Gertler. 1989. Agency costs, net wealth, and business fluctuations. *American Economic Review*, 79, 14–31

Bertola, G. and R. J. Caballero. 1994. Irreversibility and aggregate investment. *Review of Economic Studies*, 61(2), 223–46.

Blanchard, O. and A. Shleifer. 2000. Federalism with and without political centralization; China versus Russia. NBER working paper no. 7616.

Blundell, R. and S. Bond. 1998. Initial conditions and moment restrictions in dynamic panel data models. *Journal of Econometrics*, 87, 115–43.

Blundell, R. and S. Bond. 2000. GMM estimation with persistent panel data: an application to production functions. *Econometric Reviews*, 19, 321–40.

Bond, S. 2002. Dynamic panel data models: a guide to micro data methods and practice. *Portuguese Economic Journal*, 1, 141–62.

Bond, S., A. Hoeffler and J. Temple. 2001. GMM estimation of empirical growth models. CEPR discussion paper no. 3048.

Bowsher, C. G. 2002. On testing overidentifying restrictions in dynamic panel data models. *Economics Letters*, 77, 211–20.

Brock, W. and S. Durlauf. 2001. Discrete choice with social interactions. *Review of Economic Studies*, 59, 235–60.

Bruno, G. S. F. 2005. Approximating the bias of the LSDV estimator for dynamic unbalanced panel data models. *Economics Letters*, 87(3), 361–66.

Bun, M. J. G. and J. F. Kiviet. 2003. On the diminishing returns of higher order terms in asymptotic expansions of bias. *Economics Letters*, 79, 145–52.

Caballero, R. J. and R. S. Pindyck. 1996. Uncertainty, investment and industry evolution. *International Economic Review*, 37(3), 641–62.

Caselli, F., G. Esquivel and F. Lefort. 1996. Reopening the convergence debate: a new look at cross-country growth empirics. *Journal of Economic Growth*, 1(3), 363–90.

Chamberlain, G. 1984. Panel data. *Handbook of Econometrics*, vol. 2, Chapter 22, 1247–1318, North-Holland: Elsevier Science.

Chinn, M. and H. Ito. 2006. What matters for financial development? Capital controls, institutions, and interactions. *Journal of Development Economics*, 81(1), 163–92.

Bibliography

Claessens, S., A. Demirgüç-Kunt and H. Huizinga. 1998. How does foreign entry affect the domestic banking market? World Bank Policy Research Working Paper Series no. 1918.

Clague, C., P. Keefer, S. Knack and M. Olson. 1996. Property and contract rights in autocracies and democracies. *Journal of Economic Growth*, 1, 243–76.

Crafts, N. 2000. Globalization and growth in the twentieth century. IMF working paper no. 00/44

Demirgüç-Kunt, A. and E. Detragiache. 1998. Financial liberalisation and financial fragility. World bank Policy Research Working Paper Series no. 1917.

Demirgüç-Kunt, A. and R. Levine. 1996. Stock markets, corporate finance and economic growth: an overview. *World Bank Economic Review*, 10(2), 223–40.

Demirgüç-Kunt, A. and R. Levine. 1999. Bank-based and market-based financial systems: Cross-country comprisions. World Bank Policy Research working paper no. 2143.

Diamond, D.W. 1984. Financial intermediation and delegated monitoring. *Review of Economic Studies*, 51, 393–414.

Diamond, D.W. and P. Dybvig. 1983. Bank runs, deposit insurance and liquidity. *Journal of Political Economy*, 91(3), 401–19.

Diamond, J. 1997. *Guns, germs, and steel: The fates of human societies.* W. W. Norton, New York, NY.

Dixit, A. 1989. Entry and exit decisions under uncertainty. *Journal of Political Economy*, 97, 620–38.

Djankov, S., C. McLiesh, T. Nenova and A. Shleifer. 2003. Who owns the media? *Journal of Law and Economics*, 46(2), 341–82.

Do, Q. T. and A. A. Levchenko. 2004. Trade and financial development. World Bank Working Paper Series no. 3347.

Dollar, D. and A. Kraay. 2003. Institutions, trade and growth. *Journal of Monetary Economics*, 32, 459–83.

Doms, M. and T. Dunne. 1998. Capital adjustment patterns in manufacturing plants. *Review of Economic Dynamics*, 1, 409–29.

Easterly, W. and R. Levine. 2003. Tropics, germs, and crops: How endowments influence economic development. *Journal of Monetary Economics*, 50, 3–39.

Engle, R. F. and C. W. J. Granger. 1987. Cointegration and error correction: representation, estimation and testing. *Econometrica*, 55, 251–76.

Fernandez, C., E. Ley and M. Steel. 2001. Model uncertainty in cross-country growth regressions. *Journal of Applied Econometrics*, 16, 563–76.

Fernandez, R. and D. Rodrik. 1991. Resistance to Reform: Status Quo Bias in the Presence of Individual-Specific Uncertainty. *American Economic Review*, 81(5), 1146–55.

Frankel, J. A. and A. K. Rose. 1998. The endogeneity of the optimum currency area criteria. *Economic Journal*, 108, 1009–25.

Frankel, J. A. and D. Romer. 1999. Does trade cause growth? *American Economic Review*, 89, 379–98.

Freedom House. 2008. Freedom House Country Survey, available at www.freedomhouse.org.

Gale, D. H. M. 1985. Incentive-compatible debt contracts: The one-period problem. *Review of Economic Studies*, 52, 647–64.

Gale, D. and M. Hellwig. 1985. Incentive-compatible debt contracts: The one-period problem. *Review of Economic Studies*, 52, 647–64.

Gallup, J. L., J. D. Sachs and A. Mellinger. 1999. Geography and economic development. CID at Harvard working paper no. 1.
Gengenbach, C. F. C. Palm and J. Urbain. 2005. Panel cointegration testing in the presence of common factors. Maastricht Research School of Economics of Technology and Organization Research Paper no. 050.
Giavazzi, F. and G. Tabellini. 2004. Economic and political liberalization. NBER working paper no.10657.
Girma, S. and A. K. Shortland. 2008. The political economy of financial development. *Oxford Economic Papers*, 60(4), 567–96.
Gleditsch, K. S. and M. D. Ward. 2001. Measuring space: A minimum-distance database and applications to international studies. *Journal of Peace Research*, 38, 749–68.
Granger, C. W. J. and D. F. Hendry. 2005. A dialog concerning a new instrument for econometric modeling. *Econometrics Theory*, 21(1), 278–97.
Greenwood. J. and B. Jovanovic. 1990. Financial development, growth, and the distribution of income. *Journal of Political Economy*, 98, 1076–1107.
Greenwood, J. and B. D. Smith. 1997. Financial markets in development, and the development of financial markets. *Journal of Economic Dynamics and Control*, 21, 145–81.
Gregory, A. W., A. C. Head and J. Raynauld. 1997. Measuring world business cycles. *International Economic Review*, 38, 677–701.
Hall, R. and C. Jones. 1999. Why do some countries produce so much more output per worker than others? *Quarterly Journal of Economics*, 114, 83–116.
Hansen, B. E. 2005. Challenges for econometric model selection, *Econometrics Theory*, 21(1), 60–68.
Haveman, J., International trade data, Available at www.eiit.org.
Hendry, D. F. 1995. *Dynamic Econometrics*, Oxford, Oxford University Press.
Hendry, D. F. and H. Krolzig. 2005. The properties of automatic GETS modelling. *Economic Journal*, 115(502), 32–61.
Henisz, W. J. 2000. The institutional environment for economic growth. *Economics and Politics*, 12(1), 1–31.
Heston, A, R. Summers and B. Aten. 2006. Penn World Table version 6.2, Center for International Comparisons at the University of Pennsylvania (CICUP)
Goldsmith, R. W. 1969. *Financial Structure and Development*, New Haven, CT: Yale University Press.
Hicks, J. R, 1969. Automatists, Hawtreyans, and Keynesians. *Journal of Money, Credit and Banking*, 1(3), 307–17.
Hoeting, J., A. Raftery and D. Madigan. 1996. A method for simultaneous variable selection and outlier identification in linear regression. *Computational Statistics and Data Analysis*, 22, 25–70.
Holtz-Eakin, D, W. Newey and H. S. Rosen. 1988. Estimation vector autoregressions with panel data. *Econometrica*, 56(6), 1371–95.
Hoover, K. D. and S. J. Perez. 1999. Data mining reconsidered: Encompassing and the general-to-specific approach to specification search. *Econometrics Journal*, 2, 167–91.
Huybens, E. and B. D. Smith. 1999. Inflation, financial markets and long-run real activity. *Journal of Monetary Economics*, 43: 283–315.
Huang, Y. and J. Temple. 2005. Does external trade promote financial development? CEPR working paper no. 5150.

198 Bibliography

Im, K., H. Pesaran and Y. Shin. 2003. Testing for unit roots in heterogeneous panels. *Journal of Econometrics*, 115, 53–74.

Imbs, J. 2003. Trade, finance, specialization and synchronization. IMF working paper no. 03/81

IMF, 2003. *World Economic Outlook*.

Isham, J., M. Woolcock, L. Pritchett and G. Busby. 2005. The varieties of resource experience: How natural resource export structures affect the political economy of economic growth. *World Bank Economic Review*, 19(2), 141–74.

Islam, N. 1995. Growth empirics: A panel data approach. *Quarterly Journal of Economics*, 110, 1127–70.

Jaffee, D. and M. Levonian. 2001. Structure of banking systems in developed and transition economies. *European Financial Management*, 7(2), 161–81.

Judson, R. A. and A. L. Owen. 1999. Estimating dynamic panel data models: A guide for macroeconomists. *Economics Letters*, 65, 9–15.

Kamarck, A. M. 1976. *The Tropics and Economic Development*, Baltimore, MD: John Hopkins University Press.

Kaufmann, D., A. Kraay and M. Mastruzzi. 2008. Governance Matters VII: Governance Indicators for 1996–2007. World Bank Policy Research Working Paper no. 4654.

Kelejian, H. H. and I. R. Prucha and Y. Yuzefovich. 2004. Instrumental variable estimation of a spatial autoregressive model with autoregressive disturbances: Large and small sample results. In J. LeSage and K. Pace (eds.) *Advances in Econometrics: Spatial and Spatiotemporal Econometrics*. NewYork: Elsevier, 63–198.

Kelejian, H. H. and I. R. Prucha. 1998. A generalized spatial two-stage least squares procedure for estimating a spatial autoregressive model with autoregressive disturbance. *Journal of Real Estate Finance and Economics*, 17, 99–121.

Kelejian, H. H. and I. R. Prucha. 1999. A generalized moments estimator for the autoregressive parameter in a spatial model. *International Economic Review*, 40, 509–33.

Kelejian, H. H. and I. R. Prucha. 2010. Specification and estimation of spatial autoregressive models with autoregressive and heteroskedastic disturbances. *Journal of Econometrics*, 157(1), 53–67.

Kim, S. H., M. A. Kose and M. Plummer. 2003. Dynamics of business cycles in Asia. *Review of Development Economics*, 7, 462–77.

King, R. and R. Levine. 1993. Finance and growth: Schumpeter might be right. *Quarterly Journal of Economics*, 108(3), 717–37.

Kiviet, J. F. 1995. On bias, inconsistency, and efficiency of various estimators in dynamic panel data models. *Journal of Econometrics*, 68, 53–78.

Koenker, R. 1981. A note on studentizing a test for heteroskedasticity. *Journal of Econometrics*, 17, 107–12.

Kose, M. A., C. Otrok and C. H. Whiteman. 2003. International business cycles: world, region, and country-specific factors. *American Economic Review*, 93, 216–39.

Kose, M. A., E. S. Prasad and M. E. Terrones. 2003. Volatility and comovement in a globalized world economy: an empirical exploration. IMF working paper no. 03/246

Krolzig, H. M. and D. F. Hendry. 2001. Computer automation of general-to-specific model selection procedures. *Journal of Economic Dynamics and Control*, 25, 831–66.

Kruiniger, H. 2008. Maximum likelihood estimation and inference methods for the covariance stationary panel AR(1)/unit root model. *Journal of Econometrics*, 144(2), 447–64.

Laeven, L. 2000. Does Financial Liberalization Reduce Financial Constraints? World Bank Policy Research Working Paper no. 2435.

La Porta, R., F. Lopez-de-Silanes, A. Lopez-de-Silanes and R. W. Vishny. 1997. Legal determinants of external finance. *Journal of Finance*, 52(3), 1131–50.

La Porta, R., F. Lopez-de-Silanes, A. Lopez-de-Silanes and R. W. Vishny. 1998. Law and finance. *Journal of Political Economy*, 106, 1113–55.

Leahy, J. 1993. Investment in competitive equilibrium: the optimality of myopic behaviour. *Quarterly Journal of Economics*, 108, 1105–33.

Leamer, E. E. 1983. Let's take the con out of econometrics. *American Economic Review*, 73, 31–43.

Leamer, E. E. 1985. Sensitivity analysis would help. *American Economic Review*, 75, 308–13.

Lee, L. 2003. Best spatial two-stage least squares estimators for a spatial autoregressive model with autoregressive disturbances. *Econometric Reviews*, 22, 307–35.

Lee, L. 2007. GMM and 2SLS estimation of mixed regressive, spatial autoregressive models. *Journal of Econometrics*, 137, 489–514.

Lee, L. and X. Liu. 2006. Efficient GMM estimation of a spatial autoregressive model with autoregressive disturbances. Working paper, Department of Economics, Ohio State University.

Levine, R. 1997. Financial development and economic growth: views and agenda. *Journal of Economic Literature*, 35, 688–726.

Levine, R. 2003. More on finance and growth: More Finance, more growth? The Federal Reserve Bank of St. Louis. July/August.

Levine, R. 2005. Finance and growth: Theory and evidence. In: P. Aghion and S. N. Durlauf (eds.), *Handbook of Economic Growth*, North-Holland: Elsevier.

Levine, R., N. Loayza and T. Beck. 2000. Financial intermediation and growth: causality and causes. *Journal of Monetary Economics*, 46(1), 31–77.

Levine, R. and D. Renelt. 1992. A sensitivity analysis of cross-country growth regressions. *American Economic Review*, 82, 942–63.

Maddala, G. S. and S. Wu. 1999. A comparative study of unit root tests with panel data and a new simple test. *Oxford Bulletin of Economics and Statistics*, 61, 631–52.

Malik, A. and J. R. W. Temple. 2009. The geography of output volatility. *Journal of Development Economics*, 90(2), 163–78.

Mankiw, N. G., D. Romer and D. N. Weil. 1992. A contribution to the empirics of economic growth. *Quarterly Journal of Economics*, 107, 407–37.

Manski, C. F. 2000. Economic analysis of social interactions. *Journal of Economic Perspectives*, 14(3), 115–36.

Marshall, M.G. and Jaggers, K. 2008. Polity IV Project Country Reports, College Park, College Park CIDUM, University of Maryland.

Marshall, M. G. and K. Jaggers. 2009. Polity IV Project Country Reports, College Park CIDUM, University of Maryland.

Mayer, C. and O. Sussman. 2001. The assessment: finance, law and growth. *Oxford Review of Economic Policy*, 17(4), 457–66.

McKinnon, R. I. 1973. *Money and Capital in Economic Development*. Washington D.C. Brookings Institution

Minier, J. A. 1998. Democracy and growth: Alternative approaches. *Journal of Economic Growth*, 3(3), 241–66.

Moon, H. R. and B. Perron. 2004. Testing for a unit root in panels with dynamic factors. *Journal of Econometrics*, 122, 81–126.

Ndikumana, L. 2000. Financial determinants of domestic investment in Sub-Saharan Africa: evidence from panel data. *World Development*, 28(2), 381–400.

Ndikumana, L. 2005. Financial development, financial structure, and domestic investment: interanatioal evidence. *Journal of International Money and Finance*, 24, 651–73.

Newey, W. and F. Windmeijer. 2009. Generalized Method of Moments with many weak moment conditions. *Econometrica*, 77(3), 687 - 719.

Nickel, S. J. 1981. Biases in dynamic models with fixed effects. *Econometrica*, 49, 1417–26.

Olson, M. 1993. Dictatorship, democracy and development. *American Political Science Review*, 87, 567–76.

Pagano, M. and P. Volpin. 2001. The political economy of finance. *Oxford Review of Economic Policy*, 17(4), 502–19.

Papaioannou, E. and G. Siourounis. 2008. Democratization and growth. *Economic Journal*, 118(532), 1520–51.

Papke, L. E. and J. M. Wooldridge. 2005. A computational trick for delta-method standard errors. *Economic Letters*, 86, 413–17.

Pedroni, P. 1999. Critical values for cointegration tests in heterogeneous panels with multiple regressors. *Oxford Bulletin of Economics and Statistics*, 61, 653–70.

Pedroni, P. 2004. Panel cointegration, asymptotic and finite sample properties of pooled time series tests with an application to the PPP hypothesis. *Econometric Theory*, 20, 597–625.

Persson, T. 2005. Forms of democracy, policy and economic development. NBER working paper no. 11171.

Persson, T. and G. Tabellini. 1992. Growth, income distribution and democracy. *European Economic Review*, 36, 593–602.

Pesaran, M. H. 2004. General diagnostic tests for cross section dependence in panels. *CESifo Working Papers* no. 1233.

Pesaran, M. H. 2006. Estimation and inference in large heterogeneous panels with a multifactor error structure. *Econometrica*, 74 (4), 967–1012.

Pesaran, M. H. 2007. A simple panel unit root test in the presence of cross section dependence. *Journal of Applied Econometrics*, 22(2), 265–312.

Pesaran, M. H., Y. Shin and R. P. Smith. 1999. Pooled mean group estimation of dynamic heterogeneous panels. *Journal of American Statistical Association*, 94, 621–34.

Pesaran, M. H. and R. P. Smith. 1995. Estimating long-run relationships from dynamic heterogeneous panels. *Journal of Econometrics*, 68, 79–113.

Phillips, P. C. B. and D. Sul. 2003. Dynamic Panel Testing and Homogeneity Testing under Cross Section Dependence. *Econometrics Journal*, 6, 217–59.

Quinn, D. P. and C. Inclán. 1997. The origins of financial openness: A study of current and capital account liberalization. *American Journal of Political Science*, 41(3), 771–813.

Raftery, A. E. 1995. Bayesian model selection in social research. In: P.V. Marsden (ed.), *Sociological Methodology*, Cambridge: Blackwell, 111–96.

Raftery, A. E., D. Madigan and J. E. Hoeting. 1997. Bayesian model averaging for linear regression models. *Journal of American Statistical Association*, 92, 179–91.

Rajan, R. G. and L. Zingales. 1998. Financial dependence and growth. *American Economic Review*, 88(6), 559–86.

Rajan, R. G. and L. Zingales. 2003. The great reversals: The politics of financial development in the twentieth century. *Journal of Financial Economies*, 69, 5–50.

Reynal-Querol, M. and J. G. Montalvo. 2005. Ethnic polarization, potential conflict and civil war. *American Economic Review*, 95(3), 796–816.

Rodrik, D., A. Subramanian and F. Trebbi. 2004. Institutions rule: the primacy of institutions over geography and integration in economic development. *Journal of Economic growth*, 9, 131–65.

Rodrik, D. and R. Wacziarg. 2005. Do democratic transitions produce bad economic outcomes? *American Economic Review*, 95(2), 50–55.

Sachs, J. D., 2003a. Institutions don't rule: Direct effects of geography on per capita income. NBER working paper no. 9490.

Sachs, J. 2003b. Institutions matter, but not for everything. *Finance and Development*, 40(2).

Sachs, J., and A. Warner. 1995a. Economic reform and the process of global integration. *Brookings Papers on Economic Activity*, 1, 1–95.

Sachs, J. D. and A. M. Warner, 1995b. Natural resource abundance and economic growth. NBER Working Paper no. W5398.

Sachs, J. and A. Warner. 1997. Fundamental sources of long-run growth. *American Economic Review Papers and Proceedings*, 87, 184–188.

Saint-Paul, G. 1992, Technological Choice, Financial Markets and Economic Development. *European Economic Review*, 36, 763–81.

Sala-i-Martin, X. 1997a. I have just run two million regressions. *American Economic Review*, 87(2), 178–83.

Sala-i-Martin, X. 1997b. I have just run four million regressions. NBER Working Paper No. W6252.

Sala-i-Martin, X., G. Doppelhofer and R. Miller. 2004. Determinants of long-run growth: A Bayesian Averaging of Classical Estimates (BACE) approach. *American Economic Review*, 94(4), 813–35.

Schich, S. and F. Pelgrin. 2002. Financial development and investment: panel data evidence for OECD countries from 1970–1997. *Applied Economics Letters*, 9, 1–7.

Schumpeter, J. A. 1911. *The Theory of Economic Development*, Cambridge MA, Harvard University Press.

Shaw, E. S. 1973. *Financial Deepening in Economic Development*, New York, Oxford University Press

Simmons, B. A. and Z. Elkins. 2004. The globalization of liberalization: Policy diffusion in the international political economy. *American Political Science Review*, 98(1), 171–89.

Stulz, R. M. M. and R. G. Williamson, 2003. Culture, openness, and finance. *Journal of Financial Economics*, 70, 313–49.

Summers, L. H. 2000. International Financial Crises: Causes, Prevention, and Cures. *American Economic Review Papers and Proceedings*, 90(2), 1–16.

Tavares, J. and R. Wacziarg. 2001. How democracy affects growth. *European Economic Review*, 45(8), 1341–78.

Townsend, R. M. 1979. Optimal contracts and competitive markets with costly state verification. *Journal of Economic Theory*, 21, 265–93.

UNEP Risoe Centre, CDM/JI Pipeline Analysis and Database (2008).
White, H. 1980. A Heteroskedasticity-consistent covariance matrix estimator and a direct test for heteroskedasticity. *Econometrica*, 48, 817–38.
Williamson, S. D. 1986. Costly monitoring, financial intermediation, and equilibrium credit rationing. *Journal of Monetary Economics*, 18, 159–79.
Williamson, S. D. 1987. Costly monitoring, loan contracts, and equilibrium credit rationing. *Quarterly Journal of Economics*, 102, 135–45.
Windmeijer, F. 2005. A finite sample correction for the variance of linear efficient two-step GMM estimators. *Journal of Econometrics*, 126(1), 25–51.
World Bank. 1989. *World Development Report*. New York, Oxford University Press.
World Bank. 2002. Global Development Network.
World Bank. 2008. Financial Development and Financial Structure Database.

Index

accounting practices, 3, 103
adverse selection, 2
aggregate private investment, *see* private investment
Arrow–Debreu framework, 2
Assigned Amount Units (AAUs), 161, 162
asymmetric information, 2, 64
autocracy, 17, 101, 104, 188n68

banking crises, 127, 150
banking markets
  efficiency measures, 15
  opening of, 5–6
Bayesian Model Averaging (BMA), 8, 10, 12, 21–2, 29, 30, 48–9, 125
black market premium, 18, 104–5, 107, 114, 116, 121, 188n64
bond market development, 46, 50, 62–3, 183n4
Brazil, 11, 162
business cycle co-movement, 66, 67

Canada, 11
cap-and-trade regimes, 161
capital account openness, 5, 127, 144, 151
capital flows, 185n33
carbon markets, 3, 9, 161–80
Chile, 10–11
China, 162
Chinn–Ito index, 127
civil law, 17, 25, 47, 118, 192n105
civil liberties, 17, 103
Clean Development Mechanism (CDM) markets, 8, 9, 161–82, 192n112
colonization, 4, 47, 103
Commercial-Central Bank (BTOT), 15, 68, 106

common correlated effect pooled (CCEP) approach, 126–7, 134, 139
common factor approach, 78–81
common law, 4, 17, 25, 47, 188n60, 192n105
contract enforcement, 3, 4, 47, 187n59, 188n60
countries
  civil law, 17, 25, 47, 118, 192n105
  common law, 4, 17, 25, 47, 188n60
  cross-section dependence across, 67
  developing, 101–2
  landlocked, 6, 19
creditors' rights, 17, 103
culture, 7, 11, 20, 47

democracy, 9, 17, 101, 102, 104, 126–7, 149, 188n68
democracy index, 25
democratization, 102–4, 109–21, 149, 187n59, 189n78
deposit insurance, 103
deposit rate of interest, 2
developing countries
  financial development in, 101
  institutional reform in, 101–2

economic growth
  determinants of, 65
  financial development and, 1–3, 7
  geography and, 162–3
elite groups, 104
endogenous growth models, 2
economic theory, 65
ethnicity, 20, 118, 192n104
EU Allowances (EUAs), 161
EU Emissions Trading Scheme (EU ETS), 161
extractive colonizers, 4, 103
extreme bounds analysis, 12

financial depth, 13, 36–46
financial development
  carbon markets and, 161–80
  cross-country differences in, 8, 10–63
  democratization and, 102–4, 109–21, 149, 187n59, 189n78
  determinants of, 3–7, 10–63
  in developing countries, 101
  financial liberalization and, 125–60
  government reforms and, 8–9
  indicators, 68
  institutional improvement and, 8
  measures of, 14–16
  political institutions and, 101–24
  private investment and, 64–100
  role of, in economic growth, 1–3
financial development determinants, 10–63
  conclusions about, 46–8
  data on, 13–20
  descriptive statistics, 54–5
  empirical results, 24–46
  empirical strategy, 20–4
  geographic variables, 19
  institutional variables, 17–18
  policy variables, 18
  potential, 16–20
  samples, 14
financial efficiency development, 36–7, 42–3, 46, 50
financial intermediaries, 2, 64, 185n28
financial intermediary development, 36–9, 50, 65, 66
financial liberalization, 2, 5–6
  conclusions about, 149–50
  criticism of, 125
  democratization and, 149
  empirical evidence on, 133–44
  factors stimulating, 125–7
  financial development and, 125–60
  methodology of study, 127–33
  study results, 144–9
  variables, 141–52
financial market analysis, 1–2

financial markets
  development of, 3
  integration of, 66–7
financial openness, see financial liberalization
financial repression, 2, 5
financial size development, 36–7, 44–5, 50
financial systems, 1, 46
  functions of, 2
  repressive policies toward, 2
France, 10
Frankel–Romer trade share, 26
French Civil Law, 4, 47, 118, 120, 188n60

GDP per capita, 20, 29, 47
Generalized Spatial Two-Step Least Square (GS2SLS) estimator, 170
General-to-specific (Gets) approach, 8, 10, 12, 22–4, 31, 60–1, 125
geographic determinants, of carbon markets, 161–80
geographic variables, 53
geography
  economic development and, 162–3
  role of, in financial development, 6–7, 9, 11–13, 19, 27, 29, 31, 33–5, 47–8
globalization, 66, 163, 181
global shocks, 66, 67, 70, 72, 77, 168
global warming, 161
GMM estimation, 8, 67, 69–73, 108–9
government quality, 17
government reforms, 8–9, 125–7 see also financial liberalization

income levels, 7, 11, 29, 47
India, 162
industrial revolution, 1
inflation rates, 2, 5, 11, 127, 150
information asymmetry, 2, 64
information disclosure, 103
institutional improvement, 8
  conclusions about, 121–2
  evidence on, 109–21
  measures and data on, 104–9

institutional improvement – *continued*
    methodology of study, 106–9
    variables, 123–4
institutional variables, 17–18, 51–2
institutions
    democratization and, 102–4
    political, and financial
        development, 101–24
    role of, in financial
        development, 3–5, 12–13, 17–18,
        24–9, 31, 33–5, 46–8
interest groups, 104
interest rates, 1–2, 150
investment, *see* private investment
investor rights, 192n105

Joint Implementation (JI)
    schemes, 161

Kyoto Protocol, 161, 162, 178

landlocked countries, 6, 19
language, 20, 47, 192n104
Latin America, 10–11, 162
latitude, 6, 11, 19
Least Square Dummy Variable
    (LSDV), 102
legal origin theory, 4
legal system, 3–4, 10, 11, 17, 25, 47,
    103, 118, 188n60, 192n105
Liquid Liabilities (LLY), 14–15, 24–5,
    28, 68, 105, 125
logarithm of the real GDP per capita
    (LGDP), 107

macroeconomic policy, 5–6,
    10–11, 18
macroeconomic shocks, 168
Markov Chain Monte Carlo
    technique, 184n20
McKinnon–Shaw model, 2
media, state-owned, 20
Mexico, 11, 162
microeconomic lumpiness, 185n30
model uncertainty problem, 12, 20–1
moral hazard, 2

natural resources, 6–7, 19, 163,
    167, 178
Net Interest Margin (NIM), 15, 188n66
new political economy, 4–5, 103–4

Occam's Window, 184n13, 184n14,
    184n15
Ordinary Least Squares (OLS)
    technique, 107
Overhead Costs (OVC), 15, 188n66

panel cointegration tests, 84–5
panel unit root tests, 81–3
PcGets, 183n10
policy
    macroeconomic policy, 10–11
    role of, in financial
        development, 5–6, 8–9, 11–13, 29,
        31, 33–5, 46–8
policy variables, 18, 50–1
political institutions
    evidence of effect, on financial
        development, 109–21
    financial development and, 101–24
    measures and data on, 104–9
    methodology of study, 106–9
    variables, 123–4
political liberalization, 3, 8, 101
political rights, 17
political stability, 17
politics, 11
posterior inclusion probabilities
    (PIPs), 29
posterior model probabilities, 48–9
"premature" democracy, 103
principle component
    analysis, 185n35, 186n37
Private Credit (PRIVO), 15, 68,
    105–6
private credit to GDP ratio, 10,
    11, 101
private investment, 3, 8, 64–100,
    185n33
    analysis on annual data, 77–92

private investment – *continued*
  analysis on data for five-year averages, 69–77
  data on, 67–9
  determinants of, 65
  financial development and, 64–100
  financial intermediaries and, 64–5, 66
property rights, 3, 4, 10, 103, 187n59

regime change, 104
regulatory system, 3–4, 103–4
religion, 7, 20, 47, 192n104
reserve requirements, 2
resource endowment, 6–7, 19, 163, 167, 178

savings rate, 7, 11, 47
settler colonizers, 4, 103
settler mortality hypothesis, 4, 11, 47, 103
shareholders' rights, 17, 103
Solow–Swan growth model, 65

spatial error model, 192n108
state-owned media, 20
stock market capitalization, 125
Stock Market Capitalization (MCAP), 15
stock market capitalization to GDP ratio, 10, 11
stock market development, 15, 36–7, 40–1, 50
stock markets, opening of, 6

technological shocks, 168
Total Value Traded (TVT), 15
trade factors, 18
trade liberalization, 66
trade openness, 11, 107
trade policy, 24, 26
trade volume, 185n33
tropical locations, 6, 19, 163
Turnover Ratio (TOR), 15

United Kingdom, 10

MIX
Papier aus verantwortungsvollen Quellen
Paper from responsible sources
FSC® C105338

If you have any concerns about our products,
you can contact us on
ProductSafety@springernature.com

In case Publisher is established outside the EU,
the EU authorized representative is:
Springer Nature Customer Service Center GmbH
Europaplatz 3, 69115 Heidelberg, Germany

Printed by Libri Plureos GmbH
in Hamburg, Germany